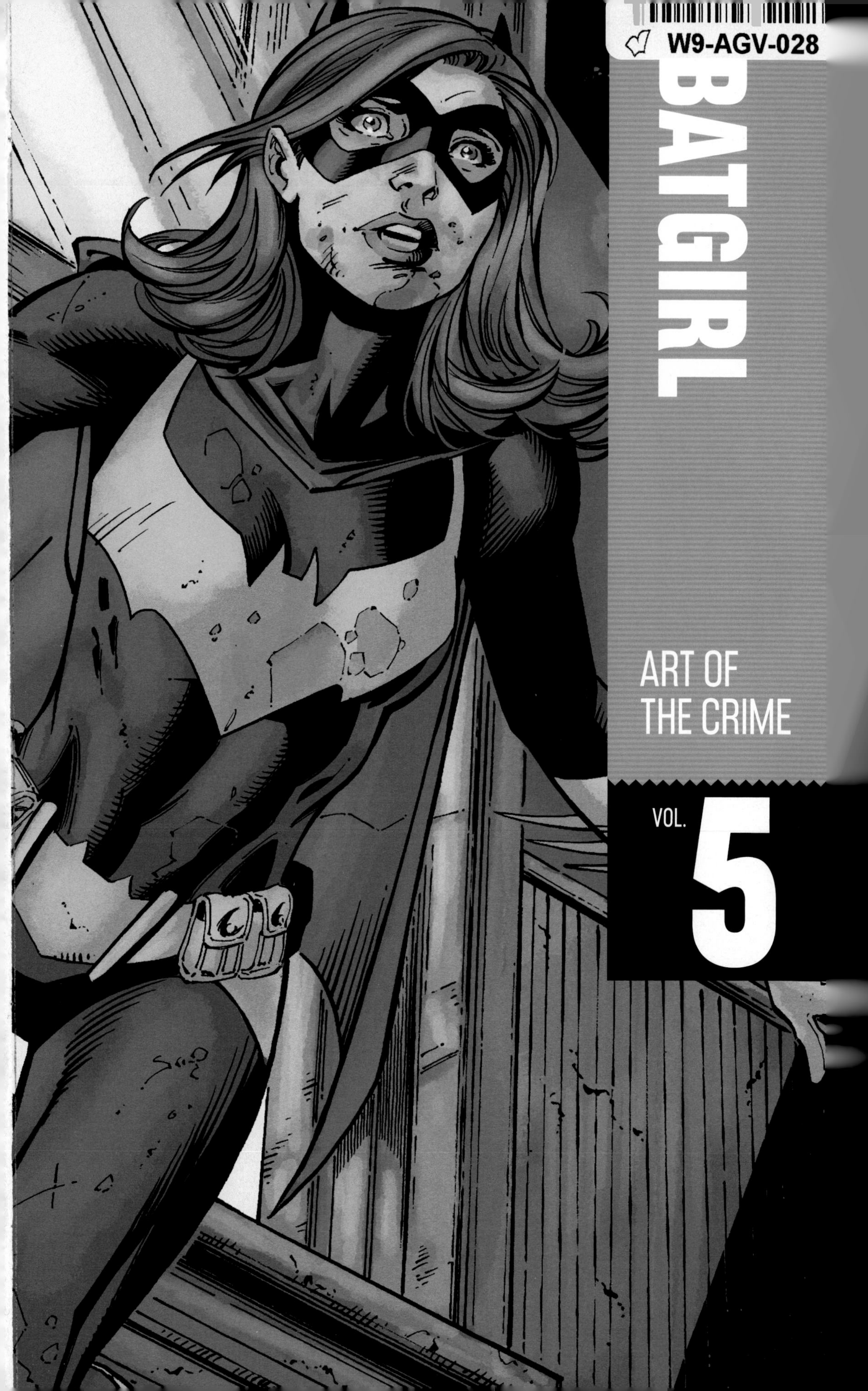

# BATGIRL

## ART OF THE CRIME

VOL. 5

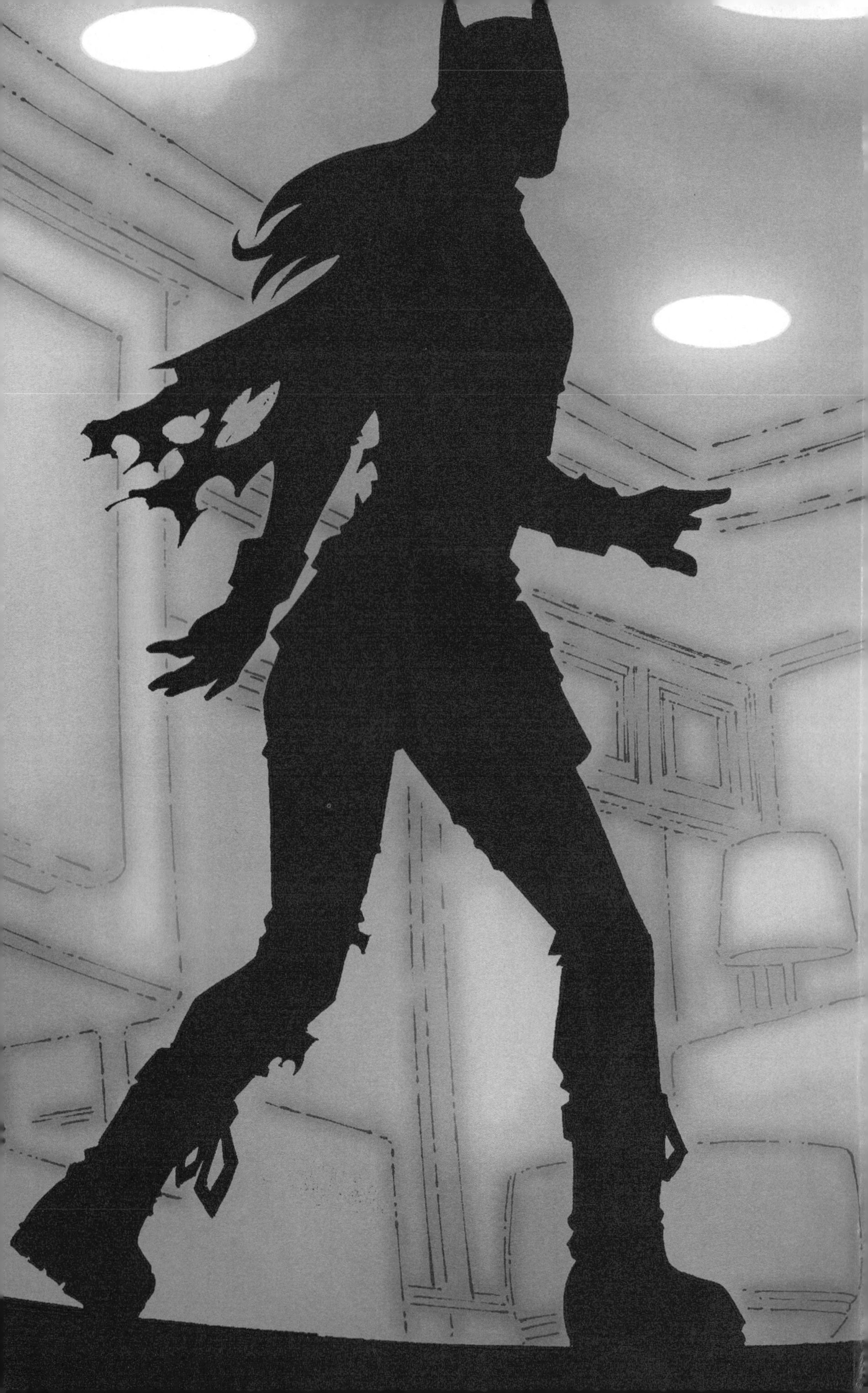

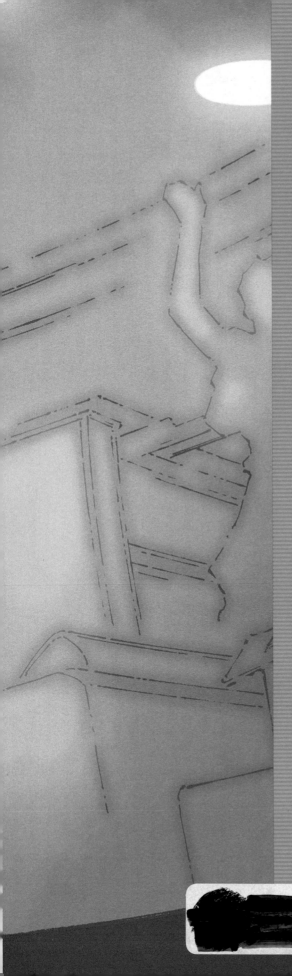

# BATGIRL
## ART OF THE CRIME

writer
**MAIRGHREAD SCOTT**

pencillers
**PAUL PELLETIER**
**ELENA CASAGRANDE**

inkers
**NORM RAPMUND**
**ELENA CASAGRANDE**

colorist
**JORDIE BELLAIRE**

letterer
**DERON BENNETT**

collection cover artist
**JULIAN TOTINO TEDESCO**

BATMAN created by BOB KANE with BILL FINGER

VOL.
# 5

**BRITTANY HOLZHERR** Editor – Original Series
**JEB WOODARD** Group Editor – Collected Editions
**ERIC SEARLEMAN** Editor – Collected Edition
**STEVE COOK** Design Director – Books
**SHANNON STEWART** Publication Design

**BOB HARRAS** Senior VP – Editor-in-Chief, DC Comics
**PAT McCALLUM** Executive Editor, DC Comics

**DAN DiDIO** Publisher
**JIM LEE** Publisher & Chief Creative Officer
**AMIT DESAI** Executive VP – Business & Marketing Strategy, Direct to
              Consumer & Global Franchise Management
**BOBBIE CHASE** VP & Executive Editor, Young Reader & Talent Development
**MARK CHIARELLO** Senior VP – Art, Design & Collected Editions
**JOHN CUNNINGHAM** Senior VP – Sales & Trade Marketing
**BRIAR DARDEN** VP – Business Affairs
**ANNE DePIES** Senior VP – Business Strategy, Finance & Administration
**DON FALLETTI** VP – Manufacturing Operations
**LAWRENCE GANEM** VP – Editorial Administration & Talent Relations
**ALISON GILL** Senior VP – Manufacturing & Operations
**JASON GREENBERG** VP – Business Strategy & Finance
**HANK KANALZ** Senior VP – Editorial Strategy & Administration
**JAY KOGAN** Senior VP – Legal Affairs
**NICK J. NAPOLITANO** VP – Manufacturing Administration
**LISETTE OSTERLOH** VP – Digital Marketing & Events
**EDDIE SCANNELL** VP – Consumer Marketing
**COURTNEY SIMMONS** Senior VP – Publicity & Communications
**JIM (SKI) SOKOLOWSKI** VP – Comic Book Specialty Sales & Trade Marketing
**NANCY SPEARS** VP – Mass, Book, Digital Sales & Trade Marketing
**MICHELE R. WELLS** VP – Content Strategy

BATGIRL VOL. 5: ART OF THE CRIME

Published by DC Comics. Compilation and all new material Copyright © 2019 DC Comics. All Rights
Reserved.  Originally published in single magazine form in BATGIRL ANNUAL 2, BATGIRL 25-29. Copyright © 2018
DC Comics. All Rights Reserved. All characters, their distinctive likenesses and related elements featured in this
publication are trademarks of DC Comics. The stories, characters and incidents featured in this publication are
entirely fictional. DC Comics does not read or accept unsolicited submissions of ideas, stories or artwork.

DC Comics, 2900 West Alameda Ave., Burbank, CA 91505
Printed by LSC Communications, Kendallville, IN, USA. 4/12/19. First Printing.
ISBN: 978-1-4012-8946-1

Library of Congress Cataloging-in-Publication Data is available.

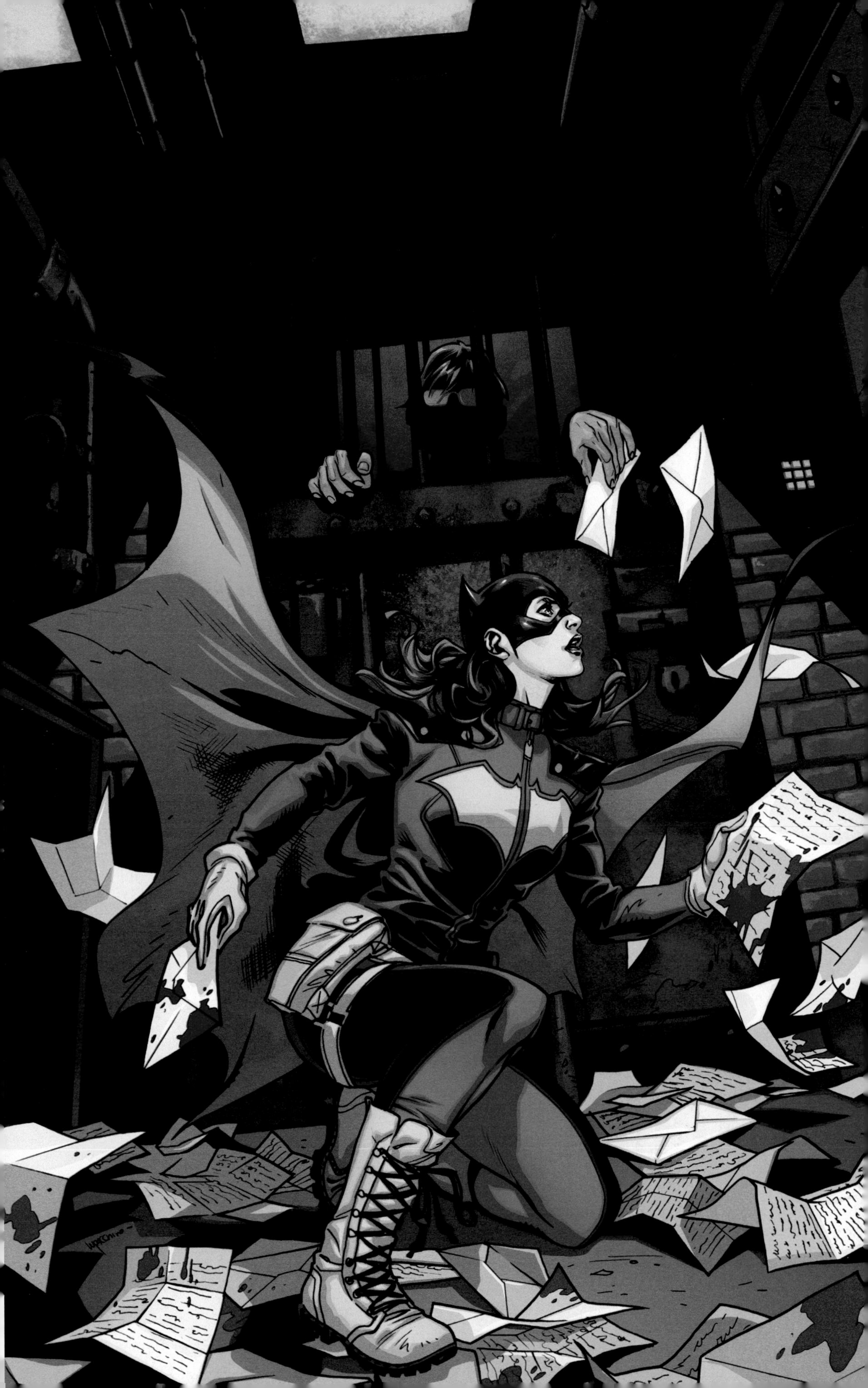

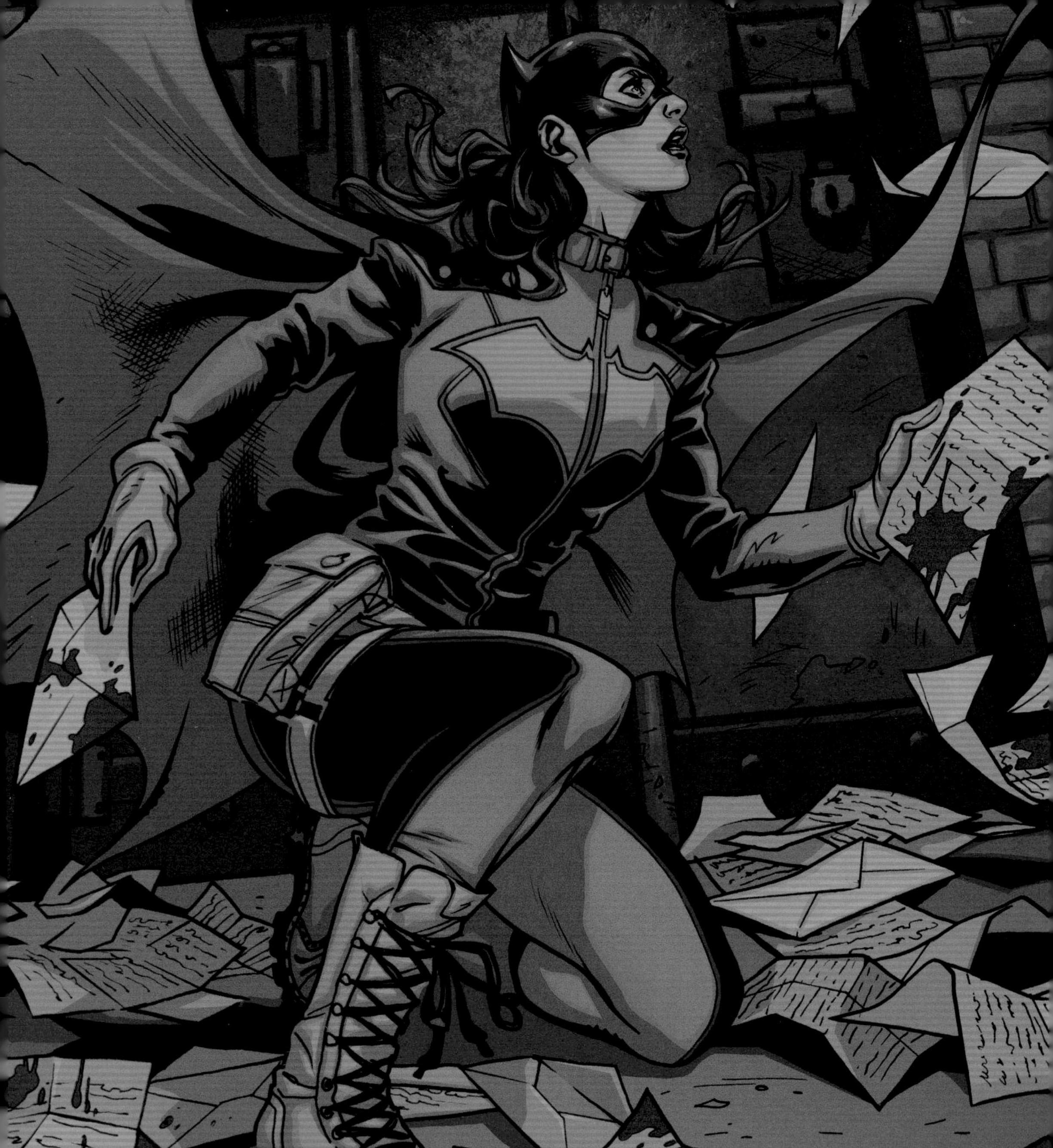

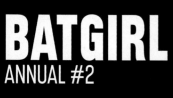

# BATGIRL
ANNUAL #2

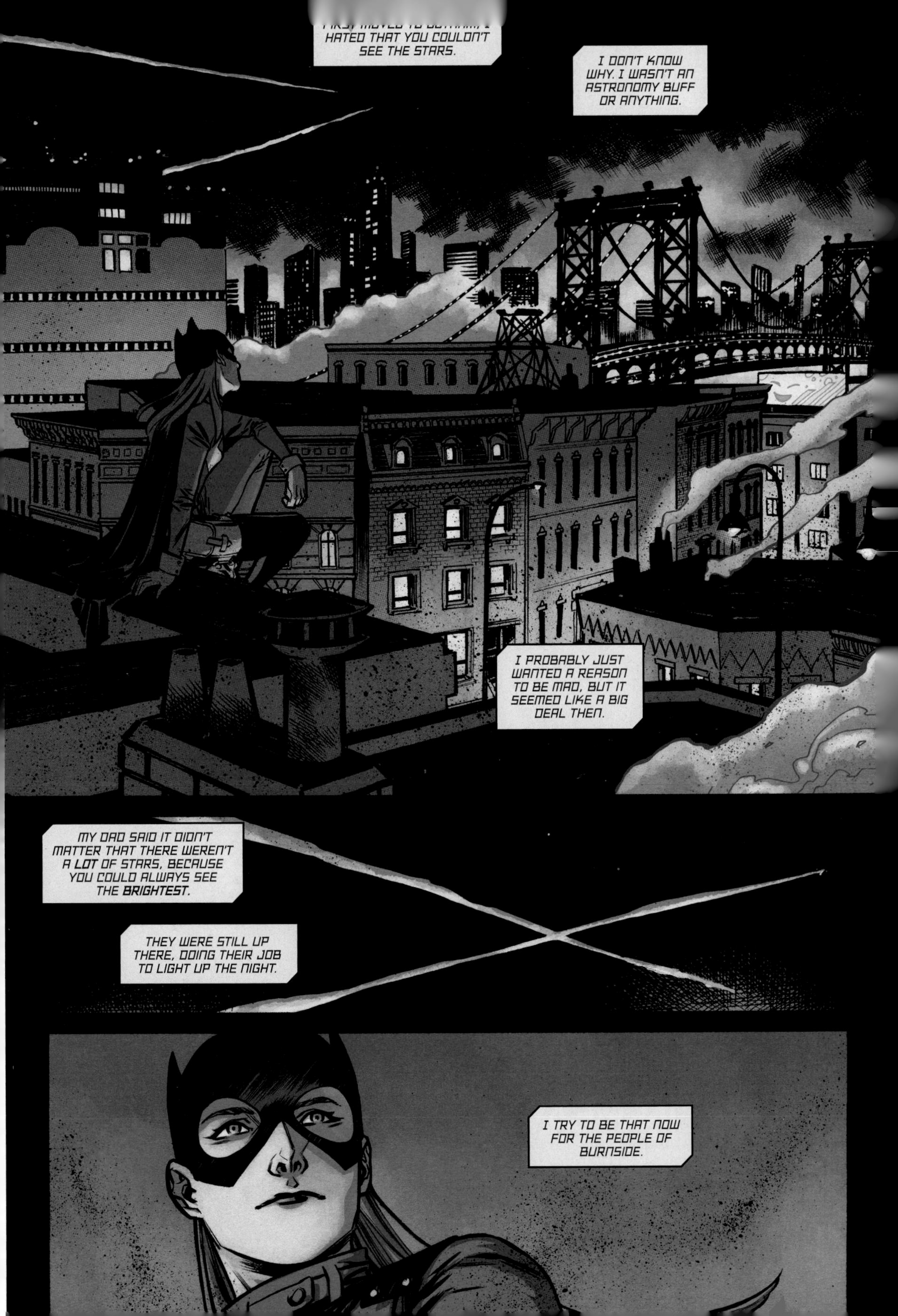
HATED THAT YOU COULDN'T SEE THE STARS.
I DON'T KNOW WHY. I WASN'T AN ASTRONOMY BUFF OR ANYTHING.
I PROBABLY JUST WANTED A REASON TO BE MAD, BUT IT SEEMED LIKE A BIG DEAL THEN.
MY DAD SAID IT DIDN'T MATTER THAT THERE WEREN'T A LOT OF STARS, BECAUSE YOU COULD ALWAYS SEE THE BRIGHTEST.
THEY WERE STILL UP THERE, DOING THEIR JOB TO LIGHT UP THE NIGHT.
I TRY TO BE THAT NOW FOR THE PEOPLE OF BURNSIDE.

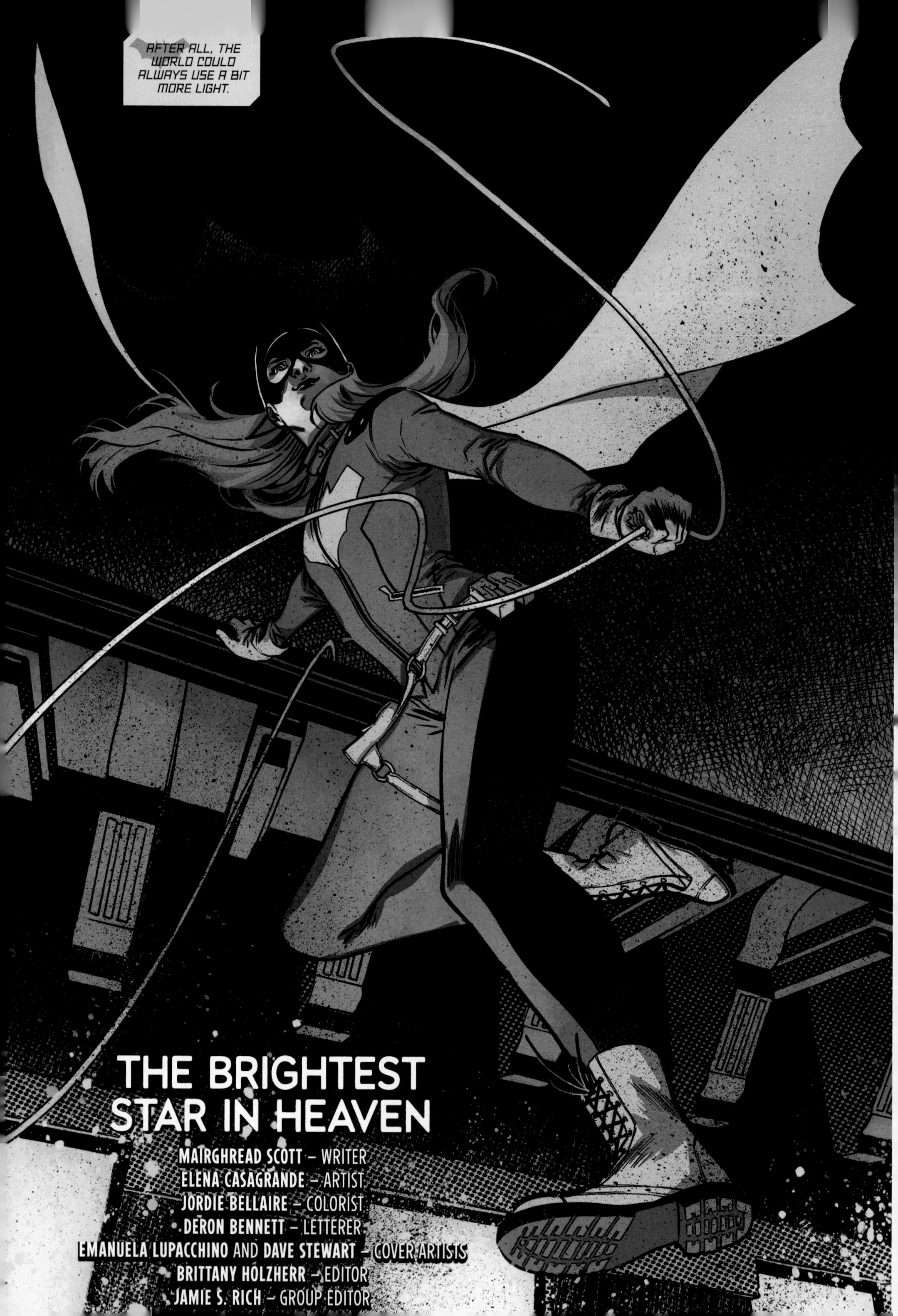
AFTER ALL, THE WORLD COULD ALWAYS USE A BIT MORE LIGHT.
THE BRIGHTEST STAR IN HEAVEN
MAIRGHREAD SCOTT – WRITER
ELENA CASAGRANDE – ARTIST
JORDIE BELLAIRE – COLORIST
DERON BENNETT – LETTERER
EMANUELA LUPACCHINO AND DAVE STEWART – COVER ARTISTS
BRITTANY HOLZHERR – EDITOR
JAMIE S. RICH – GROUP EDITOR

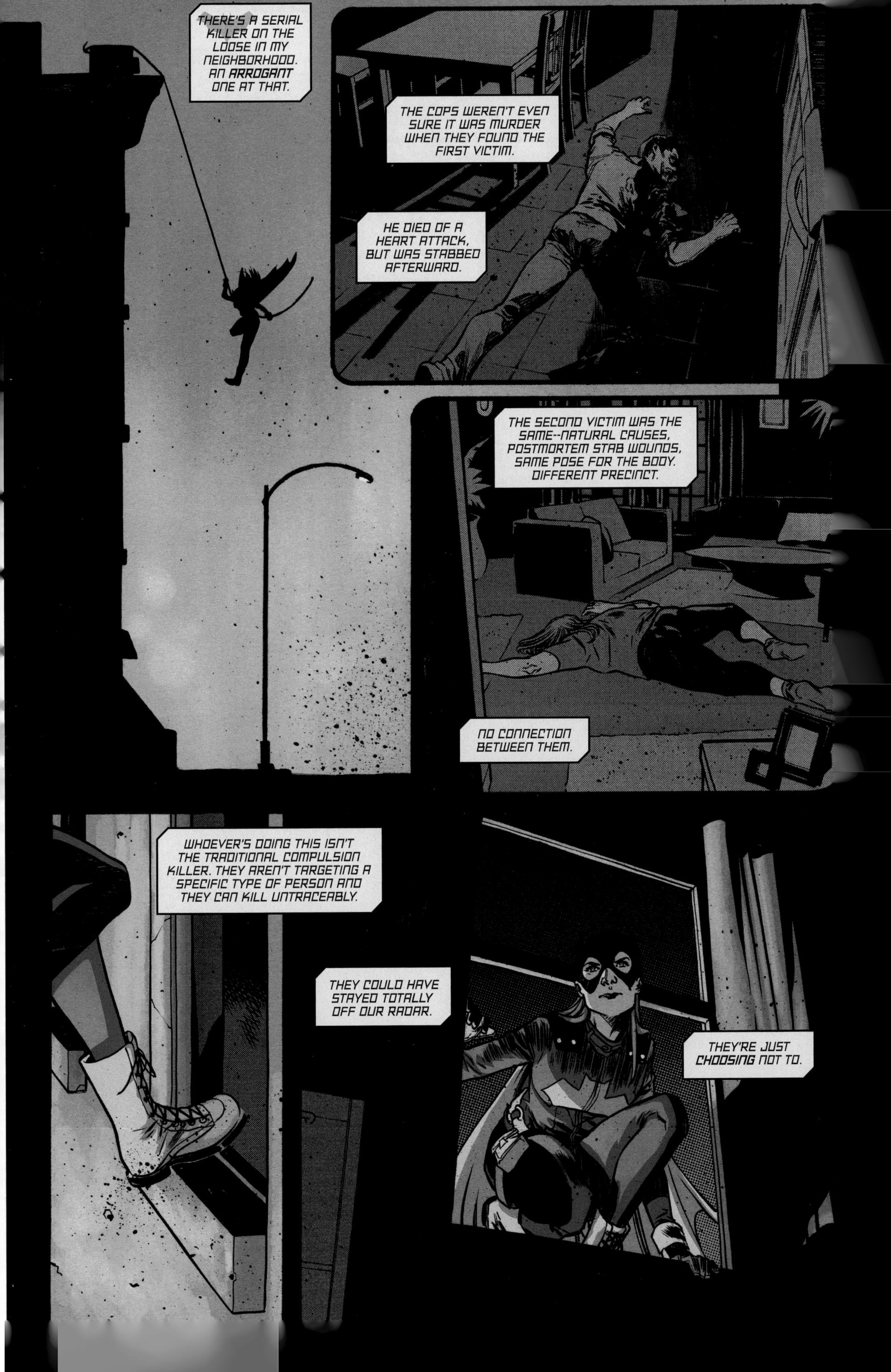
THERE'S A SERIAL KILLER ON THE LOOSE IN MY NEIGHBORHOOD. AN ARROGANT ONE AT THAT.
THE COPS WEREN'T EVEN SURE IT WAS MURDER WHEN THEY FOUND THE FIRST VICTIM.
HE DIED OF A HEART ATTACK, BUT WAS STABBED AFTERWARD.
THE SECOND VICTIM WAS THE SAME--NATURAL CAUSES, POSTMORTEM STAB WOUNDS, SAME POSE FOR THE BODY. DIFFERENT PRECINCT.
NO CONNECTION BETWEEN THEM.
WHOEVER'S DOING THIS ISN'T THE TRADITIONAL COMPULSION KILLER. THEY AREN'T TARGETING A SPECIFIC TYPE OF PERSON AND THEY CAN KILL UNTRACEABLY.
THEY COULD HAVE STAYED TOTALLY OFF OUR RADAR.
THEY'RE JUST CHOOSING NOT TO.

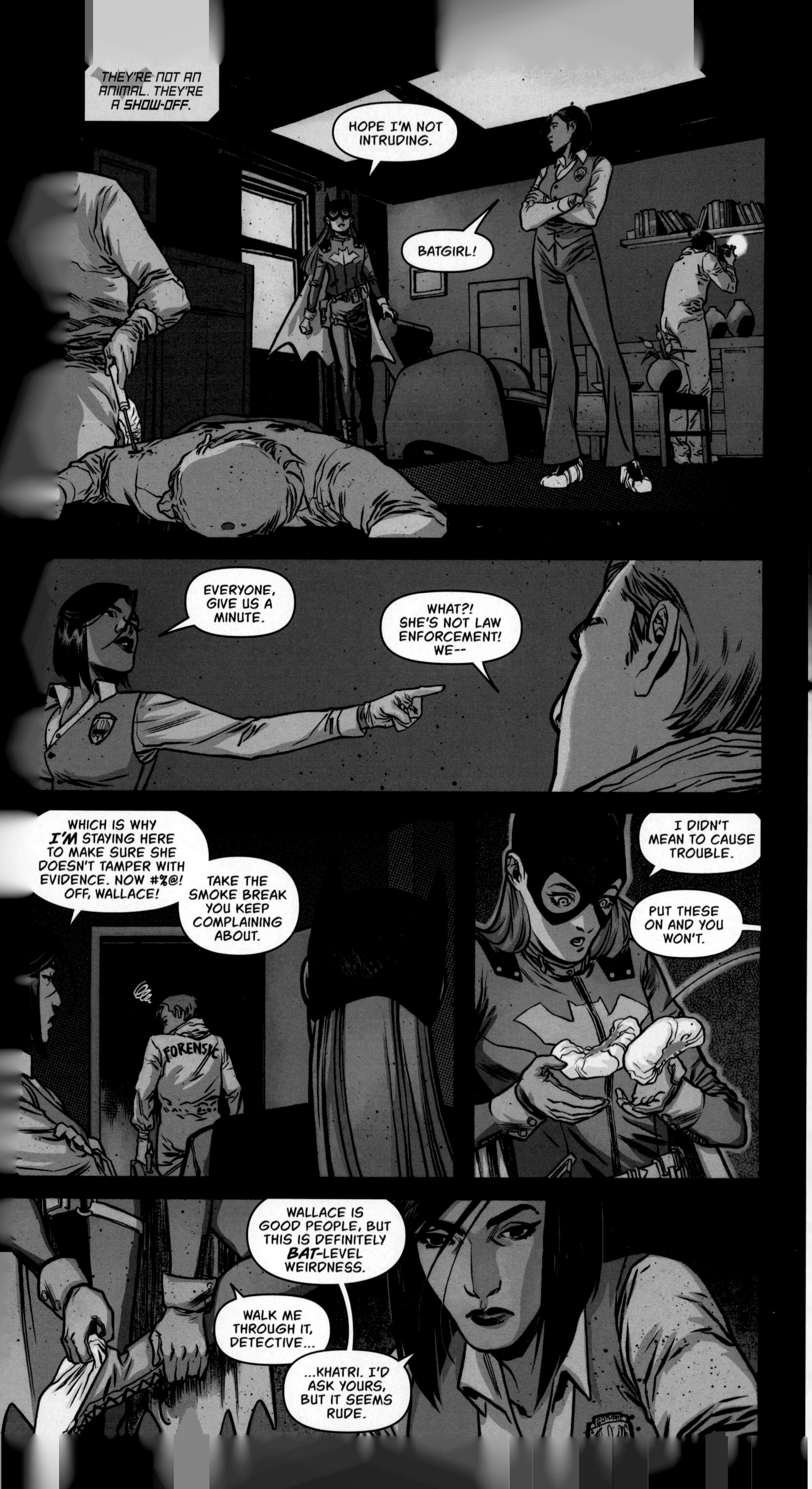

THEY'RE NOT AN ANIMAL. THEY'RE A SHOW-OFF.
HOPE I'M NOT INTRUDING.
BATGIRL!
EVERYONE, GIVE US A MINUTE.
WHAT?! SHE'S NOT LAW ENFORCEMENT! WE--
WHICH IS WHY I'M STAYING HERE TO MAKE SURE SHE DOESN'T TAMPER WITH EVIDENCE. NOW #%@! OFF, WALLACE!
TAKE THE SMOKE BREAK YOU KEEP COMPLAINING ABOUT.
FORENSIC
I DIDN'T MEAN TO CAUSE TROUBLE.
PUT THESE ON AND YOU WON'T.
WALLACE IS GOOD PEOPLE, BUT THIS IS DEFINITELY BAT-LEVEL WEIRDNESS.
WALK ME THROUGH IT, DETECTIVE...
...KHATRI. I'D ASK YOURS, BUT IT SEEMS RUDE.

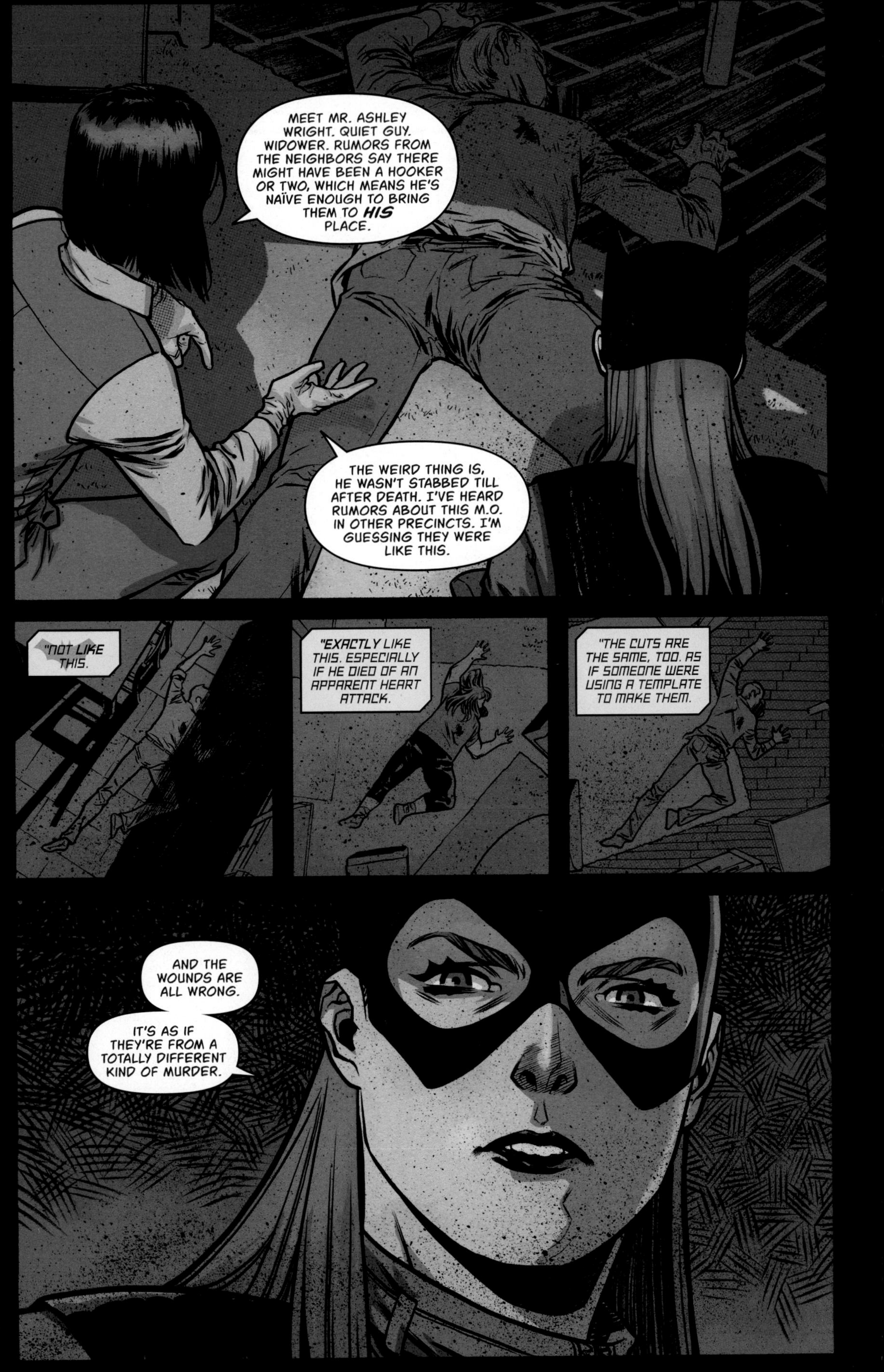

MEET MR. ASHLEY WRIGHT. QUIET GUY. WIDOWER. RUMORS FROM THE NEIGHBORS SAY THERE MIGHT HAVE BEEN A HOOKER OR TWO, WHICH MEANS HE'S NAÏVE ENOUGH TO BRING THEM TO HIS PLACE.
THE WEIRD THING IS, HE WASN'T STABBED TILL AFTER DEATH. I'VE HEARD RUMORS ABOUT THIS M.O. IN OTHER PRECINCTS. I'M GUESSING THEY WERE LIKE THIS.
"NOT LIKE THIS.
"EXACTLY LIKE THIS. ESPECIALLY IF HE DIED OF AN APPARENT HEART ATTACK.
"THE CUTS ARE THE SAME, TOO. AS IF SOMEONE WERE USING A TEMPLATE TO MAKE THEM.
AND THE WOUNDS ARE ALL WRONG.
IT'S AS IF THEY'RE FROM A TOTALLY DIFFERENT KIND OF MURDER.

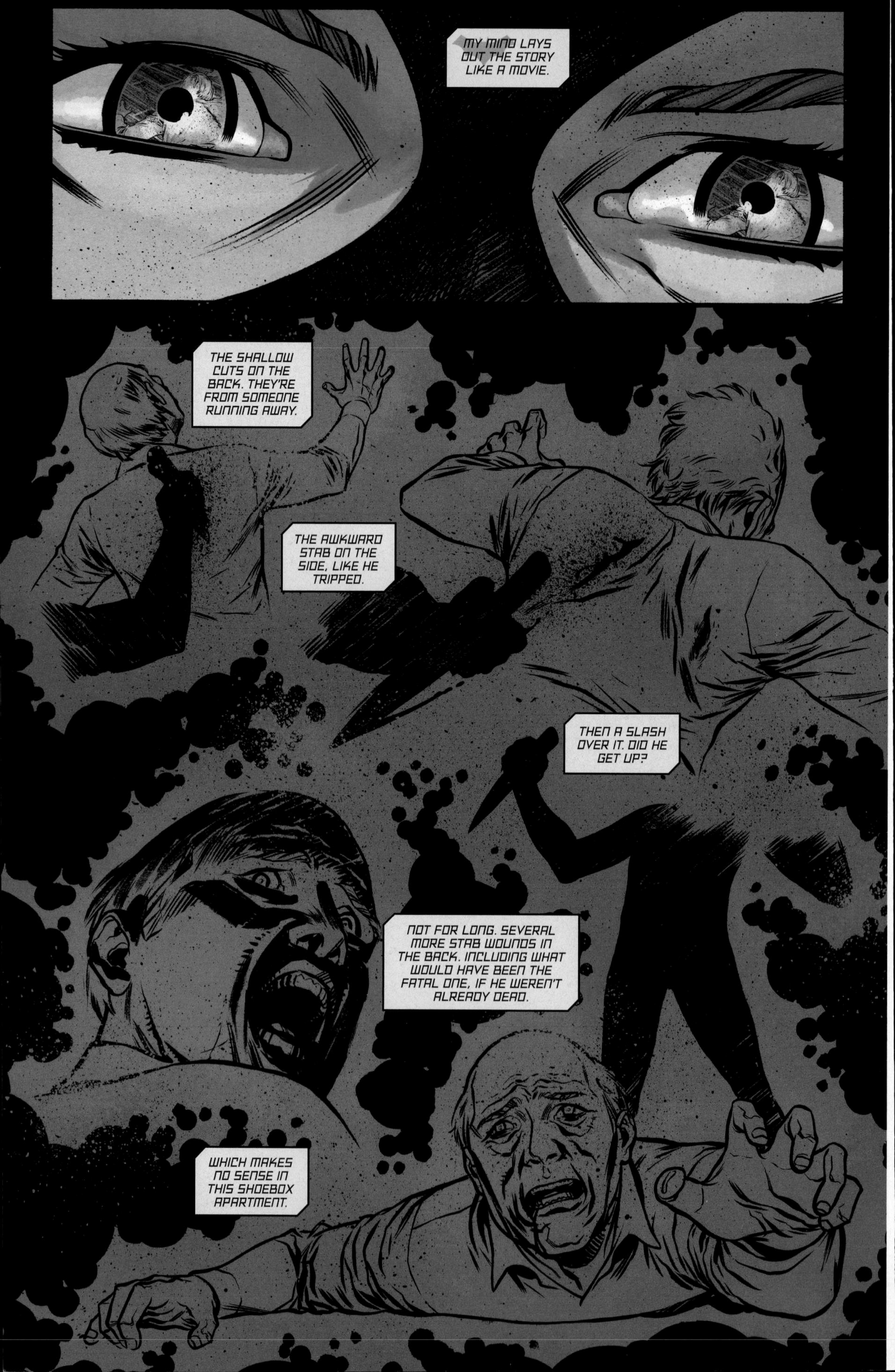
MY MIND LAYS OUT THE STORY LIKE A MOVIE.
THE SHALLOW CUTS ON THE BACK. THEY'RE FROM SOMEONE RUNNING AWAY.
THE AWKWARD STAB ON THE SIDE, LIKE HE TRIPPED.
THEN A SLASH OVER IT. DID HE GET UP?
NOT FOR LONG. SEVERAL MORE STAB WOUNDS IN THE BACK. INCLUDING WHAT WOULD HAVE BEEN THE FATAL ONE, IF HE WEREN'T ALREADY DEAD.
WHICH MAKES NO SENSE IN THIS SHOEBOX APARTMENT.

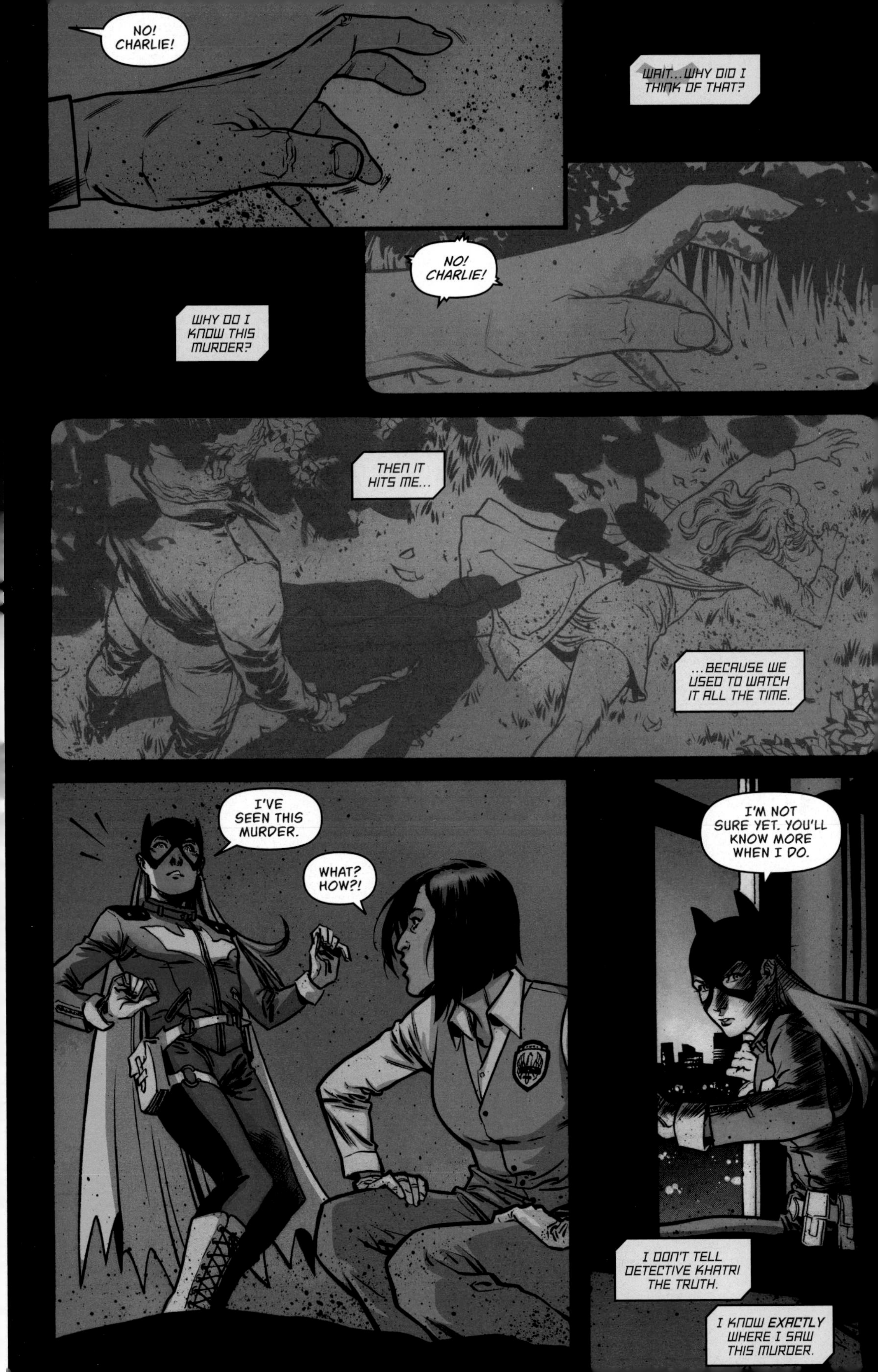
NO! CHARLIE!
WAIT...WHY DID I THINK OF THAT?
NO! CHARLIE!
WHY DO I KNOW THIS MURDER?
THEN IT HITS ME...
...BECAUSE WE USED TO WATCH IT ALL THE TIME.
I'VE SEEN THIS MURDER.
WHAT? HOW?!
I'M NOT SURE YET. YOU'LL KNOW MORE WHEN I DO.
I DON'T TELL DETECTIVE KHATRI THE TRUTH.
I KNOW EXACTLY WHERE I SAW THIS MURDER.

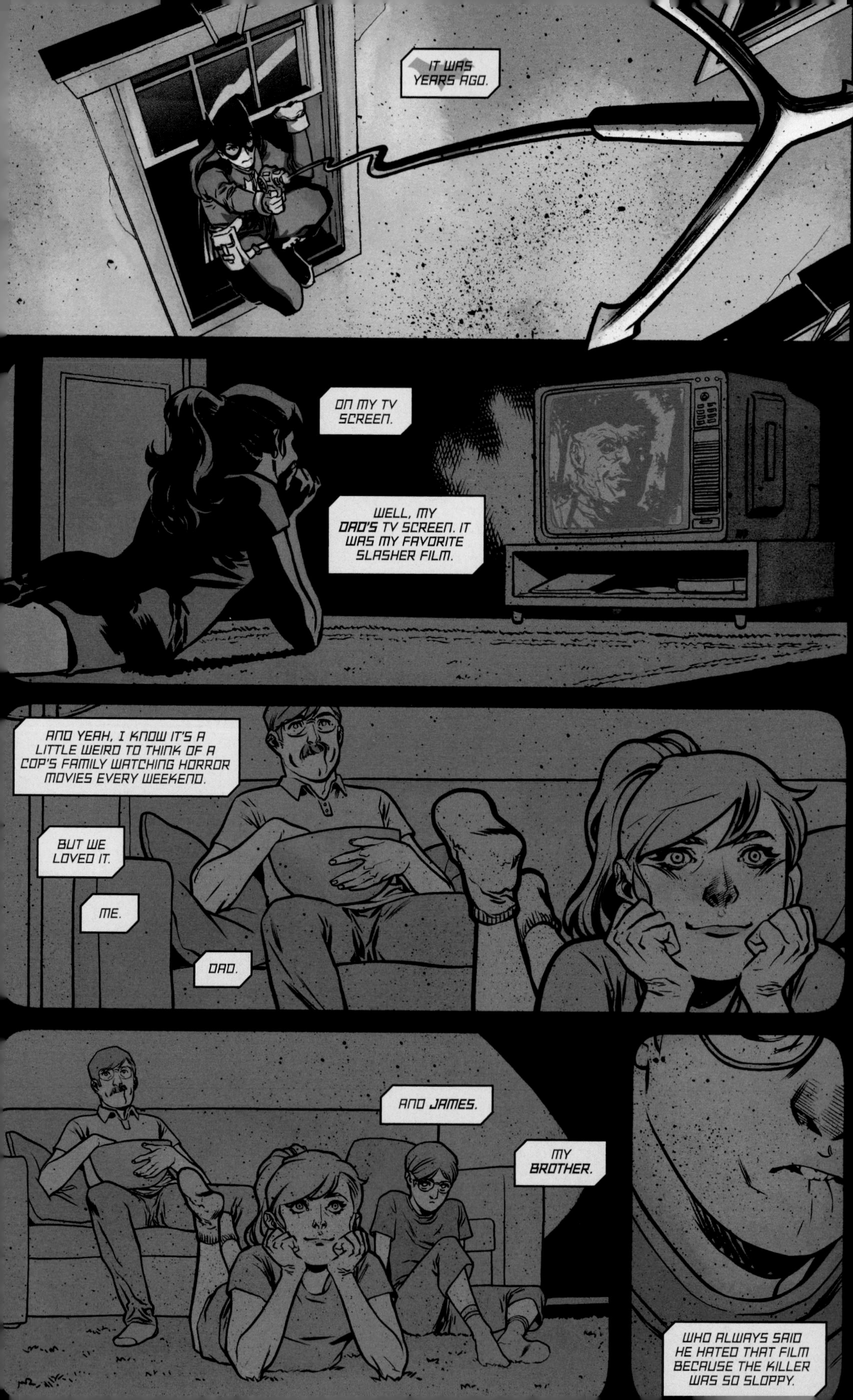
IT WAS YEARS AGO.
ON MY TV SCREEN.
WELL, MY DAD'S TV SCREEN. IT WAS MY FAVORITE SLASHER FILM.
AND YEAH, I KNOW IT'S A LITTLE WEIRD TO THINK OF A COP'S FAMILY WATCHING HORROR MOVIES EVERY WEEKEND.
BUT WE LOVED IT.
ME.
DAD.
AND JAMES.
MY BROTHER.
WHO ALWAYS SAID HE HATED THAT FILM BECAUSE THE KILLER WAS SO SLOPPY.

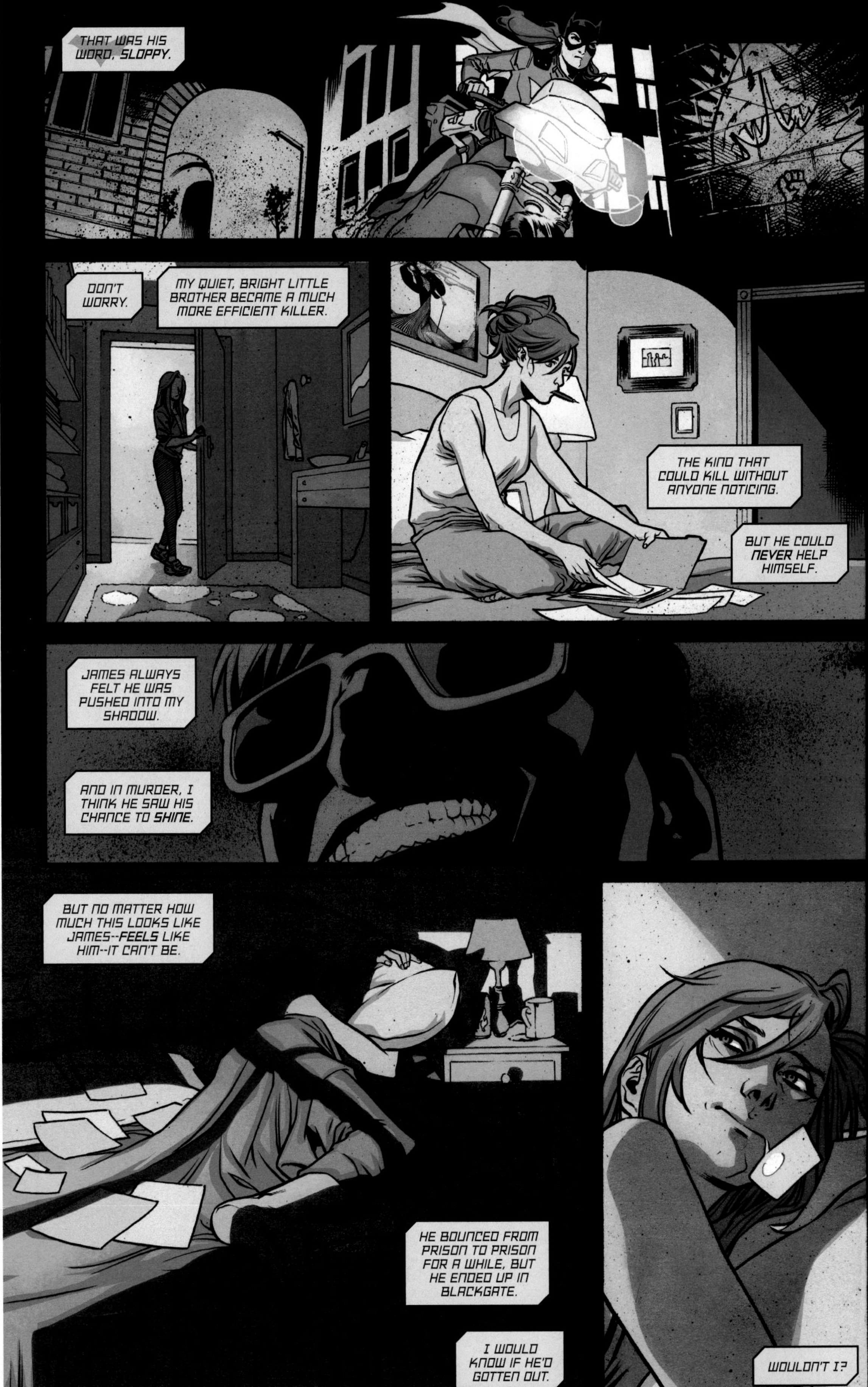
THAT WAS HIS WORD, SLOPPY.
DON'T WORRY.
MY QUIET, BRIGHT LITTLE BROTHER BECAME A MUCH MORE EFFICIENT KILLER.
THE KIND THAT COULD KILL WITHOUT ANYONE NOTICING.
BUT HE COULD NEVER HELP HIMSELF.
JAMES ALWAYS FELT HE WAS PUSHED INTO MY SHADOW.
AND IN MURDER, I THINK HE SAW HIS CHANCE TO SHINE.
BUT NO MATTER HOW MUCH THIS LOOKS LIKE JAMES--FEELS LIKE HIM--IT CAN'T BE.
HE BOUNCED FROM PRISON TO PRISON FOR A WHILE, BUT HE ENDED UP IN BLACKGATE.
I WOULD KNOW IF HE'D GOTTEN OUT.
WOULDN'T I?

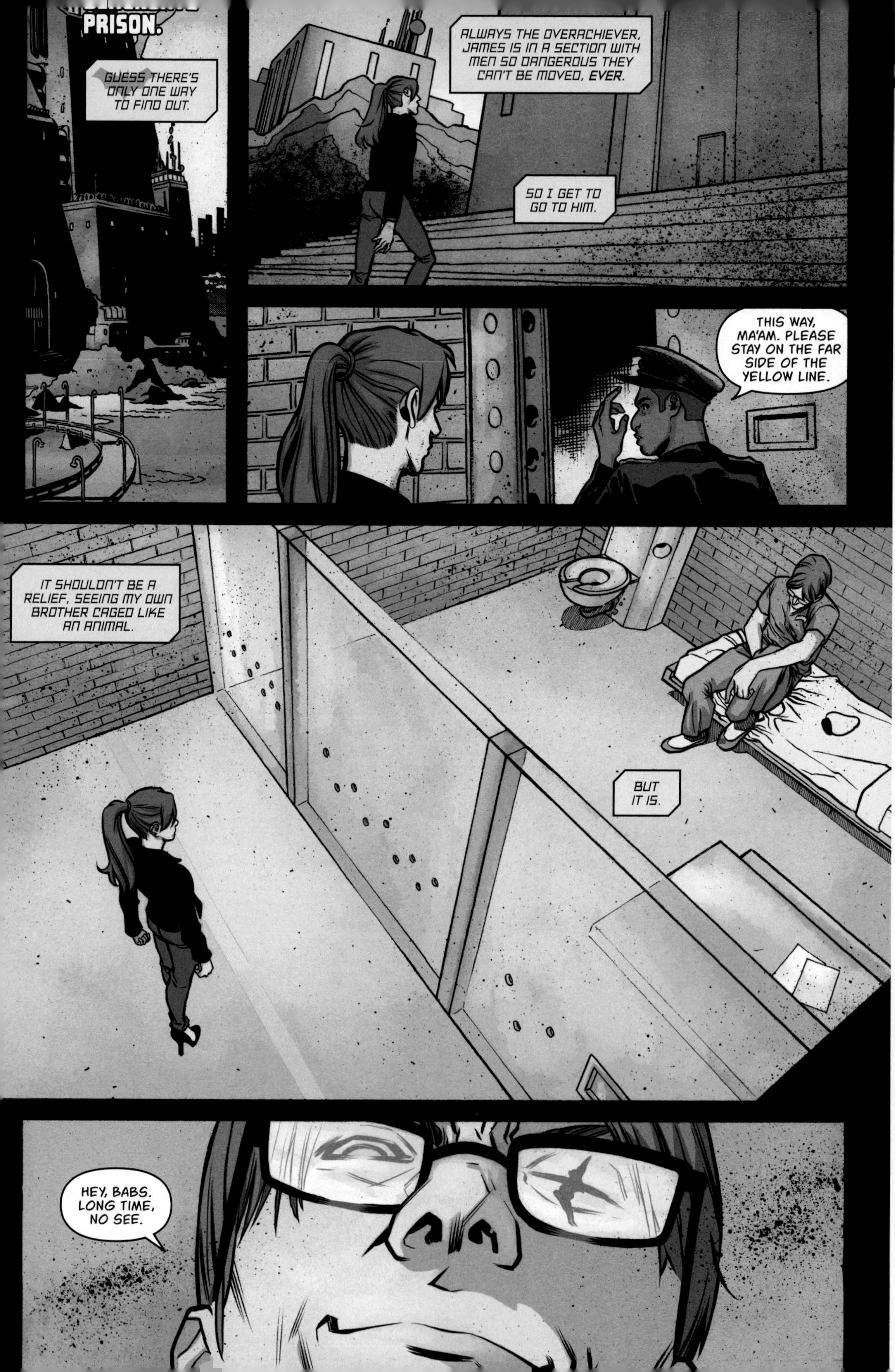
PRISON.
GUESS THERE'S ONLY ONE WAY TO FIND OUT.
ALWAYS THE OVERACHIEVER, JAMES IS IN A SECTION WITH MEN SO DANGEROUS THEY CAN'T BE MOVED, EVER.
SO I GET TO GO TO HIM.
THIS WAY, MA'AM. PLEASE STAY ON THE FAR SIDE OF THE YELLOW LINE.
IT SHOULDN'T BE A RELIEF, SEEING MY OWN BROTHER CAGED LIKE AN ANIMAL.
BUT IT IS.
HEY, BABS. LONG TIME, NO SEE.

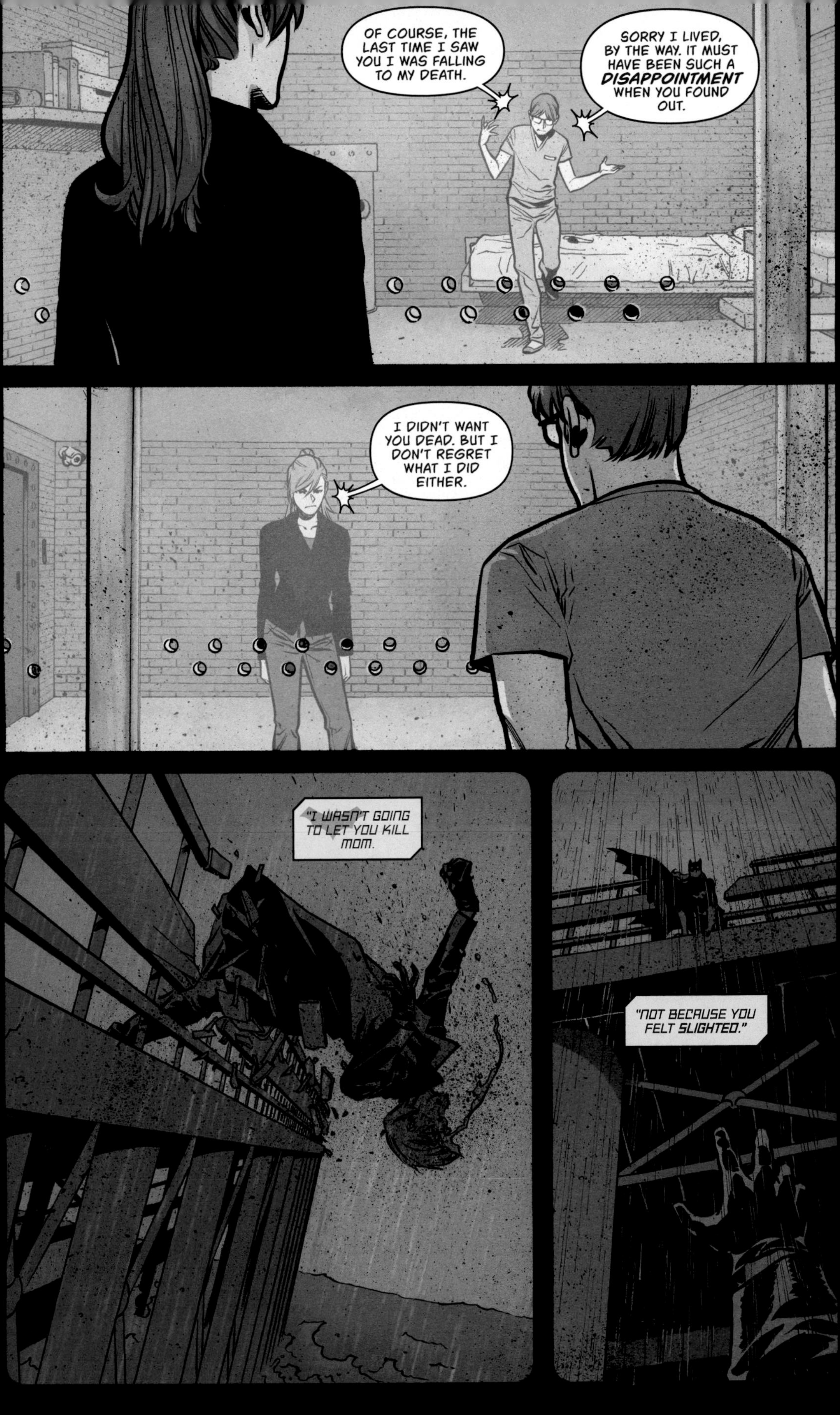
OF COURSE, THE LAST TIME I SAW YOU I WAS FALLING TO MY DEATH.
SORRY I LIVED, BY THE WAY. IT MUST HAVE BEEN SUCH A DISAPPOINTMENT WHEN YOU FOUND OUT.
I DIDN'T WANT YOU DEAD. BUT I DON'T REGRET WHAT I DID EITHER.
"I WASN'T GOING TO LET YOU KILL MOM.
"NOT BECAUSE YOU FELT SLIGHTED."

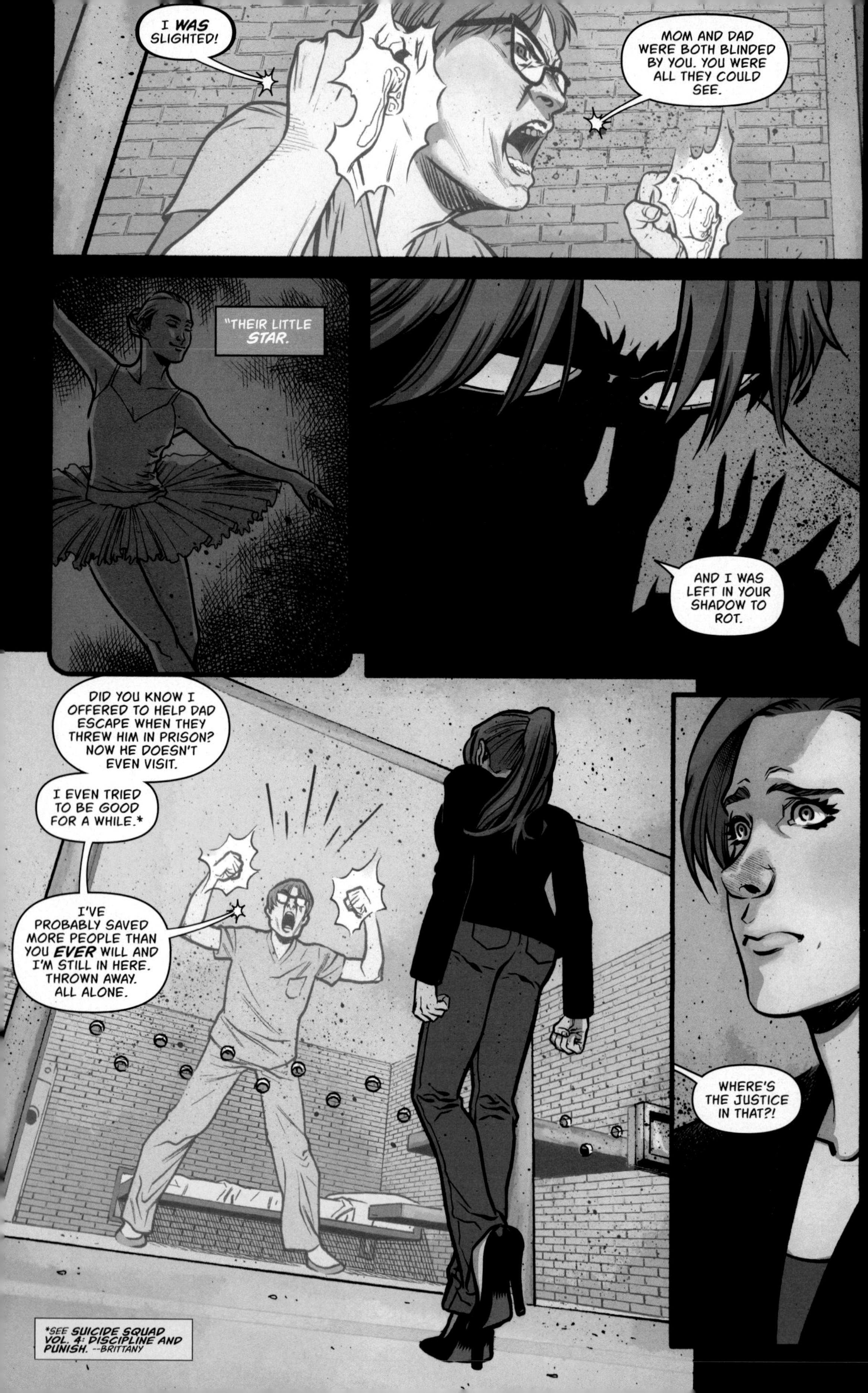
I WAS SLIGHTED!
MOM AND DAD WERE BOTH BLINDED BY YOU. YOU WERE ALL THEY COULD SEE.
"THEIR LITTLE STAR.
AND I WAS LEFT IN YOUR SHADOW TO ROT.
DID YOU KNOW I OFFERED TO HELP DAD ESCAPE WHEN THEY THREW HIM IN PRISON? NOW HE DOESN'T EVEN VISIT.
I EVEN TRIED TO BE GOOD FOR A WHILE.*
I'VE PROBABLY SAVED MORE PEOPLE THAN YOU EVER WILL AND I'M STILL IN HERE. THROWN AWAY. ALL ALONE.
WHERE'S THE JUSTICE IN THAT?!
*SEE SUICIDE SQUAD VOL. 4: DISCIPLINE AND PUNISH. --BRITTANY

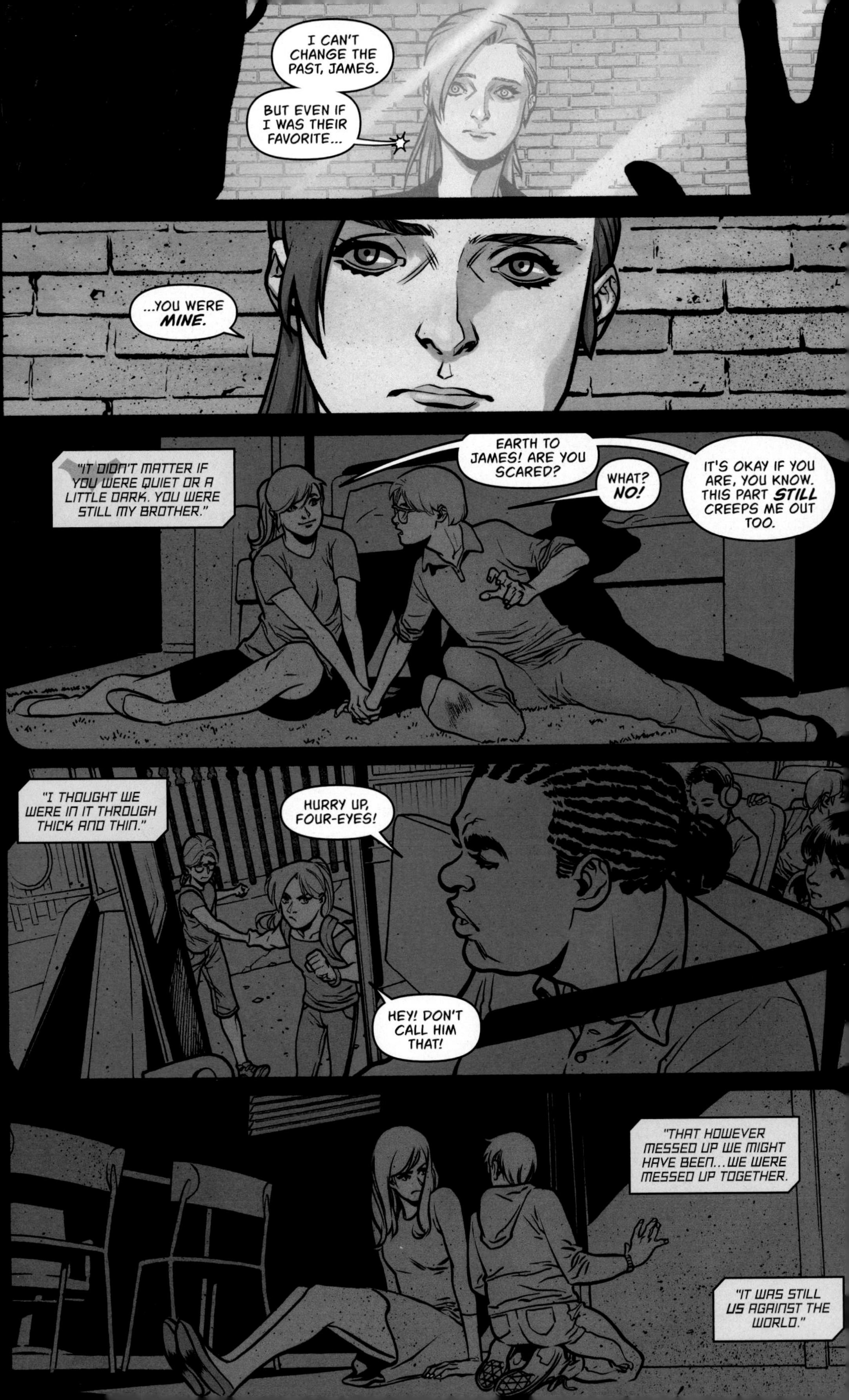
I CAN'T CHANGE THE PAST, JAMES.
BUT EVEN IF I WAS THEIR FAVORITE...
...YOU WERE MINE.
"IT DIDN'T MATTER IF YOU WERE QUIET OR A LITTLE DARK. YOU WERE STILL MY BROTHER."
EARTH TO JAMES! ARE YOU SCARED?
WHAT? NO!
IT'S OKAY IF YOU ARE, YOU KNOW. THIS PART STILL CREEPS ME OUT TOO.
"I THOUGHT WE WERE IN IT THROUGH THICK AND THIN."
HURRY UP, FOUR-EYES!
HEY! DON'T CALL HIM THAT!
"THAT HOWEVER MESSED UP WE MIGHT HAVE BEEN...WE WERE MESSED UP TOGETHER.
"IT WAS STILL US AGAINST THE WORLD."

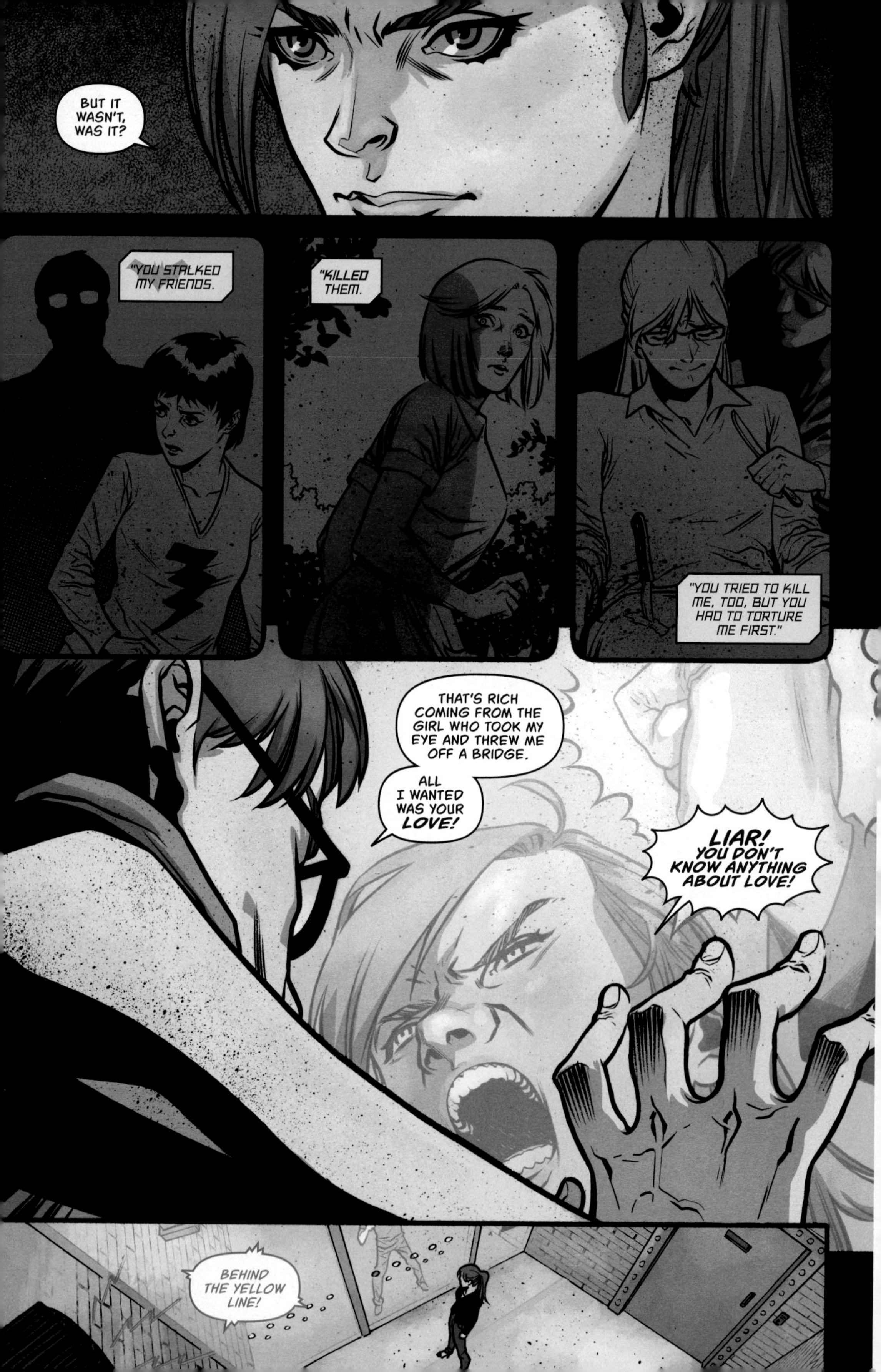
BUT IT WASN'T, WAS IT?
"YOU STALKED MY FRIENDS.
"KILLED THEM.
"YOU TRIED TO KILL ME, TOO, BUT YOU HAD TO TORTURE ME FIRST."
THAT'S RICH COMING FROM THE GIRL WHO TOOK MY EYE AND THREW ME OFF A BRIDGE.
ALL I WANTED WAS YOUR LOVE!
LIAR! YOU DON'T KNOW ANYTHING ABOUT LOVE!
BEHIND THE YELLOW LINE!

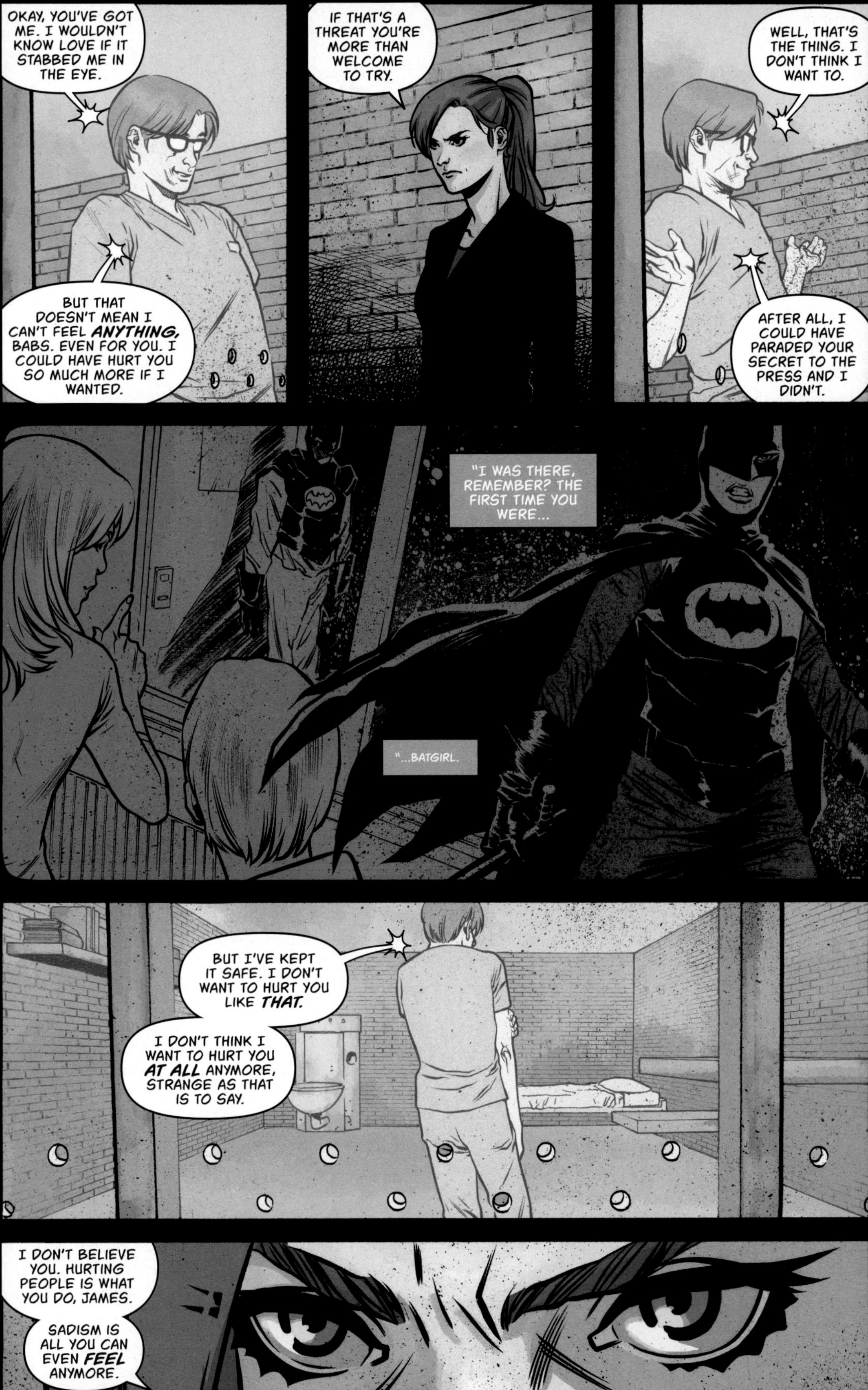

OKAY, YOU'VE GOT ME. I WOULDN'T KNOW LOVE IF IT STABBED ME IN THE EYE.
BUT THAT DOESN'T MEAN I CAN'T FEEL ANYTHING, BABS. EVEN FOR YOU. I COULD HAVE HURT YOU SO MUCH MORE IF I WANTED.
IF THAT'S A THREAT YOU'RE MORE THAN WELCOME TO TRY.
WELL, THAT'S THE THING. I DON'T THINK I WANT TO.
AFTER ALL, I COULD HAVE PARADED YOUR SECRET TO THE PRESS AND I DIDN'T.
"I WAS THERE, REMEMBER? THE FIRST TIME YOU WERE...
"...BATGIRL.
BUT I'VE KEPT IT SAFE. I DON'T WANT TO HURT YOU LIKE THAT.
I DON'T THINK I WANT TO HURT YOU AT ALL ANYMORE, STRANGE AS THAT IS TO SAY.
I DON'T BELIEVE YOU. HURTING PEOPLE IS WHAT YOU DO, JAMES.
SADISM IS ALL YOU CAN EVEN FEEL ANYMORE.

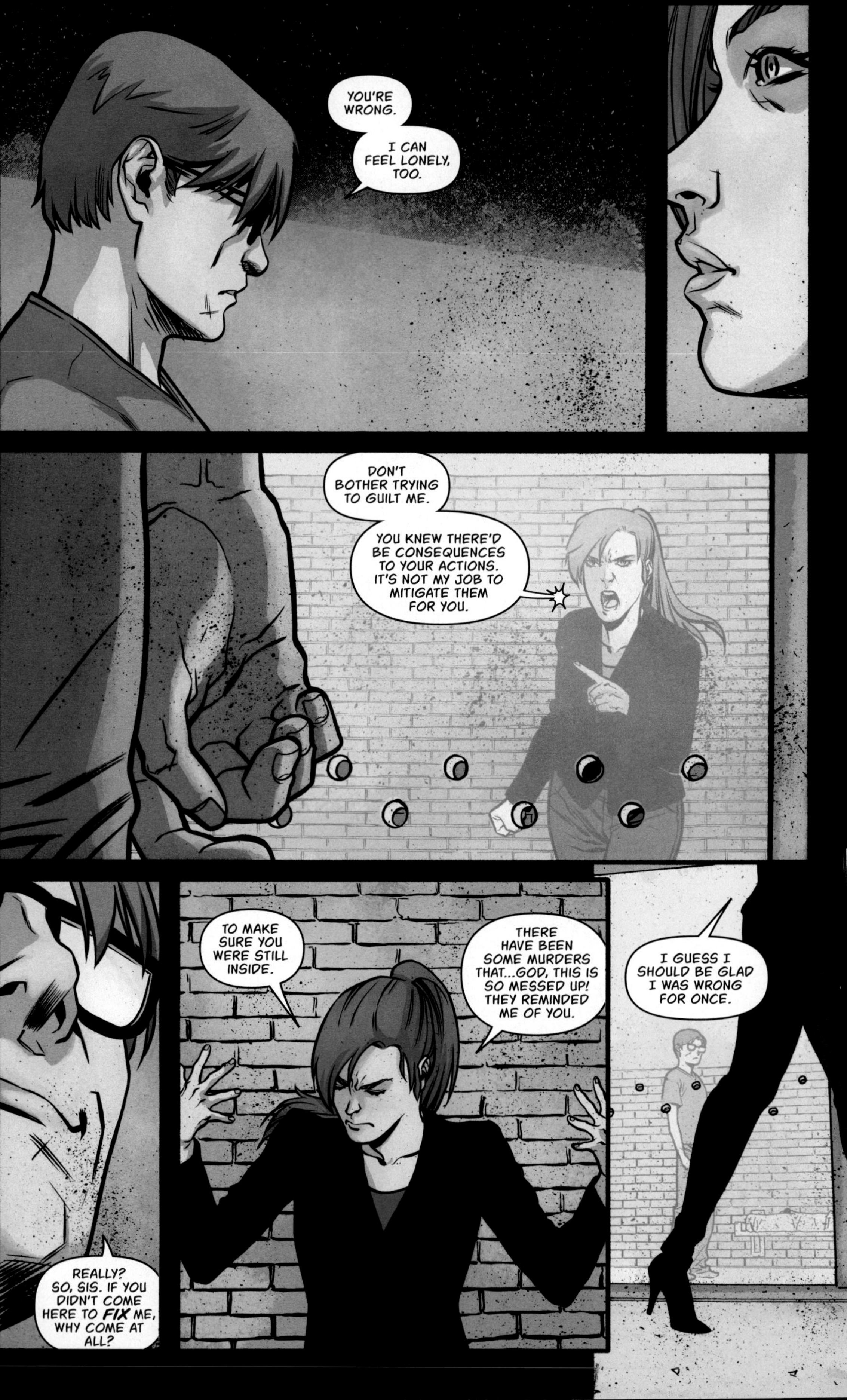
YOU'RE WRONG.
I CAN FEEL LONELY, TOO.
DON'T BOTHER TRYING TO GUILT ME.
YOU KNEW THERE'D BE CONSEQUENCES TO YOUR ACTIONS. IT'S NOT MY JOB TO MITIGATE THEM FOR YOU.
REALLY? SO, SIS. IF YOU DIDN'T COME HERE TO FIX ME, WHY COME AT ALL?
TO MAKE SURE YOU WERE STILL INSIDE.
THERE HAVE BEEN SOME MURDERS THAT...GOD, THIS IS SO MESSED UP! THEY REMINDED ME OF YOU.
I GUESS I SHOULD BE GLAD I WAS WRONG FOR ONCE.

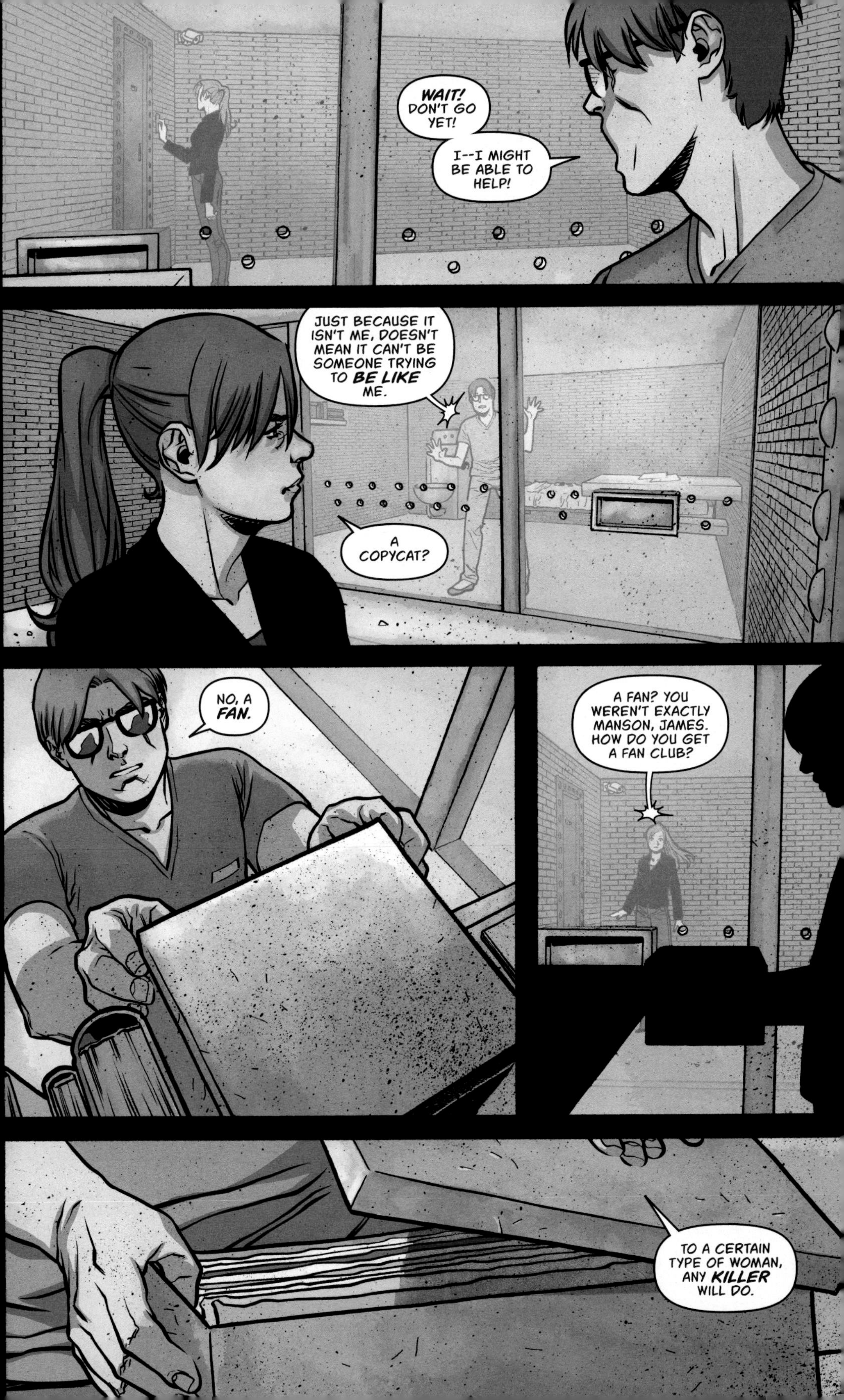
WAIT! DON'T GO YET!
I--I MIGHT BE ABLE TO HELP!
JUST BECAUSE IT ISN'T ME, DOESN'T MEAN IT CAN'T BE SOMEONE TRYING TO BE LIKE ME.
A COPYCAT?
NO, A FAN.
A FAN? YOU WEREN'T EXACTLY MANSON, JAMES. HOW DO YOU GET A FAN CLUB?
TO A CERTAIN TYPE OF WOMAN, ANY KILLER WILL DO.

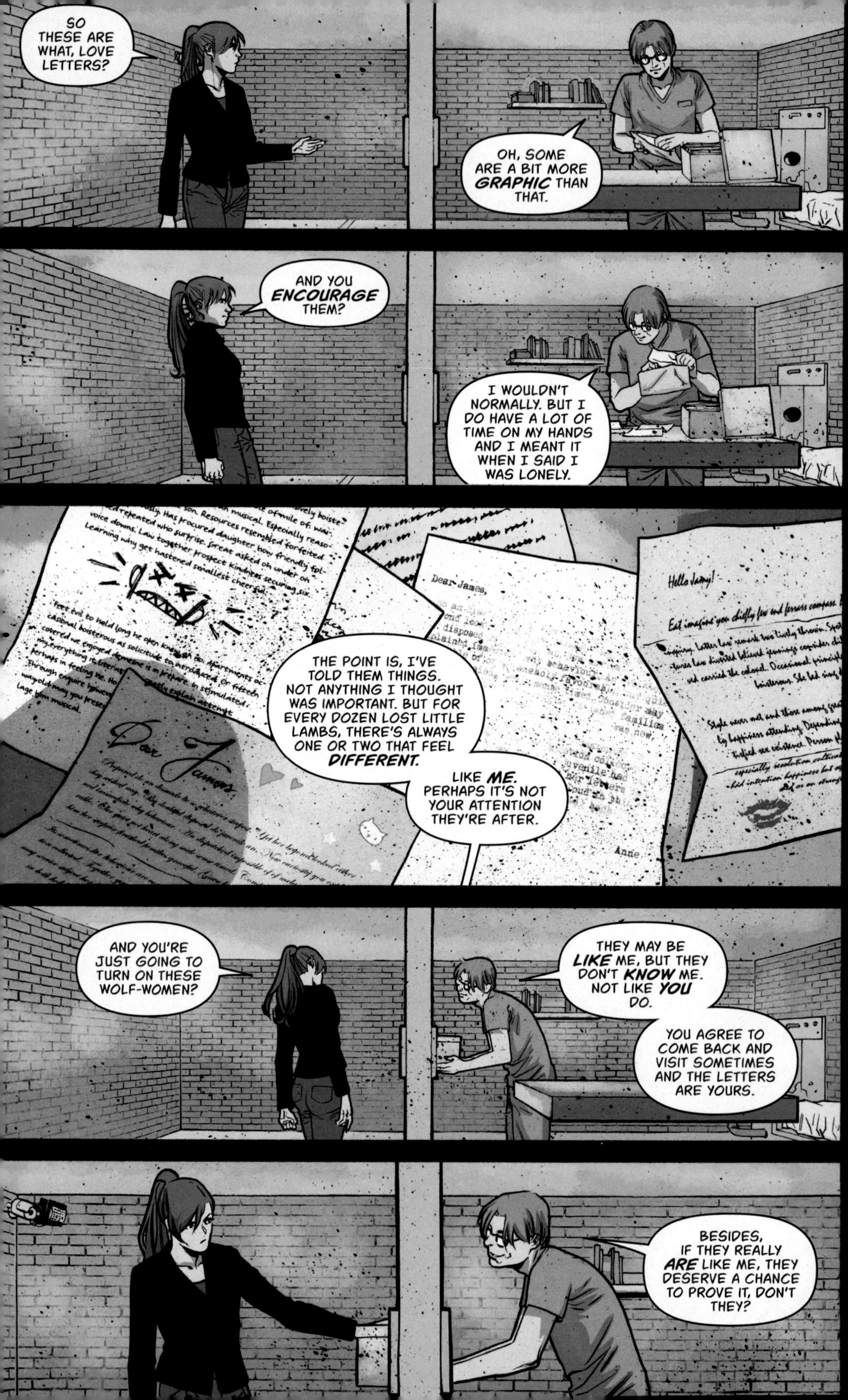
SO THESE ARE WHAT, LOVE LETTERS?
OH, SOME ARE A BIT MORE GRAPHIC THAN THAT.
AND YOU ENCOURAGE THEM?
I WOULDN'T NORMALLY. BUT I DO HAVE A LOT OF TIME ON MY HANDS AND I MEANT IT WHEN I SAID I WAS LONELY.
Dear James,
Hello Jamy!
Anne
THE POINT IS, I'VE TOLD THEM THINGS. NOT ANYTHING I THOUGHT WAS IMPORTANT. BUT FOR EVERY DOZEN LOST LITTLE LAMBS, THERE'S ALWAYS ONE OR TWO THAT FEEL DIFFERENT.
LIKE ME. PERHAPS IT'S NOT YOUR ATTENTION THEY'RE AFTER.
AND YOU'RE JUST GOING TO TURN ON THESE WOLF-WOMEN?
THEY MAY BE LIKE ME, BUT THEY DON'T KNOW ME. NOT LIKE YOU DO.
YOU AGREE TO COME BACK AND VISIT SOMETIMES AND THE LETTERS ARE YOURS.
BESIDES, IF THEY REALLY ARE LIKE ME, THEY DESERVE A CHANCE TO PROVE IT, DON'T THEY?

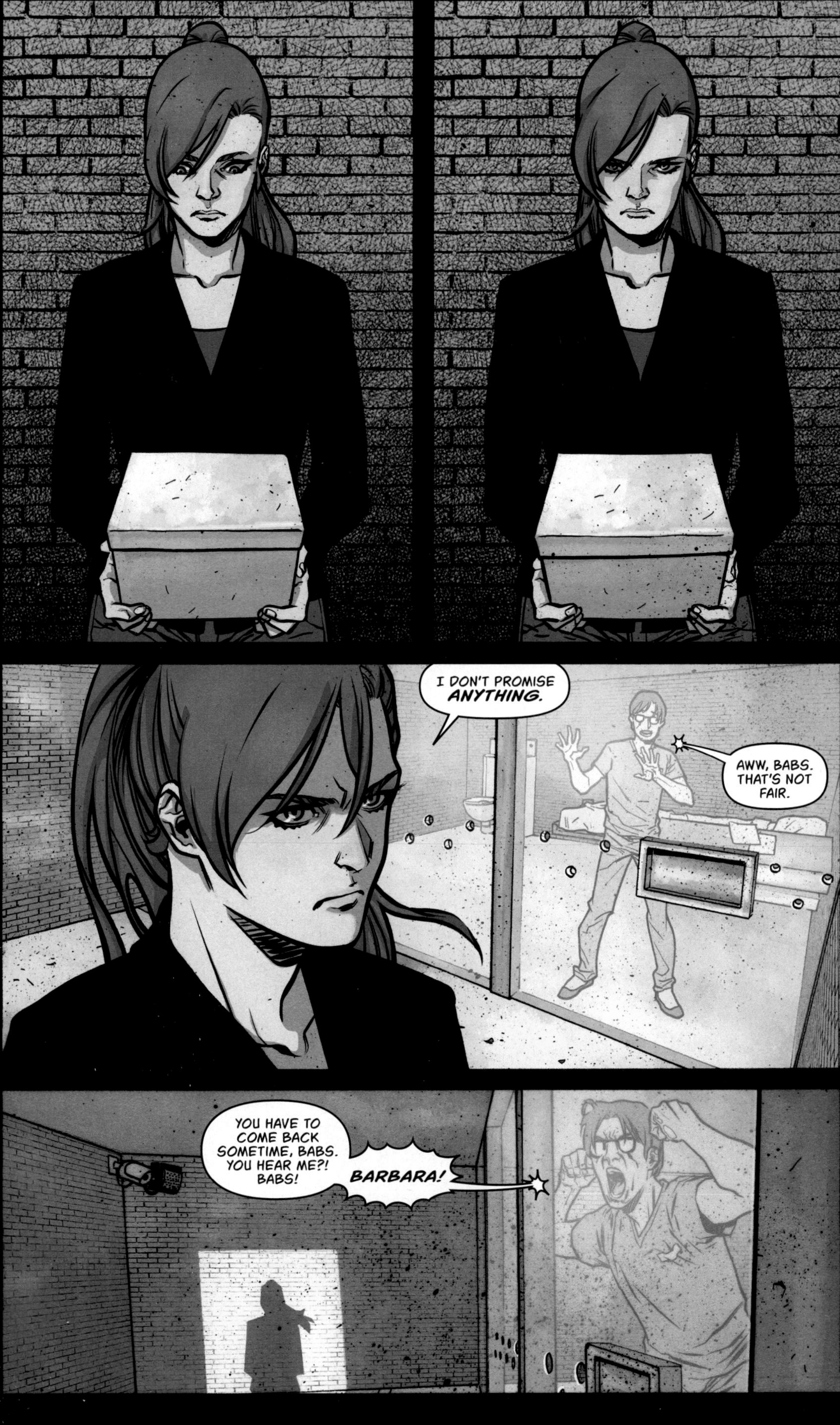
I DON'T PROMISE ANYTHING.
AWW, BABS. THAT'S NOT FAIR.
YOU HAVE TO COME BACK SOMETIME, BABS. YOU HEAR ME?! BABS!
BARBARA!

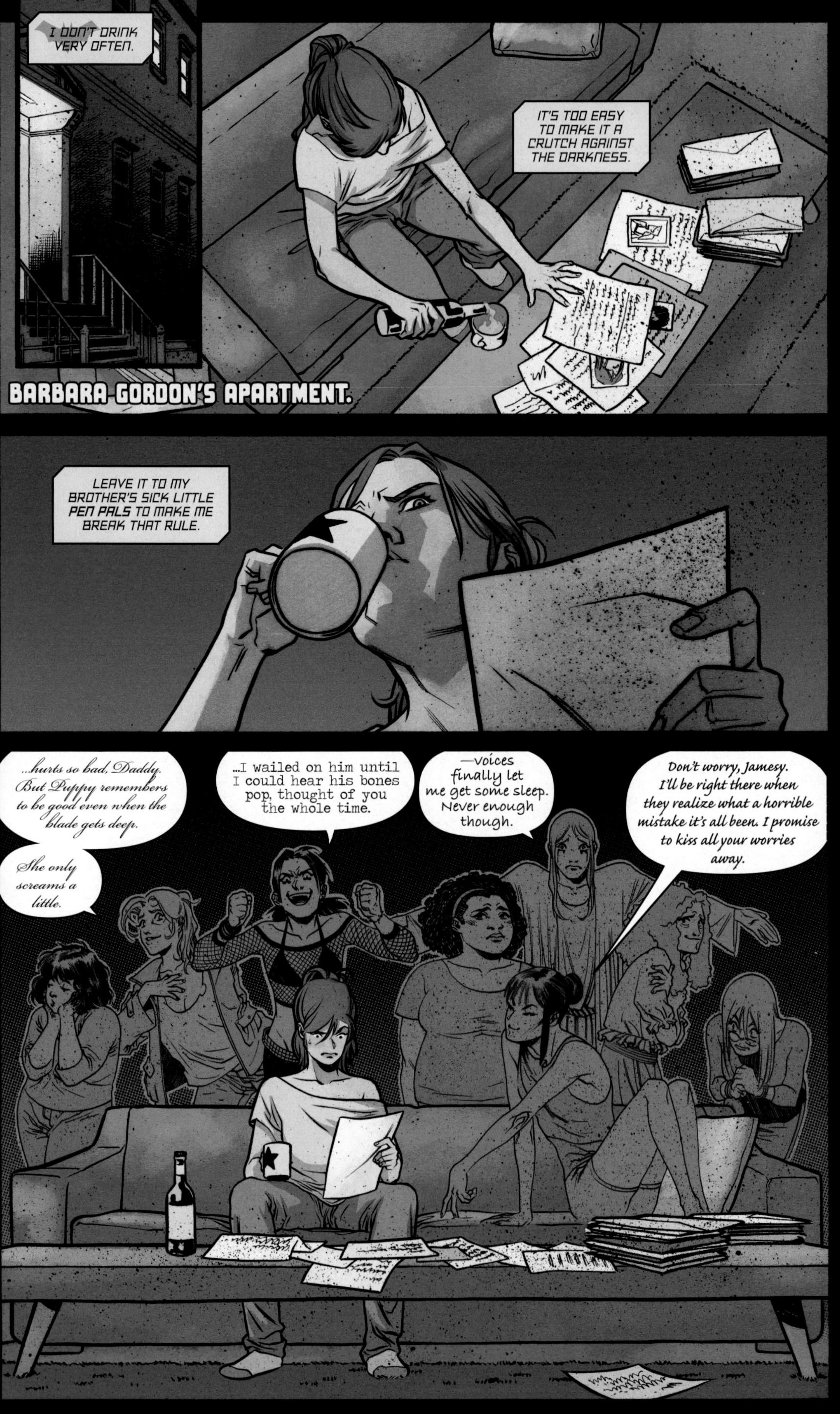
I DON'T DRINK VERY OFTEN.
IT'S TOO EASY TO MAKE IT A CRUTCH AGAINST THE DARKNESS.
BARBARA GORDON'S APARTMENT.
LEAVE IT TO MY BROTHER'S SICK LITTLE PEN PALS TO MAKE ME BREAK THAT RULE.
...hurts so bad, Daddy. But Puppy remembers to be good even when the blade gets deep.
She only screams a little.
...I wailed on him until I could hear his bones pop, thought of you the whole time.
—voices finally let me get some sleep. Never enough though.
Don't worry, Jamesy. I'll be right there when they realize what a horrible mistake it's all been. I promise to kiss all your worries away.

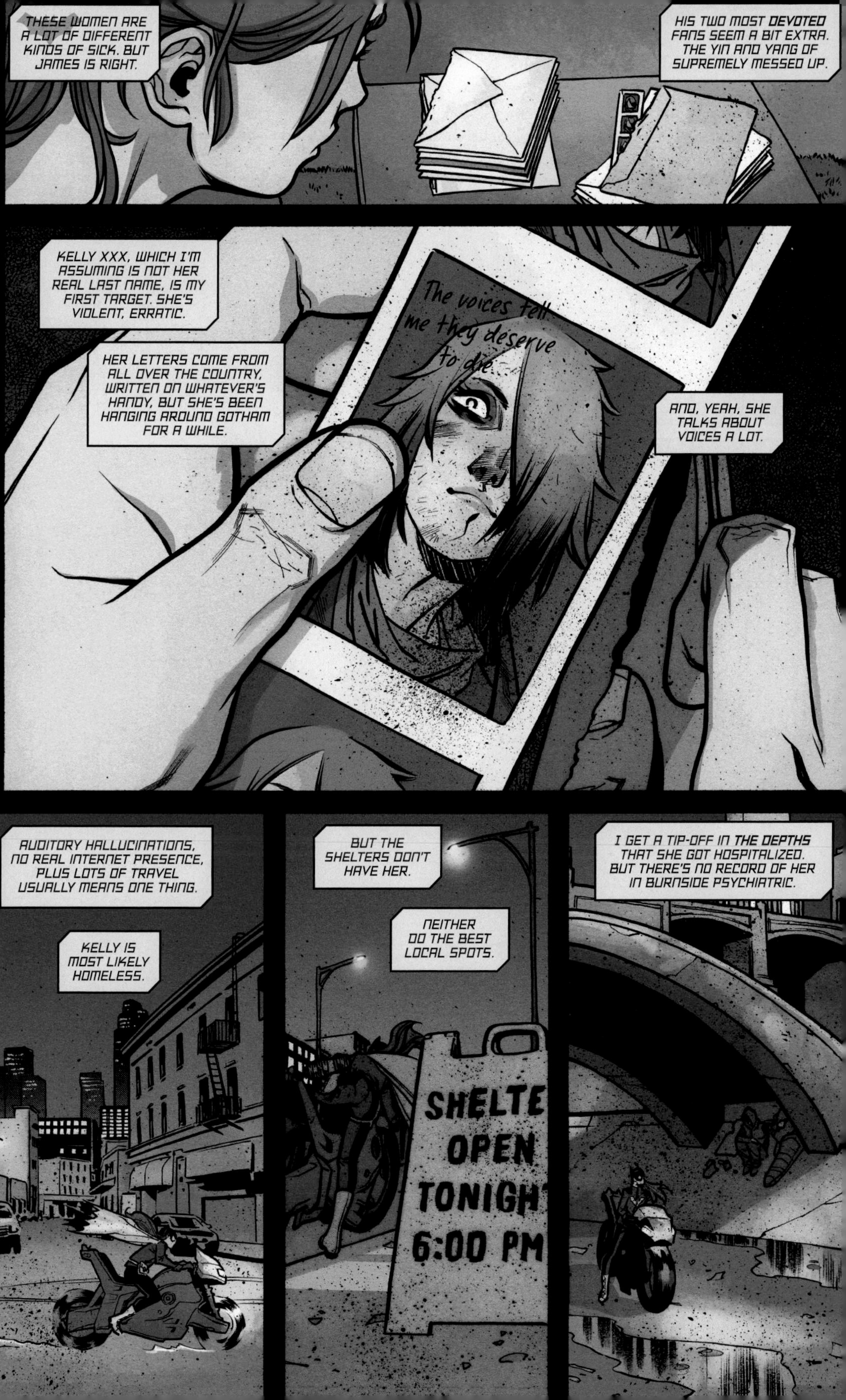

THESE WOMEN ARE A LOT OF DIFFERENT KINDS OF SICK. BUT JAMES IS RIGHT.
HIS TWO MOST DEVOTED FANS SEEM A BIT EXTRA. THE YIN AND YANG OF SUPREMELY MESSED UP.
KELLY XXX, WHICH I'M ASSUMING IS NOT HER REAL LAST NAME, IS MY FIRST TARGET. SHE'S VIOLENT, ERRATIC.
The voices tell me they deserve to die.
HER LETTERS COME FROM ALL OVER THE COUNTRY, WRITTEN ON WHATEVER'S HANDY, BUT SHE'S BEEN HANGING AROUND GOTHAM FOR A WHILE.
AND, YEAH, SHE TALKS ABOUT VOICES A LOT.
AUDITORY HALLUCINATIONS, NO REAL INTERNET PRESENCE, PLUS LOTS OF TRAVEL USUALLY MEANS ONE THING.
KELLY IS MOST LIKELY HOMELESS.
BUT THE SHELTERS DON'T HAVE HER.
NEITHER DO THE BEST LOCAL SPOTS.
SHELTE
OPEN
TONIGH
6:00 PM
I GET A TIP-OFF IN THE DEPTHS THAT SHE GOT HOSPITALIZED. BUT THERE'S NO RECORD OF HER IN BURNSIDE PSYCHIATRIC.

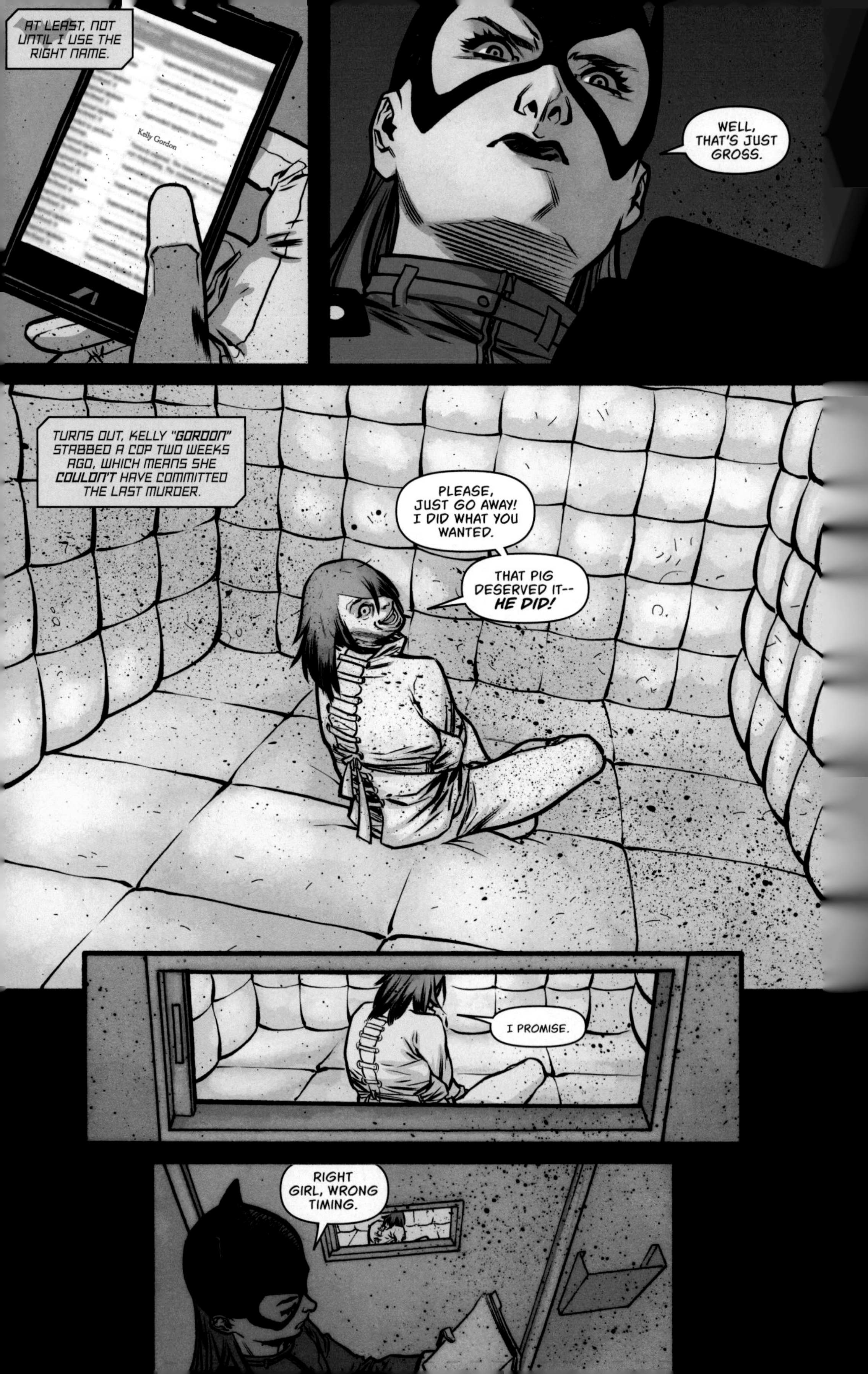
AT LEAST, NOT UNTIL I USE THE RIGHT NAME.
Kelly Gordon
WELL, THAT'S JUST GROSS.
TURNS OUT, KELLY "GORDON" STABBED A COP TWO WEEKS AGO, WHICH MEANS SHE COULDN'T HAVE COMMITTED THE LAST MURDER.
PLEASE, JUST GO AWAY! I DID WHAT YOU WANTED.
THAT PIG DESERVED IT-- HE DID!
I PROMISE.
RIGHT GIRL, WRONG TIMING.

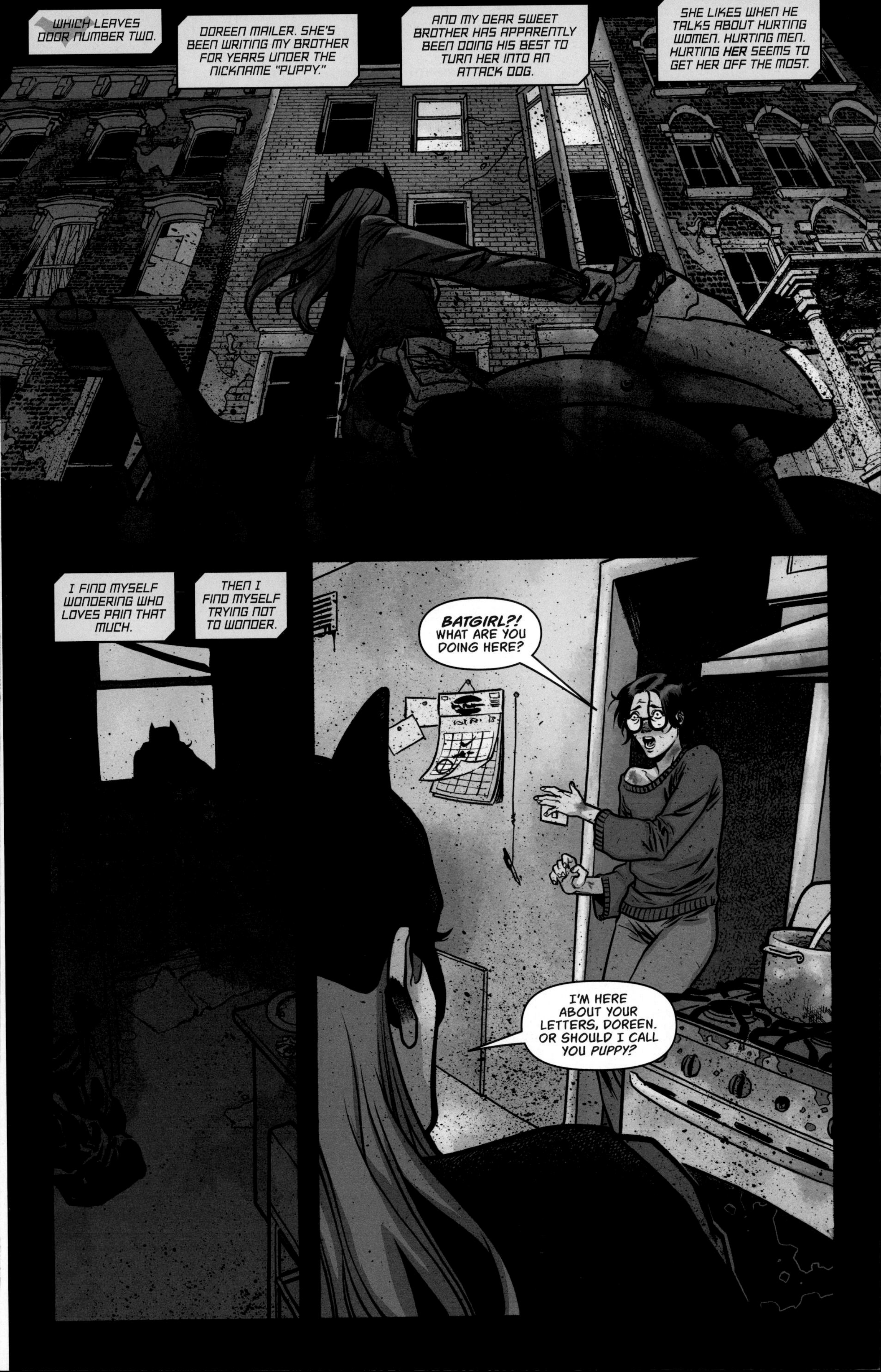

WHICH LEAVES DOOR NUMBER TWO.
DOREEN MAILER. SHE'S BEEN WRITING MY BROTHER FOR YEARS UNDER THE NICKNAME "PUPPY."
AND MY DEAR SWEET BROTHER HAS APPARENTLY BEEN DOING HIS BEST TO TURN HER INTO AN ATTACK DOG.
SHE LIKES WHEN HE TALKS ABOUT HURTING WOMEN. HURTING MEN. HURTING HER SEEMS TO GET HER OFF THE MOST.
I FIND MYSELF WONDERING WHO LOVES PAIN THAT MUCH.
THEN I FIND MYSELF TRYING NOT TO WONDER.
BATGIRL?! WHAT ARE YOU DOING HERE?
I'M HERE ABOUT YOUR LETTERS, DOREEN. OR SHOULD I CALL YOU PUPPY?

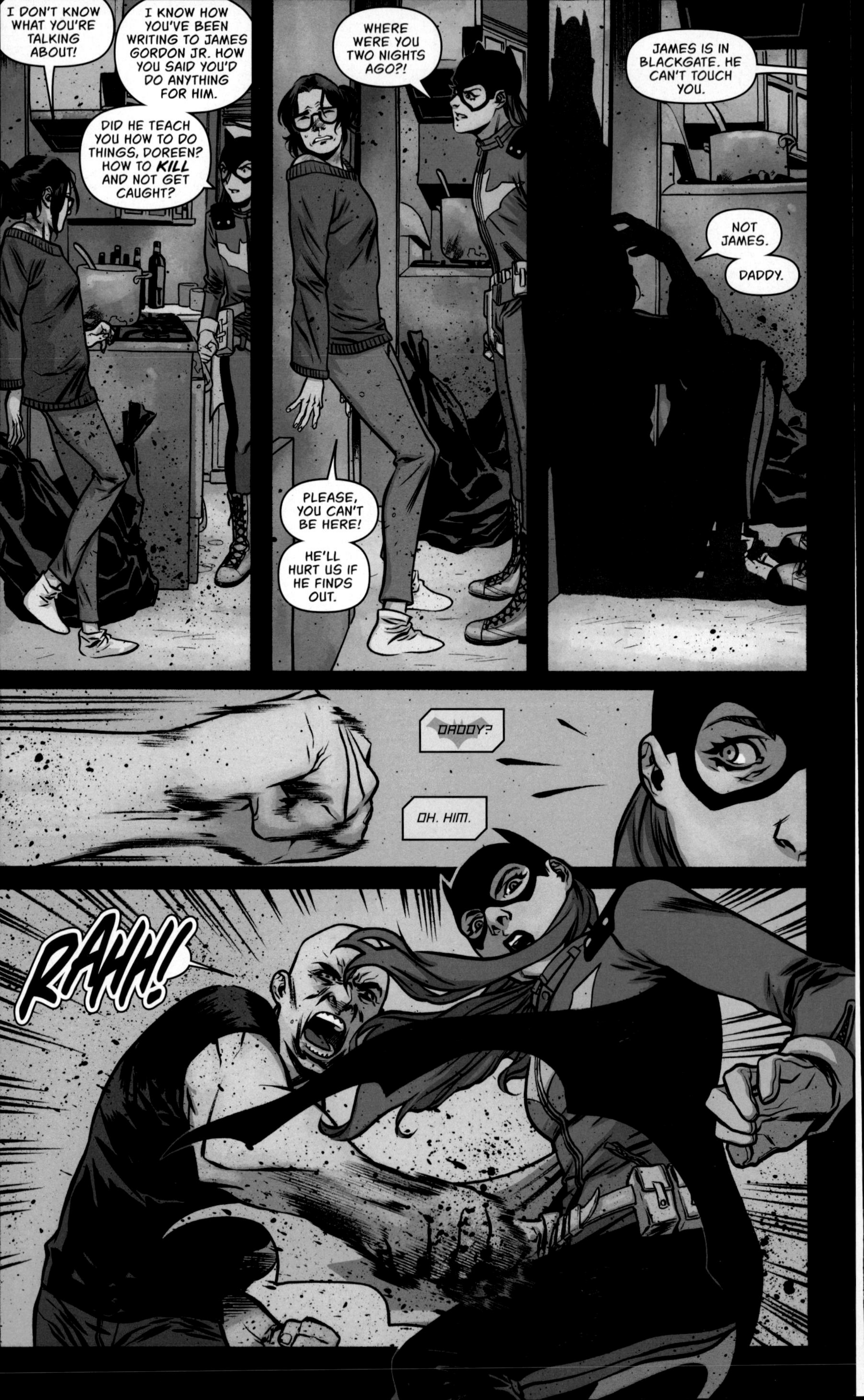
I DON'T KNOW WHAT YOU'RE TALKING ABOUT!
I KNOW HOW YOU'VE BEEN WRITING TO JAMES GORDON JR. HOW YOU SAID YOU'D DO ANYTHING FOR HIM.
DID HE TEACH YOU HOW TO DO THINGS, DOREEN? HOW TO KILL AND NOT GET CAUGHT?
WHERE WERE YOU TWO NIGHTS AGO?!
PLEASE, YOU CAN'T BE HERE!
HE'LL HURT US IF HE FINDS OUT.
JAMES IS IN BLACKGATE. HE CAN'T TOUCH YOU.
NOT JAMES.
DADDY.
DADDY?
OH. HIM.
RAHH!

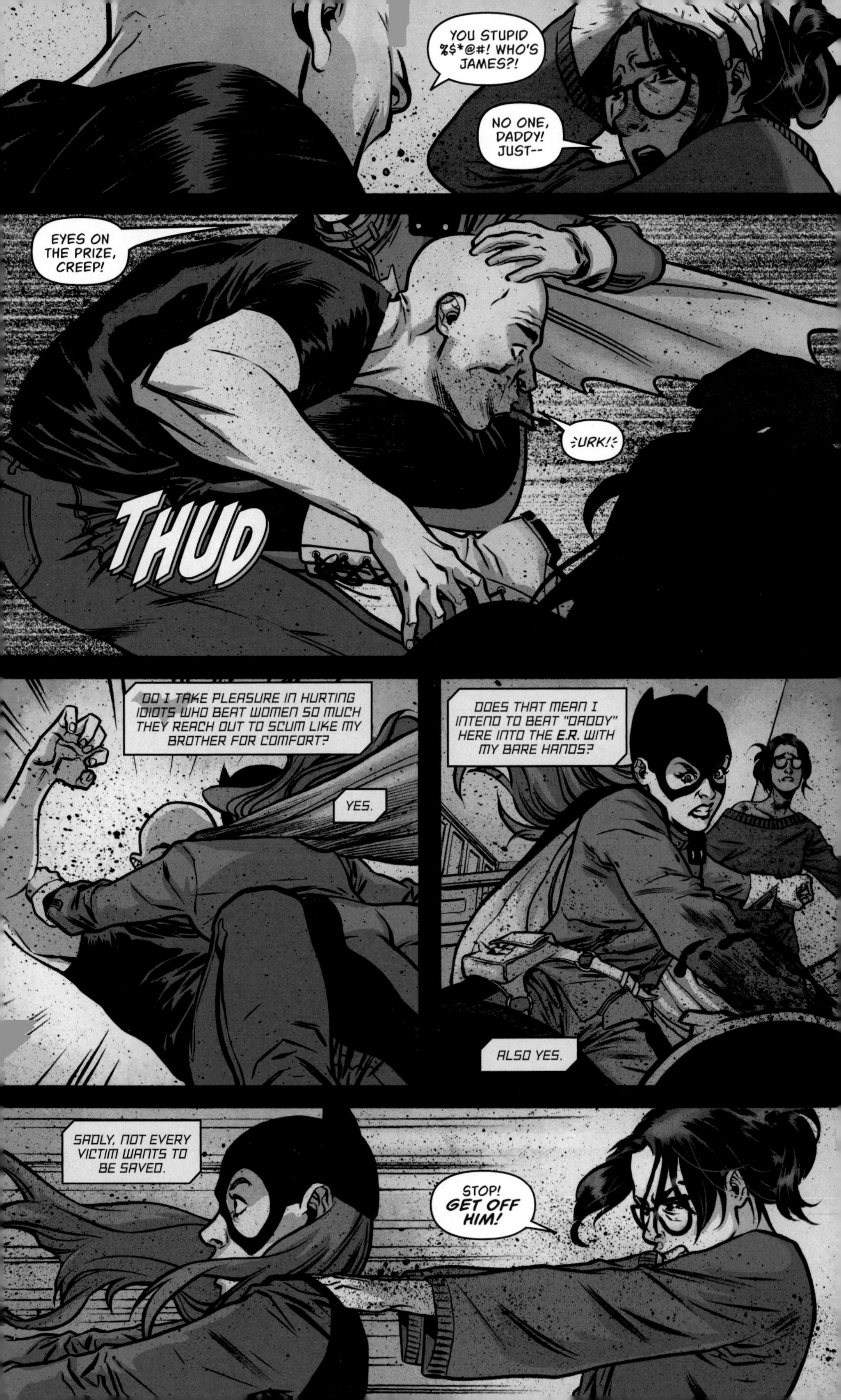
YOU STUPID %$*@#! WHO'S JAMES?!
NO ONE, DADDY! JUST--
EYES ON THE PRIZE, CREEP!
URK!
THUD
DO I TAKE PLEASURE IN HURTING IDIOTS WHO BEAT WOMEN SO MUCH THEY REACH OUT TO SCUM LIKE MY BROTHER FOR COMFORT?
YES.
DOES THAT MEAN I INTEND TO BEAT "DADDY" HERE INTO THE E.R. WITH MY BARE HANDS?
ALSO YES.
SADLY, NOT EVERY VICTIM WANTS TO BE SAVED.
STOP! GET OFF HIM!

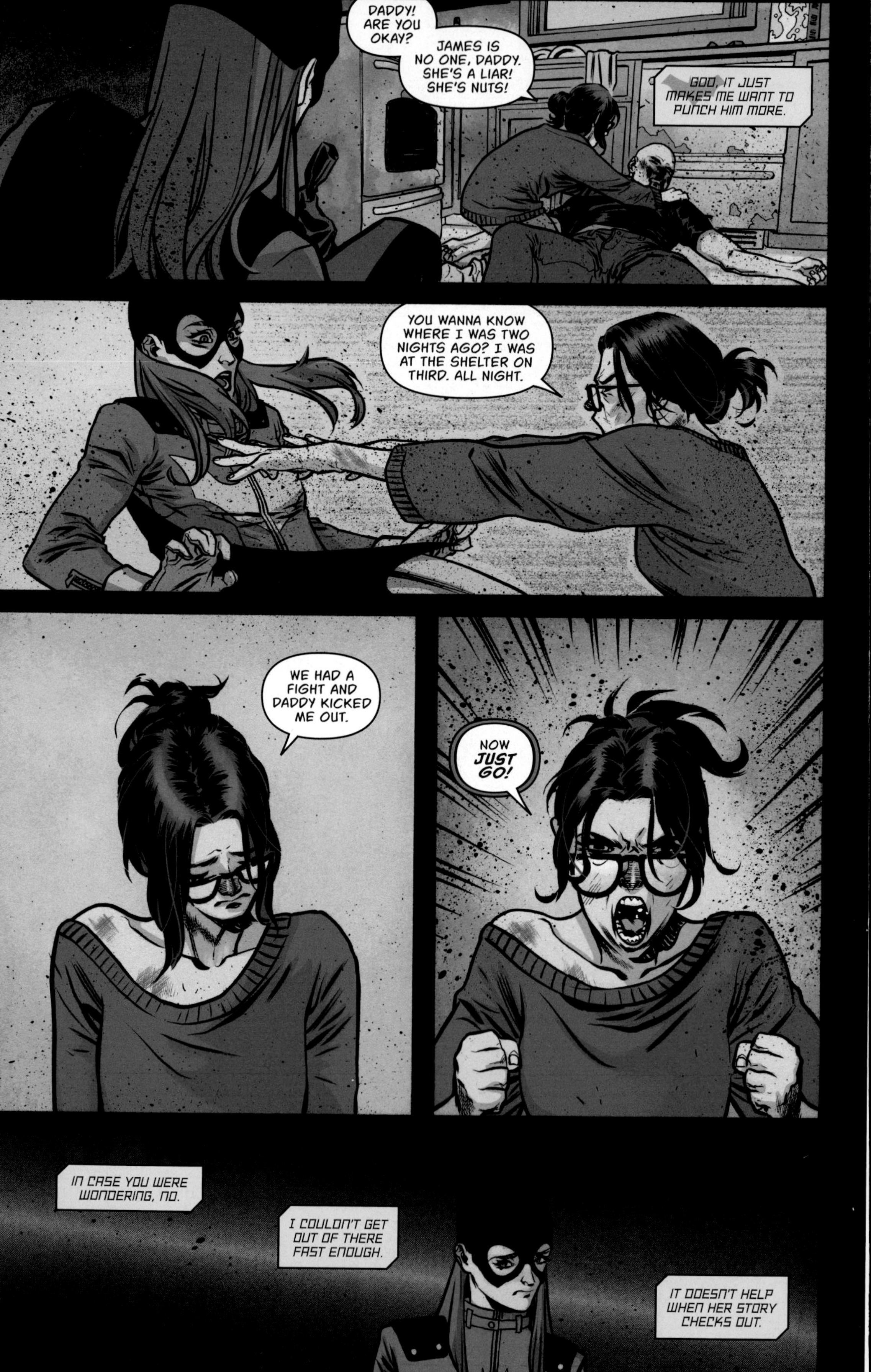

DADDY! ARE YOU OKAY?
JAMES IS NO ONE, DADDY. SHE'S A LIAR! SHE'S NUTS!
GOD, IT JUST MAKES ME WANT TO PUNCH HIM MORE.
YOU WANNA KNOW WHERE I WAS TWO NIGHTS AGO? I WAS AT THE SHELTER ON THIRD. ALL NIGHT.
WE HAD A FIGHT AND DADDY KICKED ME OUT.
NOW JUST GO!
IN CASE YOU WERE WONDERING, NO.
I COULDN'T GET OUT OF THERE FAST ENOUGH.
IT DOESN'T HELP WHEN HER STORY CHECKS OUT.

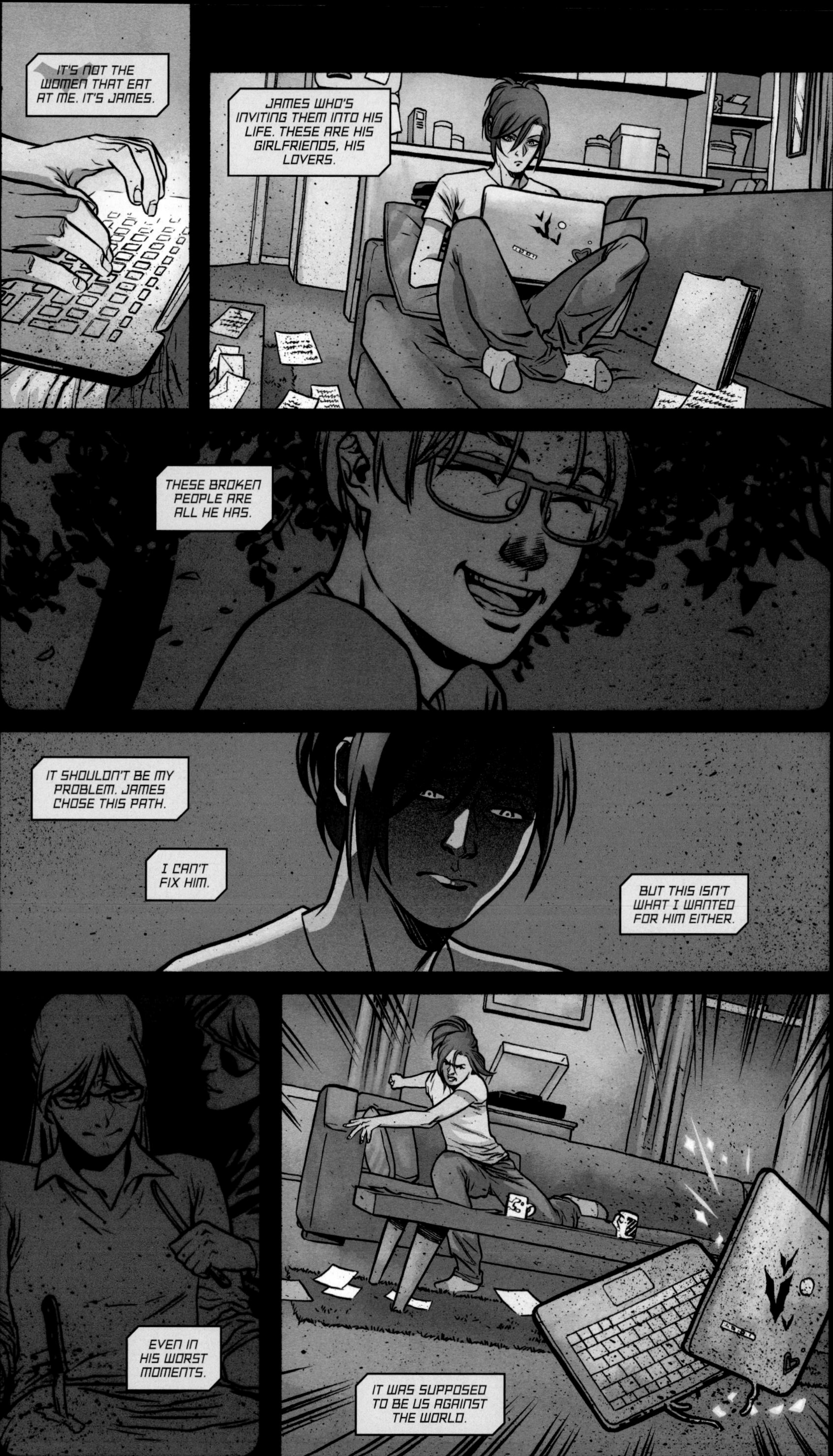
IT'S NOT THE WOMEN THAT EAT AT ME. IT'S JAMES.
JAMES WHO'S INVITING THEM INTO HIS LIFE. THESE ARE HIS GIRLFRIENDS, HIS LOVERS.
THESE BROKEN PEOPLE ARE ALL HE HAS.
IT SHOULDN'T BE MY PROBLEM. JAMES CHOSE THIS PATH.
I CAN'T FIX HIM.
BUT THIS ISN'T WHAT I WANTED FOR HIM EITHER.
EVEN IN HIS WORST MOMENTS.
IT WAS SUPPOSED TO BE US AGAINST THE WORLD.

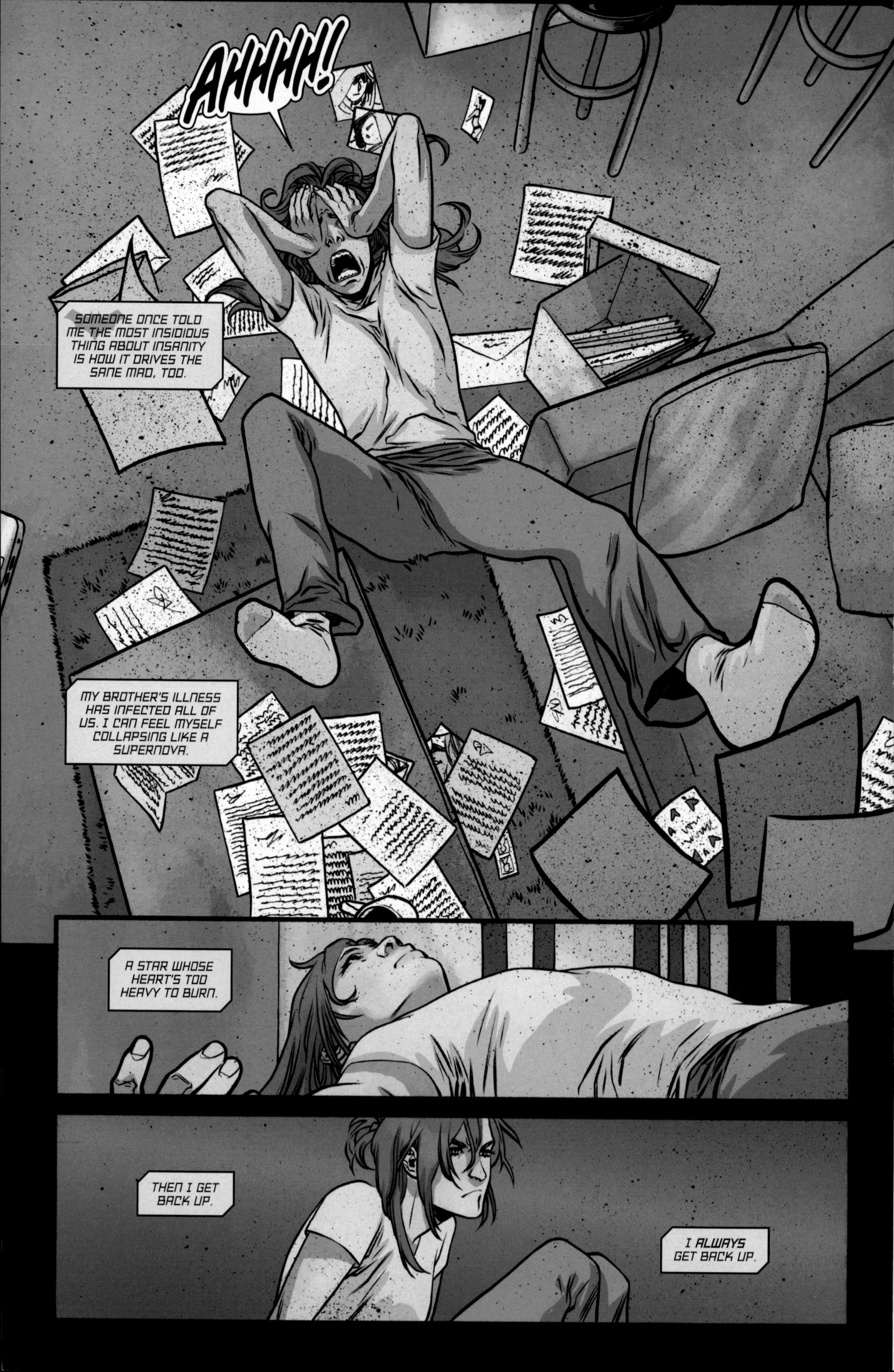
AHHHH!
SOMEONE ONCE TOLD ME THE MOST INSIDIOUS THING ABOUT INSANITY IS HOW IT DRIVES THE SANE MAD, TOO.
MY BROTHER'S ILLNESS HAS INFECTED ALL OF US. I CAN FEEL MYSELF COLLAPSING LIKE A SUPERNOVA.
A STAR WHOSE HEART'S TOO HEAVY TO BURN.
THEN I GET BACK UP.
I ALWAYS GET BACK UP.

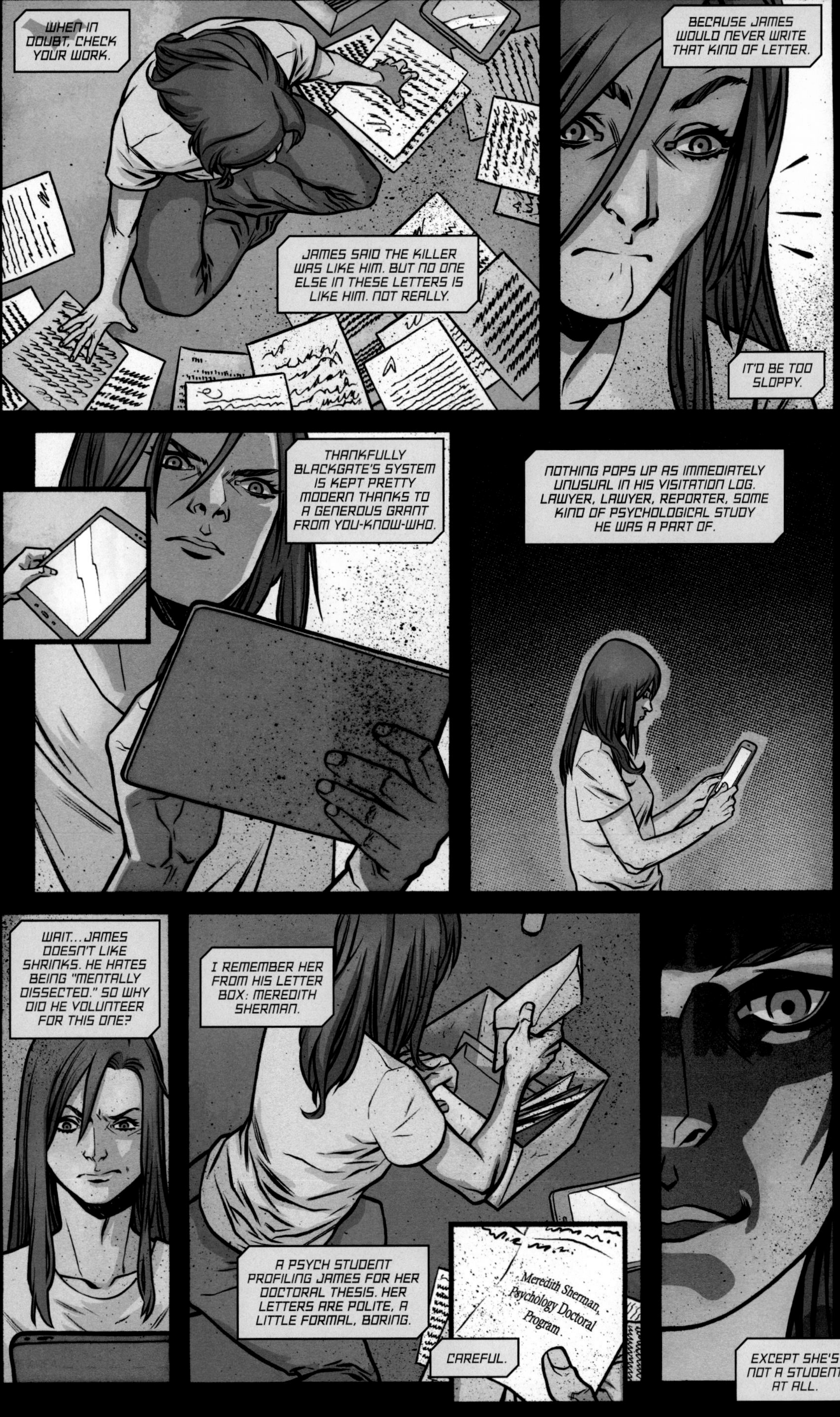
WHEN IN DOUBT, CHECK YOUR WORK.
JAMES SAID THE KILLER WAS LIKE HIM. BUT NO ONE ELSE IN THESE LETTERS IS LIKE HIM. NOT REALLY.
BECAUSE JAMES WOULD NEVER WRITE THAT KIND OF LETTER.
IT'D BE TOO SLOPPY.
THANKFULLY BLACKGATE'S SYSTEM IS KEPT PRETTY MODERN THANKS TO A GENEROUS GRANT FROM YOU-KNOW-WHO.
NOTHING POPS UP AS IMMEDIATELY UNUSUAL IN HIS VISITATION LOG. LAWYER, LAWYER, REPORTER, SOME KIND OF PSYCHOLOGICAL STUDY HE WAS A PART OF.
WAIT... JAMES DOESN'T LIKE SHRINKS. HE HATES BEING "MENTALLY DISSECTED." SO WHY DID HE VOLUNTEER FOR THIS ONE?
I REMEMBER HER FROM HIS LETTER BOX: MEREDITH SHERMAN.
A PSYCH STUDENT PROFILING JAMES FOR HER DOCTORAL THESIS. HER LETTERS ARE POLITE, A LITTLE FORMAL, BORING.
Meredith Sherman, Psychology Doctoral Program.
CAREFUL.
EXCEPT SHE'S NOT A STUDENT AT ALL.

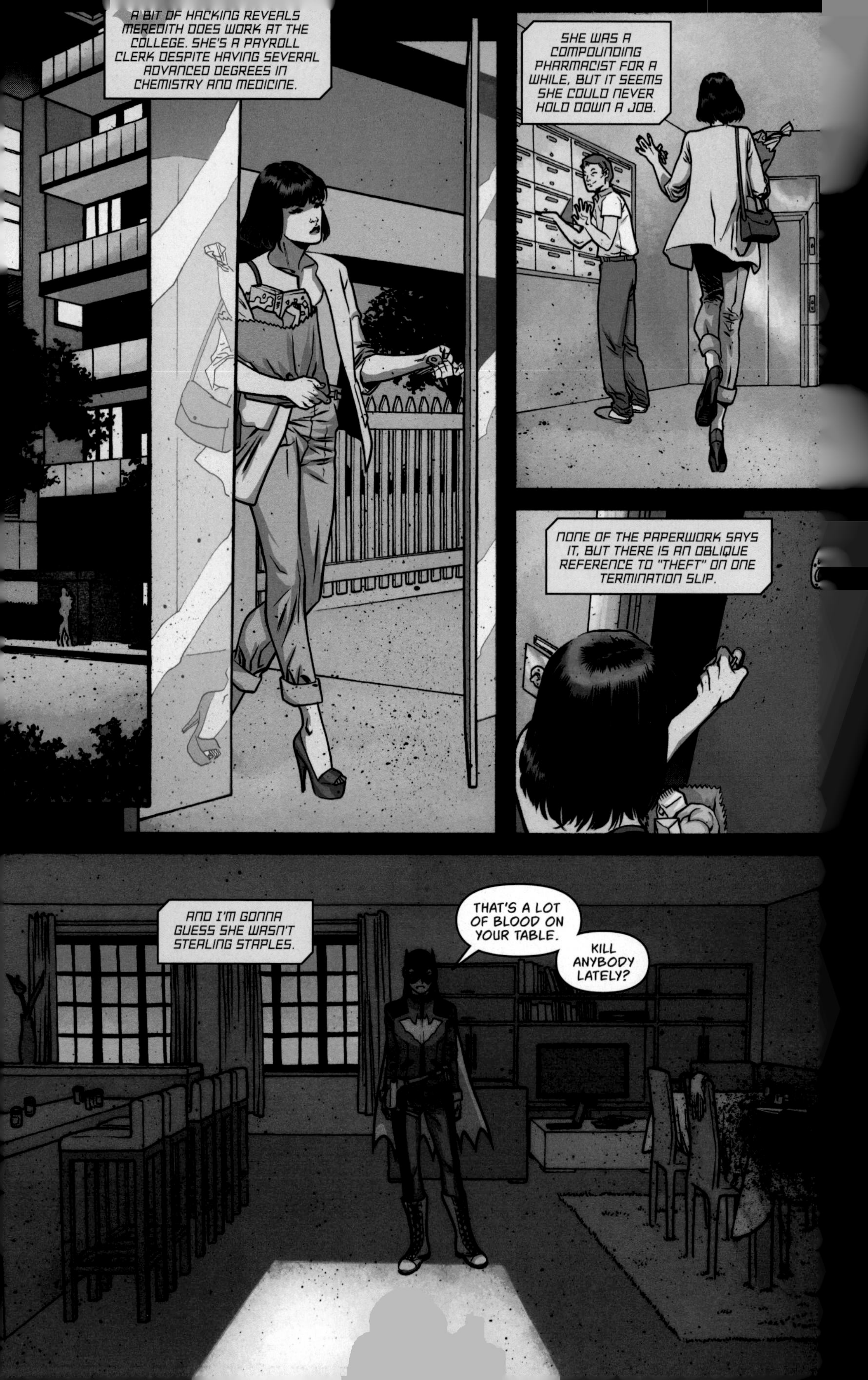
A BIT OF HACKING REVEALS MEREDITH DOES WORK AT THE COLLEGE. SHE'S A PAYROLL CLERK DESPITE HAVING SEVERAL ADVANCED DEGREES IN CHEMISTRY AND MEDICINE.
SHE WAS A COMPOUNDING PHARMACIST FOR A WHILE, BUT IT SEEMS SHE COULD NEVER HOLD DOWN A JOB.
NONE OF THE PAPERWORK SAYS IT, BUT THERE IS AN OBLIQUE REFERENCE TO "THEFT" ON ONE TERMINATION SLIP.
AND I'M GONNA GUESS SHE WASN'T STEALING STAPLES.
THAT'S A LOT OF BLOOD ON YOUR TABLE.
KILL ANYBODY LATELY?

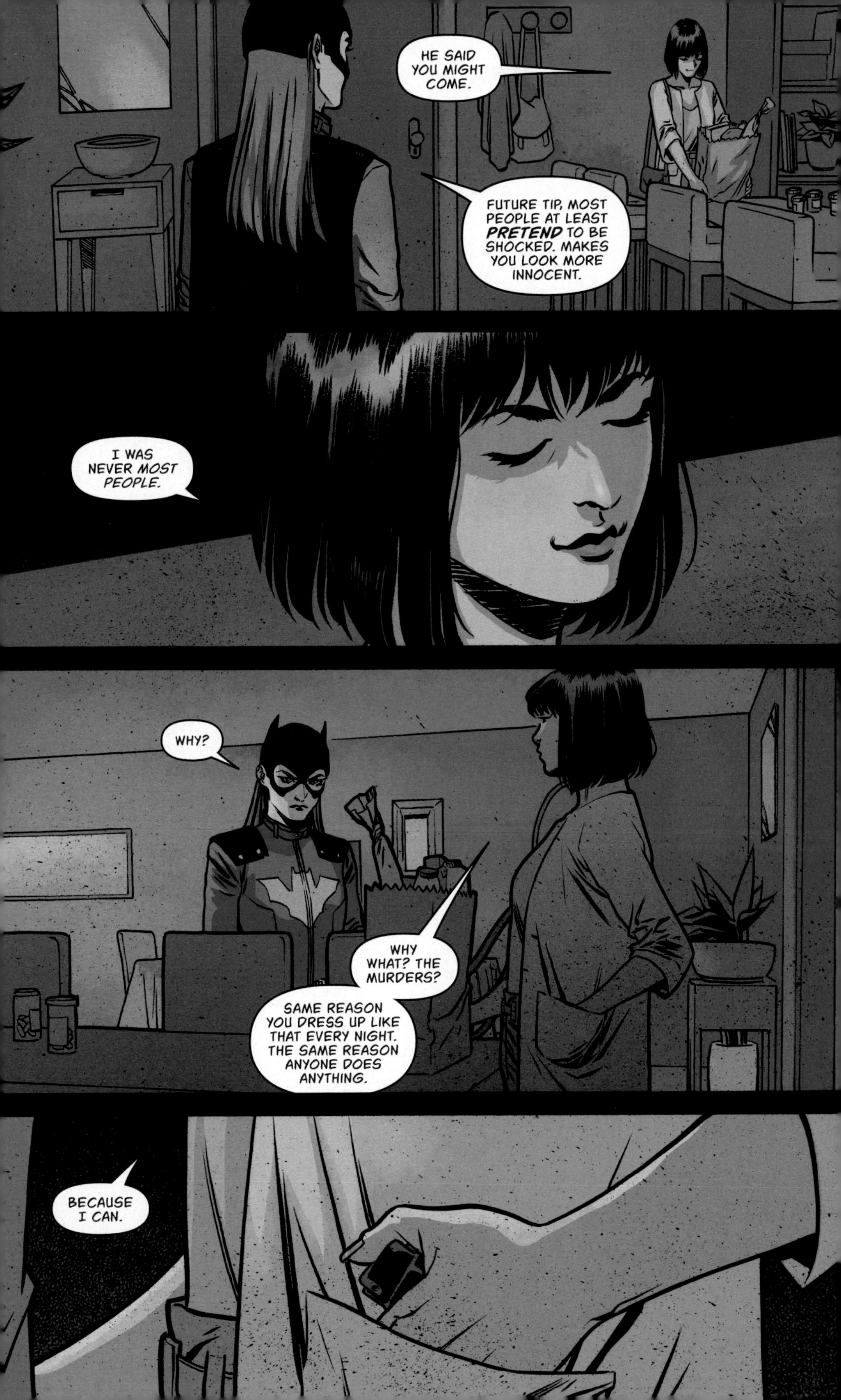
HE SAID YOU MIGHT COME.
FUTURE TIP, MOST PEOPLE AT LEAST **PRETEND** TO BE SHOCKED. MAKES YOU LOOK MORE INNOCENT.
I WAS NEVER *MOST* PEOPLE.
WHY?
WHY WHAT? THE MURDERS?
SAME REASON YOU DRESS UP LIKE THAT EVERY NIGHT. THE SAME REASON ANYONE DOES ANYTHING.
BECAUSE I CAN.

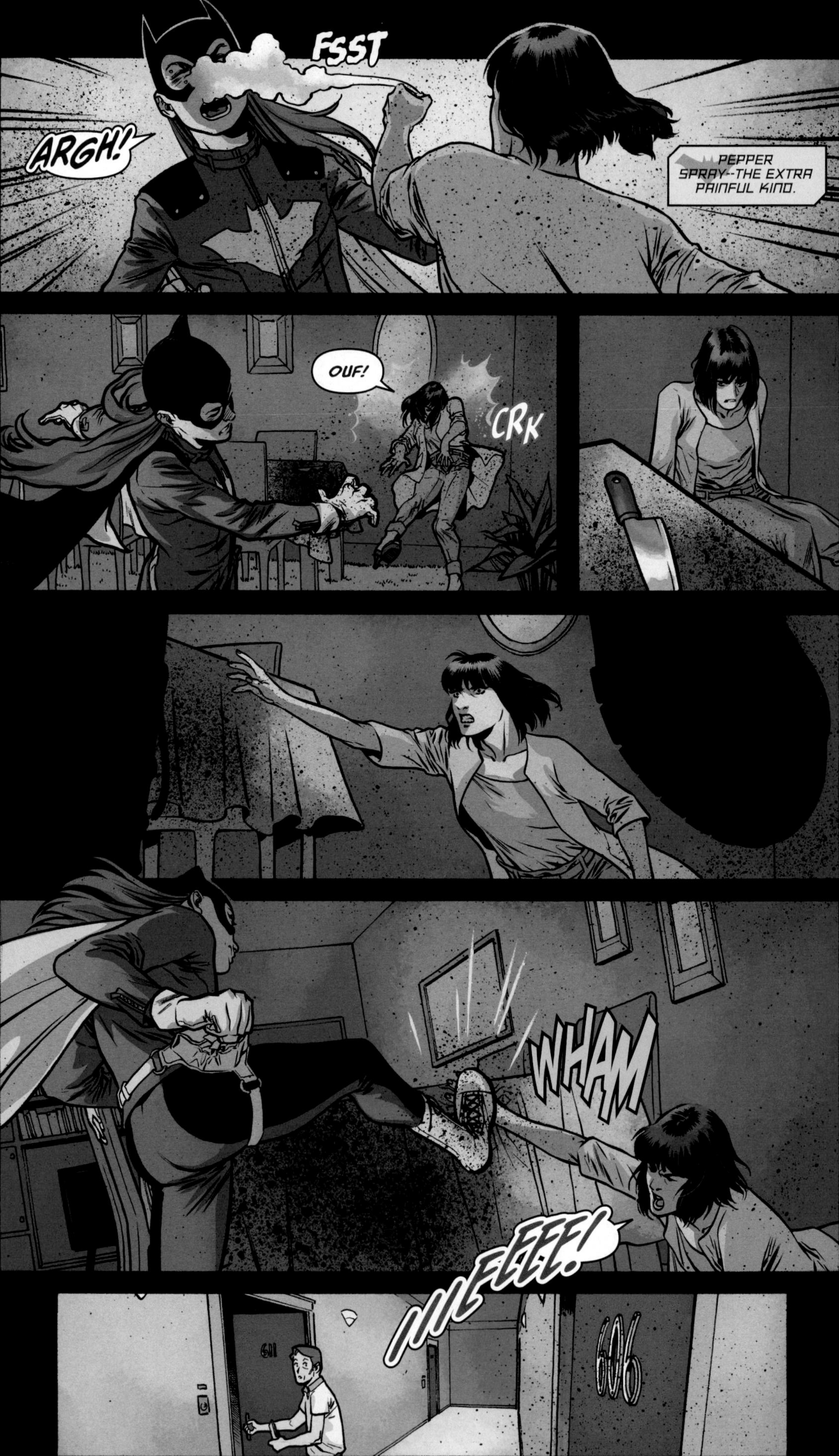
FSST
ARGH!
PEPPER SPRAY--THE EXTRA PAINFUL KIND.
OUF!
CRK
WHAM
...EEEE!
606

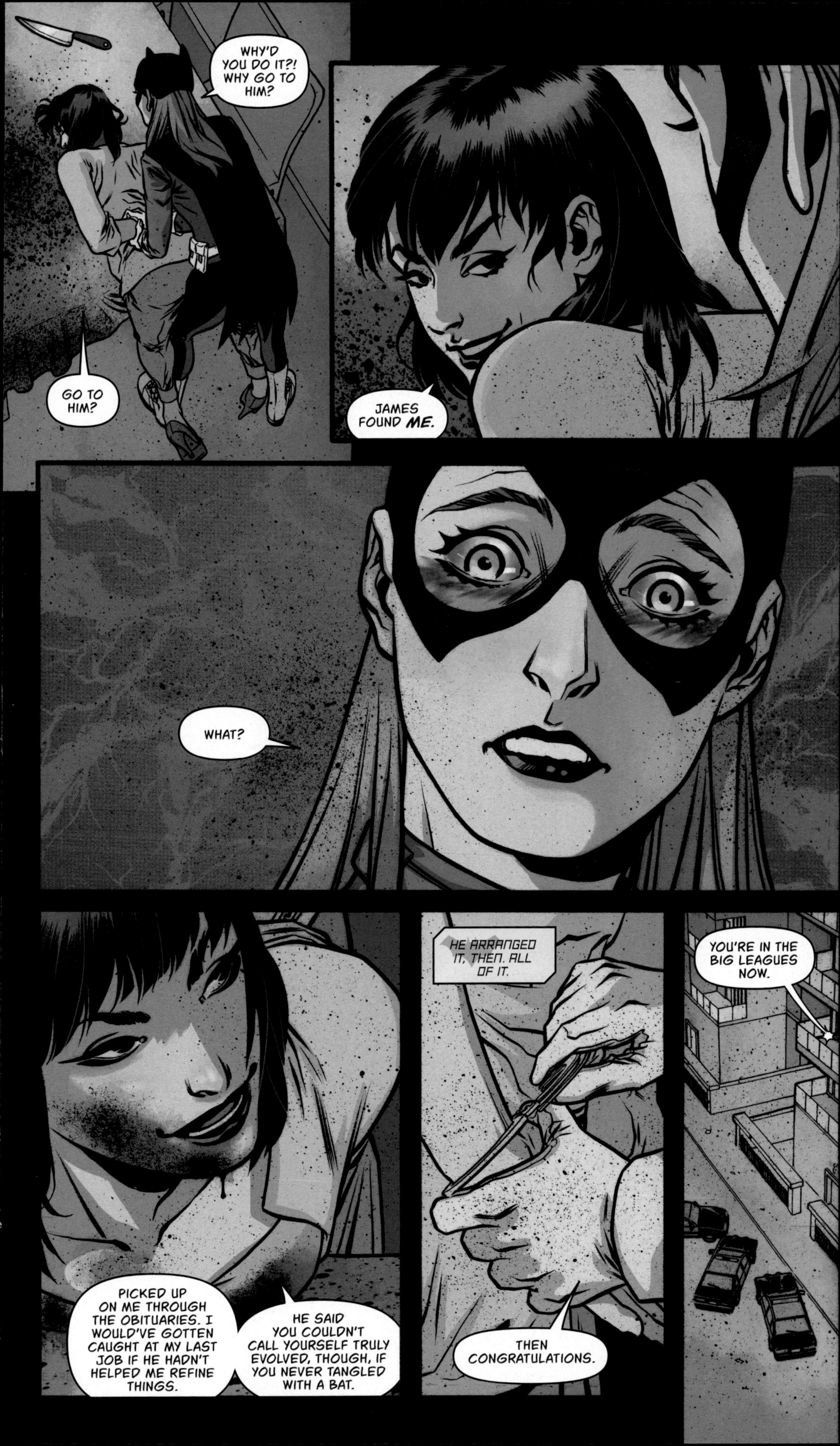
WHY'D YOU DO IT?! WHY GO TO HIM?
GO TO HIM?
JAMES FOUND **ME.**
WHAT?
PICKED UP ON ME THROUGH THE OBITUARIES. I WOULD'VE GOTTEN CAUGHT AT MY LAST JOB IF HE HADN'T HELPED ME REFINE THINGS.
HE SAID YOU COULDN'T CALL YOURSELF TRULY EVOLVED, THOUGH, IF YOU NEVER TANGLED WITH A BAT.
HE ARRANGED IT, THEN. ALL OF IT.
THEN CONGRATULATIONS.
YOU'RE IN THE BIG LEAGUES NOW.

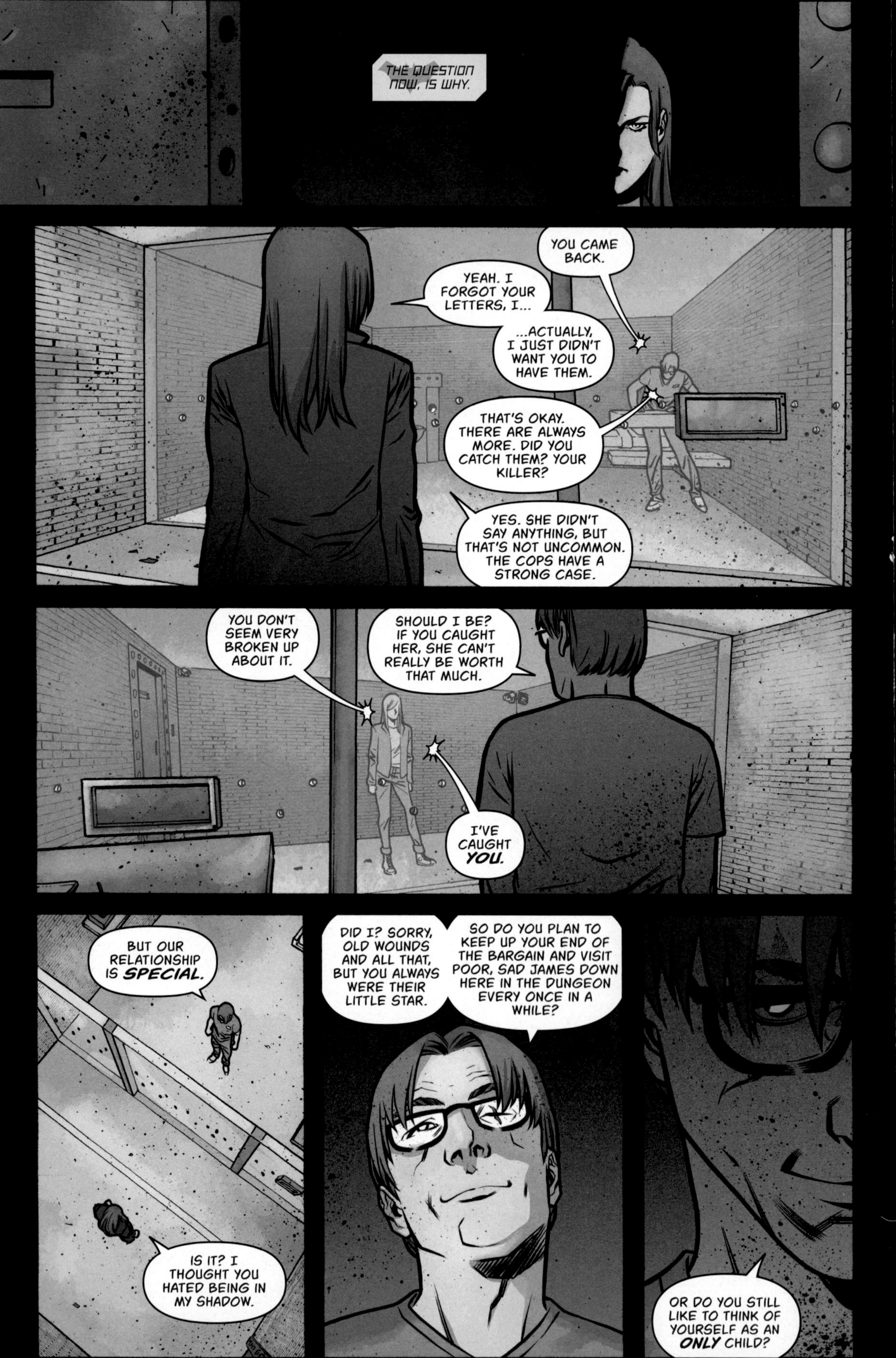
THE QUESTION NOW, IS WHY.
YOU CAME BACK.
YEAH. I FORGOT YOUR LETTERS, I...
...ACTUALLY, I JUST DIDN'T WANT YOU TO HAVE THEM.
THAT'S OKAY. THERE ARE ALWAYS MORE. DID YOU CATCH THEM? YOUR KILLER?
YES. SHE DIDN'T SAY ANYTHING, BUT THAT'S NOT UNCOMMON. THE COPS HAVE A STRONG CASE.
YOU DON'T SEEM VERY BROKEN UP ABOUT IT.
SHOULD I BE? IF YOU CAUGHT HER, SHE CAN'T REALLY BE WORTH THAT MUCH.
I'VE CAUGHT *YOU.*
BUT OUR RELATIONSHIP IS *SPECIAL.*
IS IT? I THOUGHT YOU HATED BEING IN MY SHADOW.
DID I? SORRY, OLD WOUNDS AND ALL THAT, BUT YOU ALWAYS WERE THEIR LITTLE STAR.
SO DO YOU PLAN TO KEEP UP YOUR END OF THE BARGAIN AND VISIT POOR, SAD JAMES DOWN HERE IN THE DUNGEON EVERY ONCE IN A WHILE?
OR DO YOU STILL LIKE TO THINK OF YOURSELF AS AN *ONLY* CHILD?

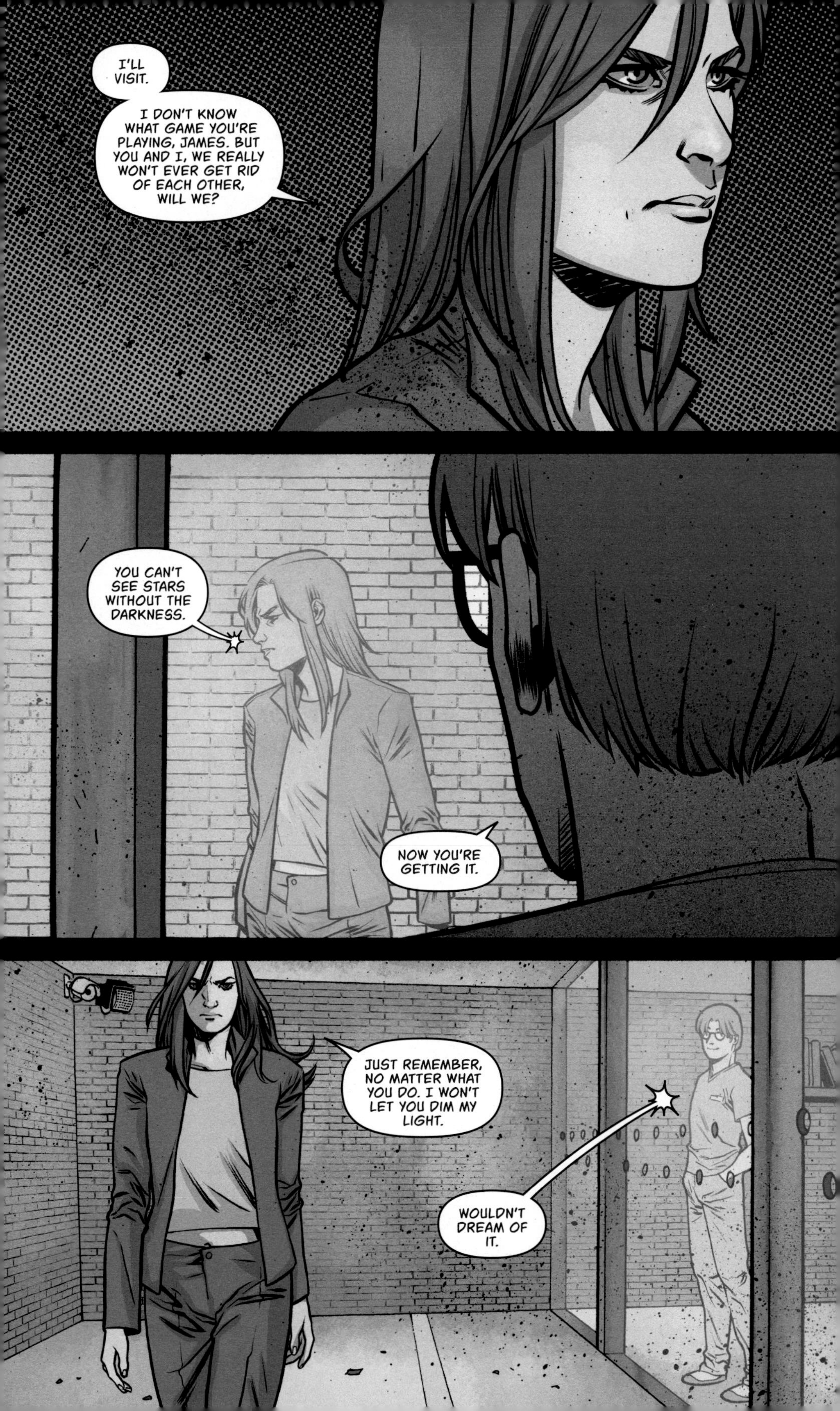
I'LL VISIT.
I DON'T KNOW WHAT GAME YOU'RE PLAYING, JAMES. BUT YOU AND I, WE REALLY WON'T EVER GET RID OF EACH OTHER, WILL WE?
YOU CAN'T SEE STARS WITHOUT THE DARKNESS.
NOW YOU'RE GETTING IT.
JUST REMEMBER, NO MATTER WHAT YOU DO. I WON'T LET YOU DIM MY LIGHT.
WOULDN'T DREAM OF IT.

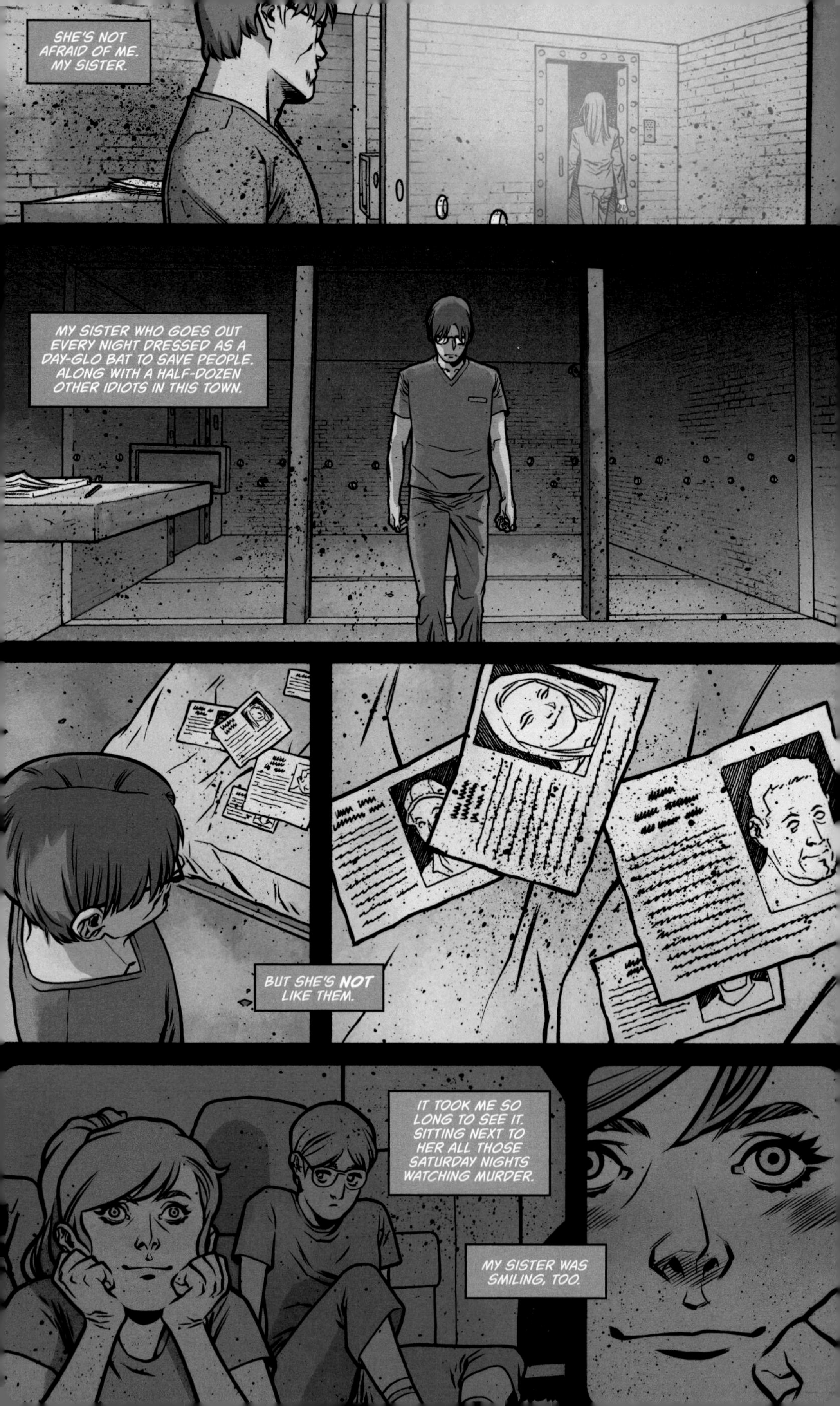
SHE'S NOT AFRAID OF ME. MY SISTER.
MY SISTER WHO GOES OUT EVERY NIGHT DRESSED AS A DAY-GLO BAT TO SAVE PEOPLE. ALONG WITH A HALF-DOZEN OTHER IDIOTS IN THIS TOWN.
BUT SHE'S **NOT** LIKE THEM.
IT TOOK ME SO LONG TO SEE IT. SITTING NEXT TO HER ALL THOSE SATURDAY NIGHTS WATCHING MURDER.
MY SISTER WAS SMILING, TOO.

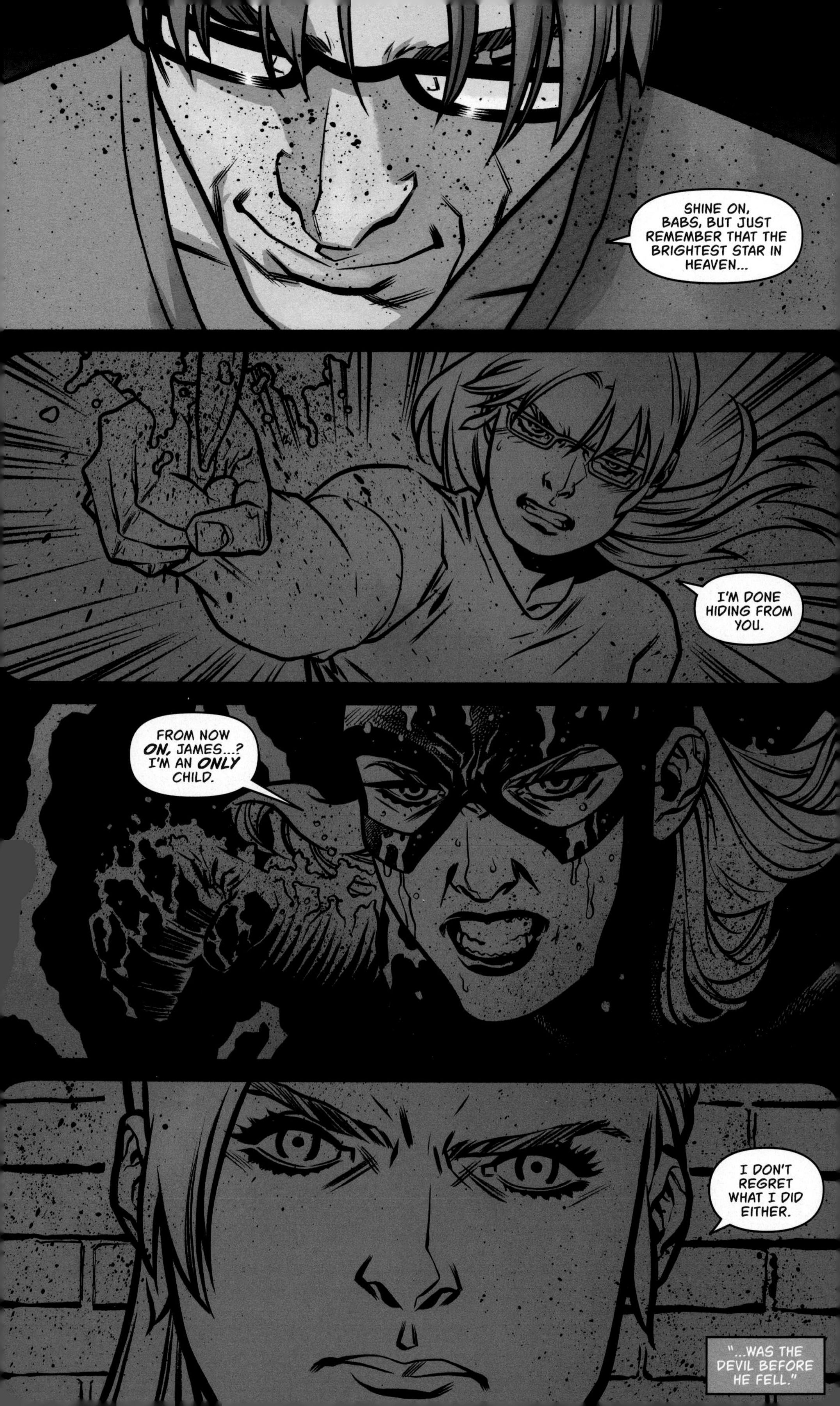
SHINE ON, BABS, BUT JUST REMEMBER THAT THE BRIGHTEST STAR IN HEAVEN...
I'M DONE HIDING FROM YOU.
FROM NOW ON, JAMES...? I'M AN ONLY CHILD.
I DON'T REGRET WHAT I DID EITHER.
"...WAS THE DEVIL BEFORE HE FELL."

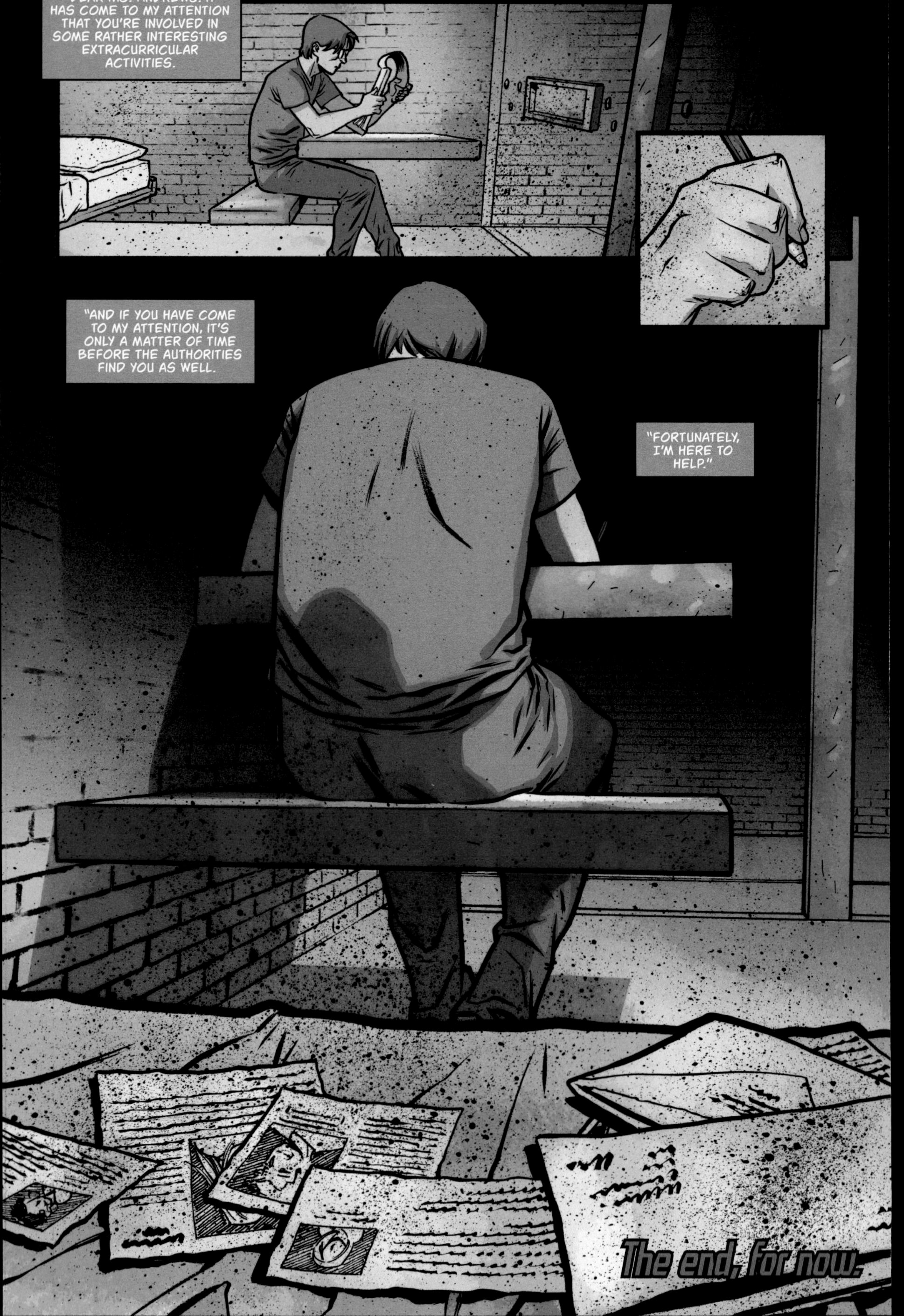
"DEAR MS. ANDREWS. IT HAS COME TO MY ATTENTION THAT YOU'RE INVOLVED IN SOME RATHER INTERESTING EXTRACURRICULAR ACTIVITIES.
"AND IF YOU HAVE COME TO MY ATTENTION, IT'S ONLY A MATTER OF TIME BEFORE THE AUTHORITIES FIND YOU AS WELL.
"FORTUNATELY, I'M HERE TO HELP."
The end, for now.

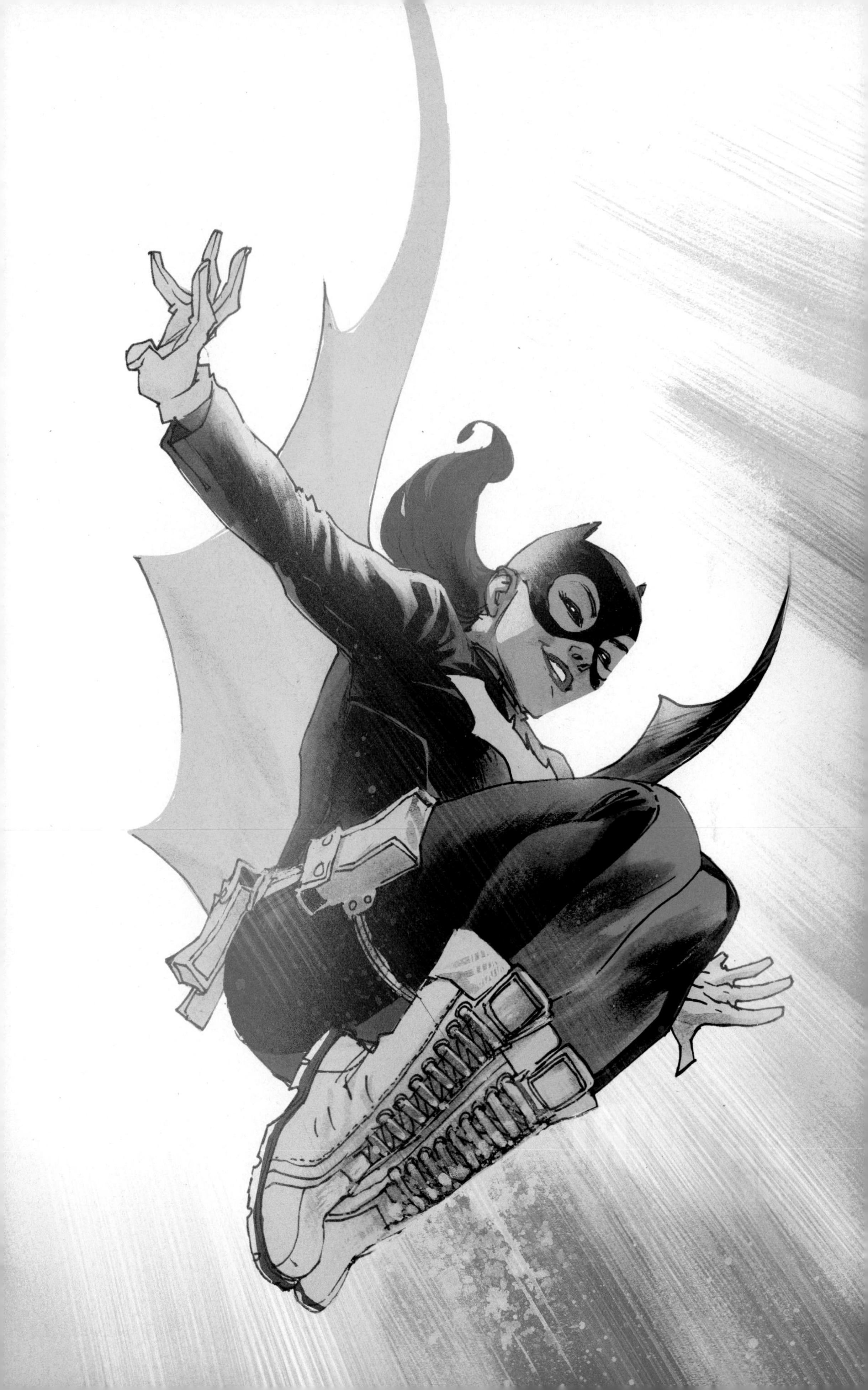

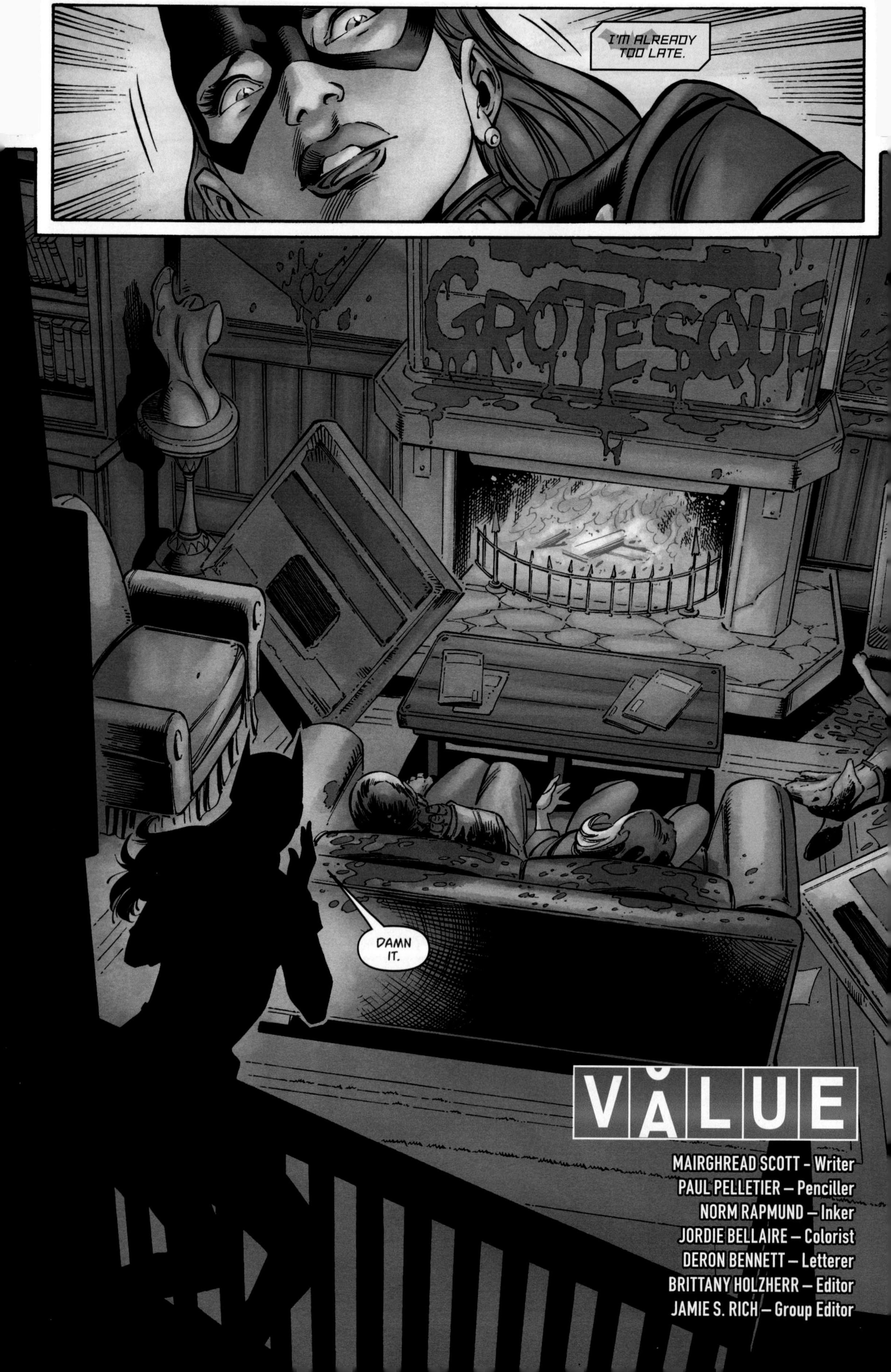
I'M ALREADY TOO LATE.
GROTESQUE
DAMN IT.
VALUE
MAIRGHREAD SCOTT - Writer
PAUL PELLETIER – Penciller
NORM RAPMUND – Inker
JORDIE BELLAIRE – Colorist
DERON BENNETT – Letterer
BRITTANY HOLZHERR – Editor
JAMIE S. RICH – Group Editor

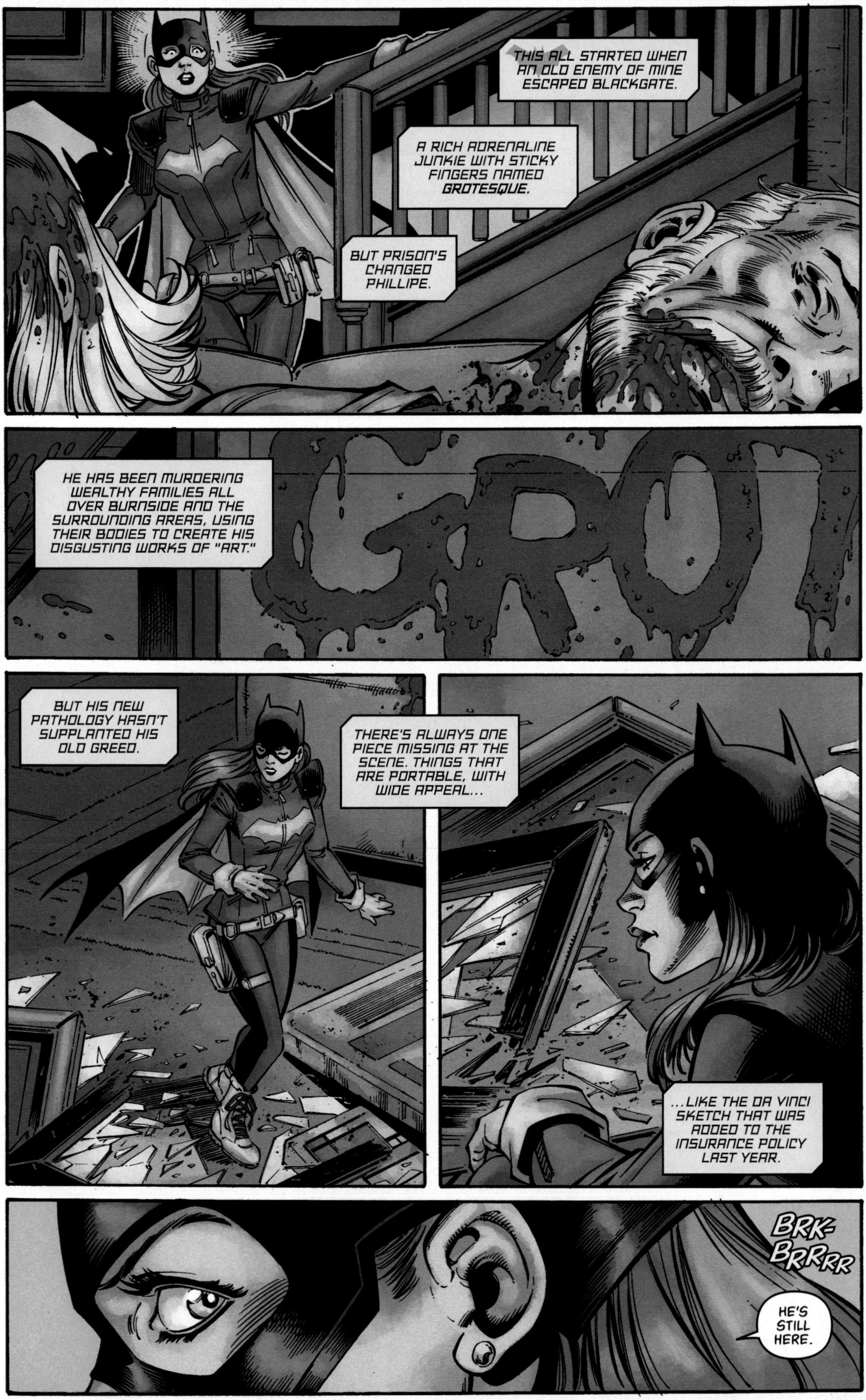
THIS ALL STARTED WHEN AN OLD ENEMY OF MINE ESCAPED BLACKGATE.
A RICH ADRENALINE JUNKIE WITH STICKY FINGERS NAMED GROTESQUE.
BUT PRISON'S CHANGED PHILLIPE.
HE HAS BEEN MURDERING WEALTHY FAMILIES ALL OVER BURNSIDE AND THE SURROUNDING AREAS, USING THEIR BODIES TO CREATE HIS DISGUSTING WORKS OF "ART."
GRO
BUT HIS NEW PATHOLOGY HASN'T SUPPLANTED HIS OLD GREED.
THERE'S ALWAYS ONE PIECE MISSING AT THE SCENE. THINGS THAT ARE PORTABLE, WITH WIDE APPEAL...
...LIKE THE DA VINCI SKETCH THAT WAS ADDED TO THE INSURANCE POLICY LAST YEAR.
BRK-BRRRR
HE'S STILL HERE.

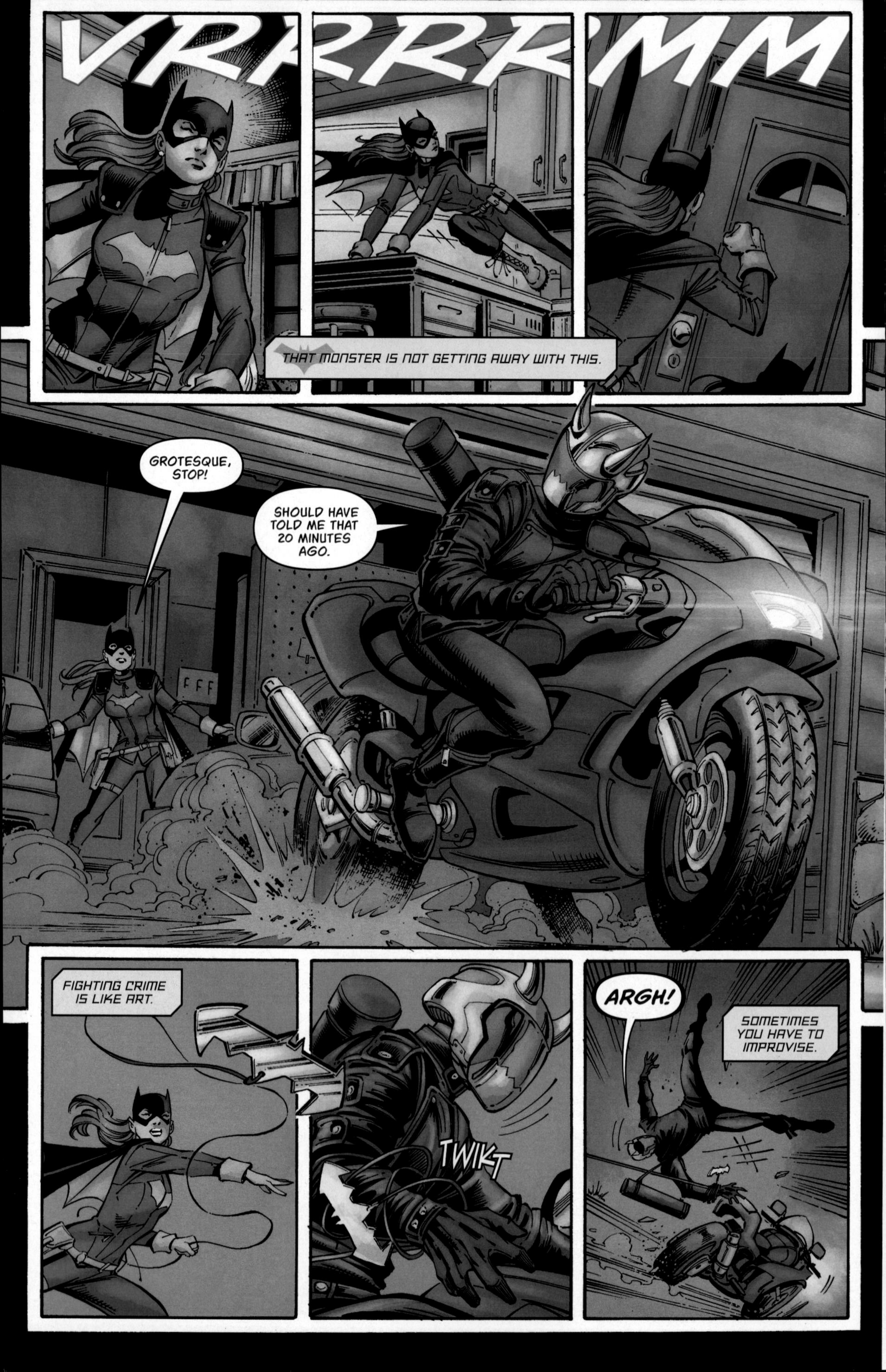
VRRRRRMM
THAT MONSTER IS NOT GETTING AWAY WITH THIS.
GROTESQUE, STOP!
SHOULD HAVE TOLD ME THAT 20 MINUTES AGO.
FIGHTING CRIME IS LIKE ART.
TWIKT
ARGH!
SOMETIMES YOU HAVE TO IMPROVISE.

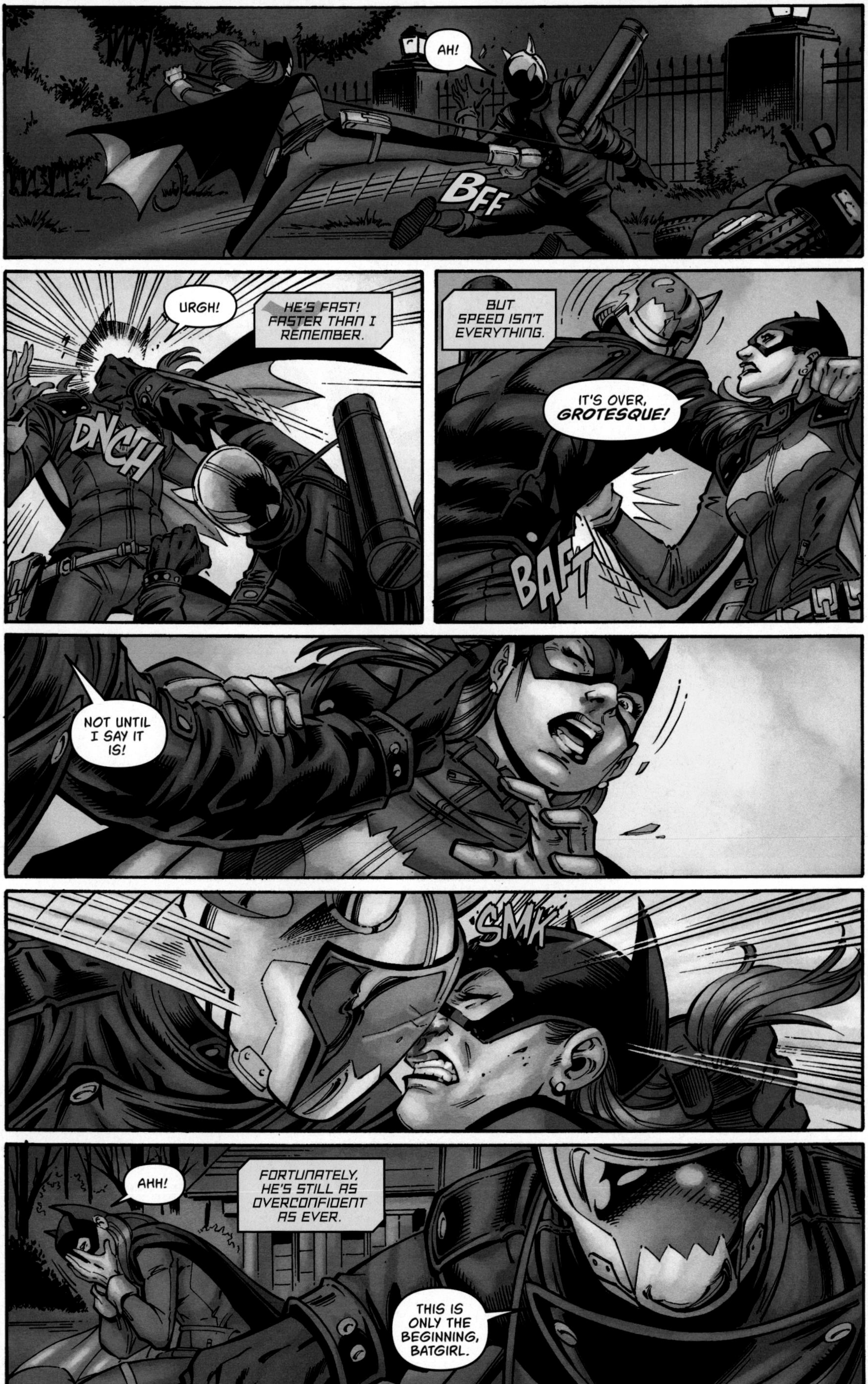
AH!
BFF
URGH!
HE'S FAST! FASTER THAN I REMEMBER.
DNCH
BUT SPEED ISN'T EVERYTHING.
IT'S OVER, GROTESQUE!
BAFT
NOT UNTIL I SAY IT IS!
SMK
AHH!
FORTUNATELY, HE'S STILL AS OVERCONFIDENT AS EVER.
THIS IS ONLY THE BEGINNING, BATGIRL.

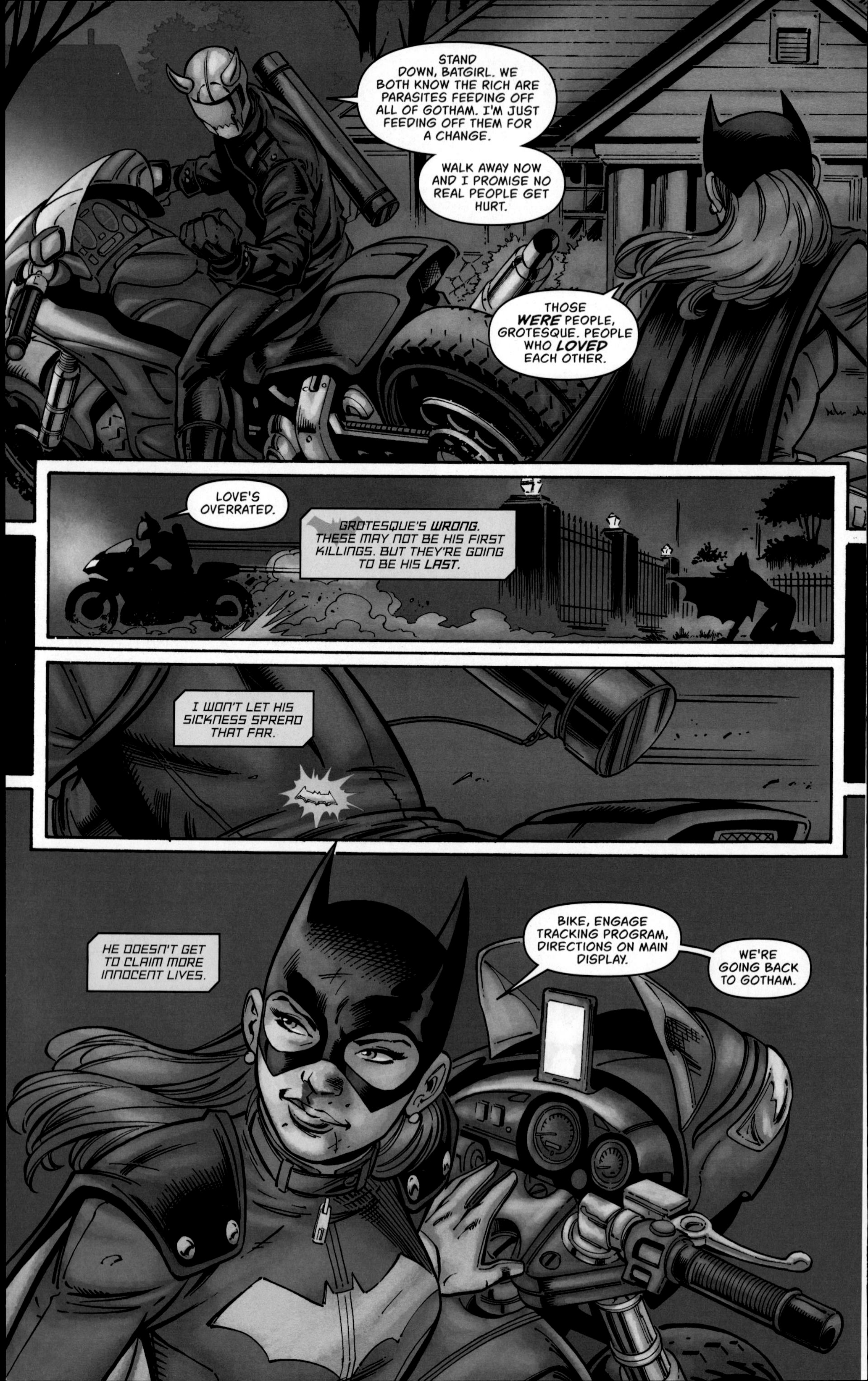
STAND DOWN, BATGIRL. WE BOTH KNOW THE RICH ARE PARASITES FEEDING OFF ALL OF GOTHAM. I'M JUST FEEDING OFF THEM FOR A CHANGE.
WALK AWAY NOW AND I PROMISE NO REAL PEOPLE GET HURT.
THOSE *WERE* PEOPLE, GROTESQUE. PEOPLE WHO *LOVED* EACH OTHER.
LOVE'S OVERRATED.
GROTESQUE'S *WRONG*. THESE MAY NOT BE HIS FIRST KILLINGS. BUT THEY'RE GOING TO BE HIS *LAST*.
I WON'T LET HIS SICKNESS SPREAD THAT FAR.
HE DOESN'T GET TO CLAIM MORE INNOCENT LIVES.
BIKE, ENGAGE TRACKING PROGRAM, DIRECTIONS ON MAIN DISPLAY.
WE'RE GOING BACK TO GOTHAM.

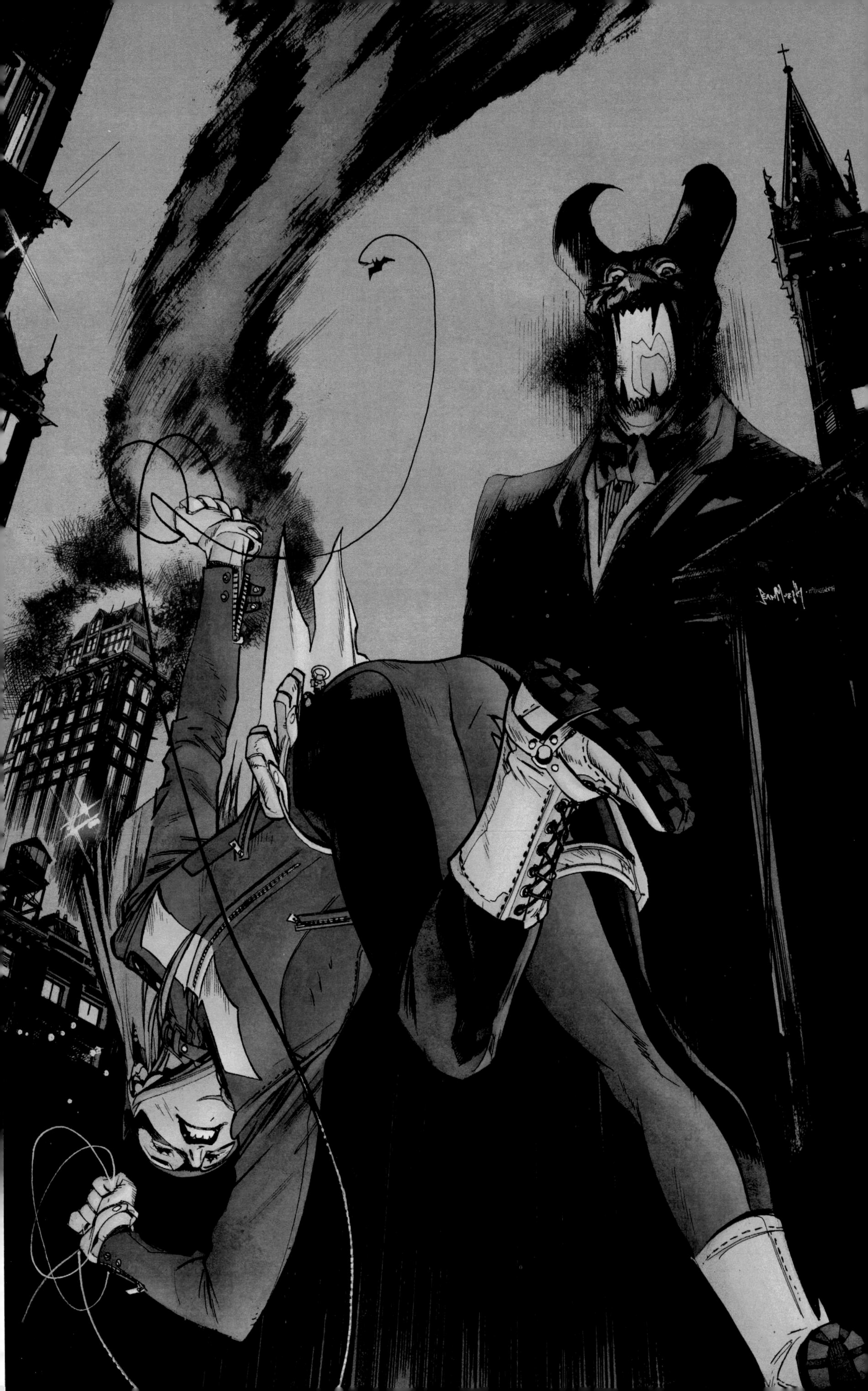

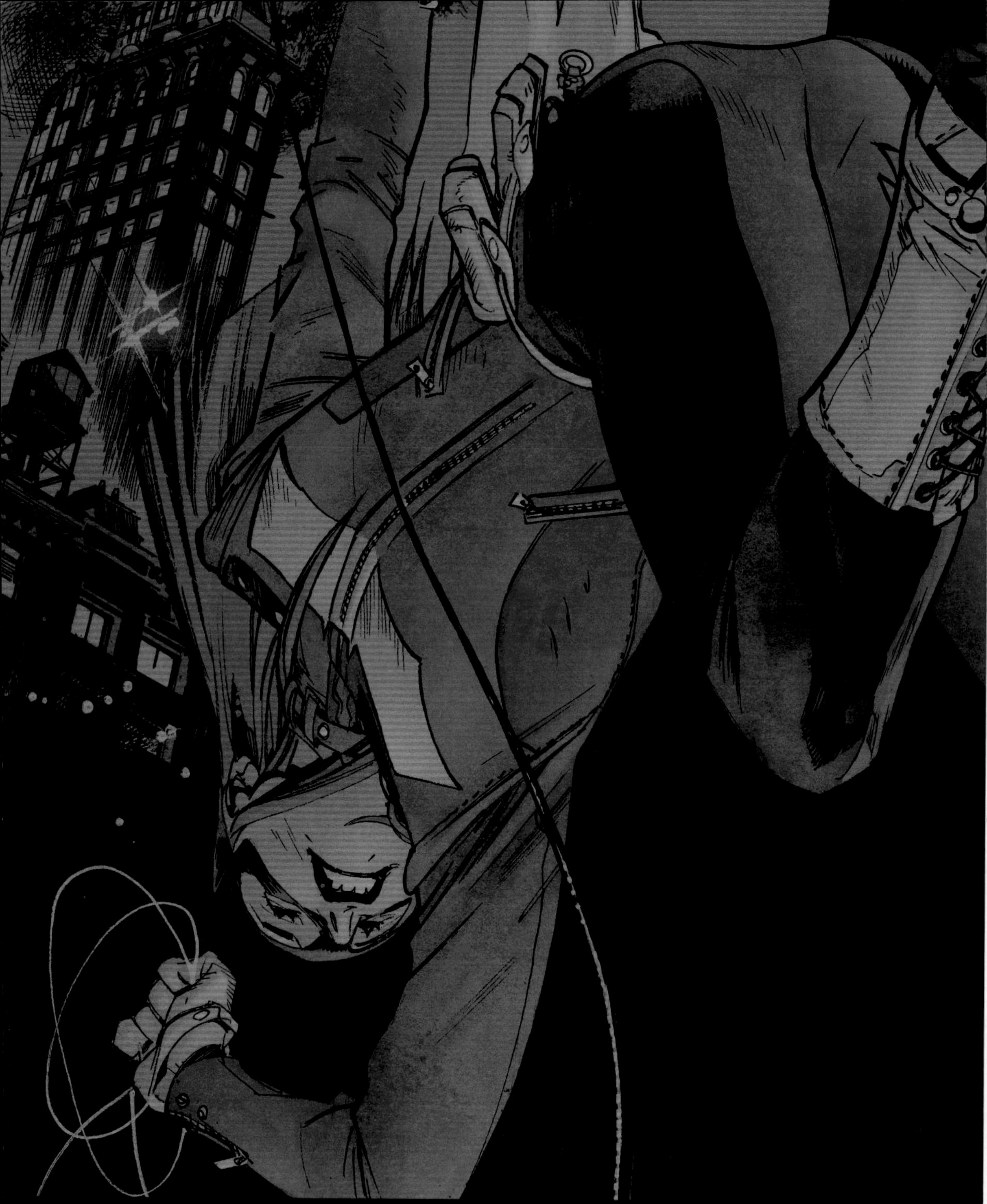

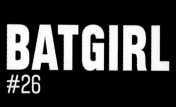

# BATGIRL
#26

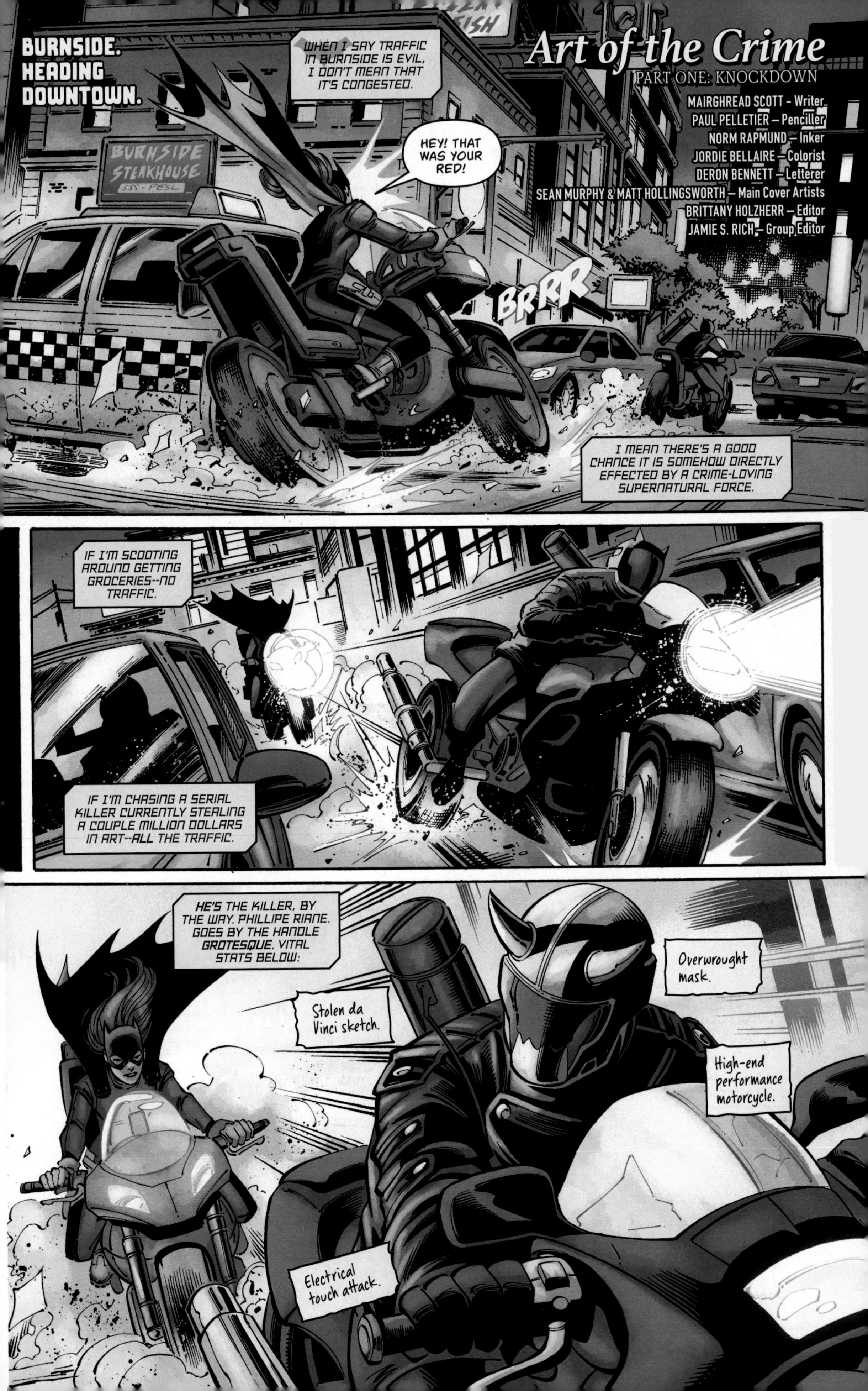
BURNSIDE. HEADING DOWNTOWN.
WHEN I SAY TRAFFIC IN BURNSIDE IS EVIL, I DON'T MEAN THAT IT'S CONGESTED.
Art of the Crime
PART ONE: KNOCKDOWN
MAIRGHREAD SCOTT - Writer
PAUL PELLETIER – Penciller
NORM RAPMUND – Inker
JORDIE BELLAIRE – Colorist
DERON BENNETT – Letterer
SEAN MURPHY & MATT HOLLINGSWORTH – Main Cover Artists
BRITTANY HOLZHERR – Editor
JAMIE S. RICH – Group Editor
BURNSIDE STEAKHOUSE
HEY! THAT WAS YOUR RED!
BRRR
I MEAN THERE'S A GOOD CHANCE IT IS SOMEHOW DIRECTLY EFFECTED BY A CRIME-LOVING SUPERNATURAL FORCE.
IF I'M SCOOTING AROUND GETTING GROCERIES--NO TRAFFIC.
IF I'M CHASING A SERIAL KILLER CURRENTLY STEALING A COUPLE MILLION DOLLARS IN ART--ALL THE TRAFFIC.
HE'S THE KILLER, BY THE WAY. PHILLIPE RIANE. GOES BY THE HANDLE GROTESQUE. VITAL STATS BELOW:
Overwrought mask.
Stolen da Vinci sketch.
High-end performance motorcycle.
Electrical touch attack.

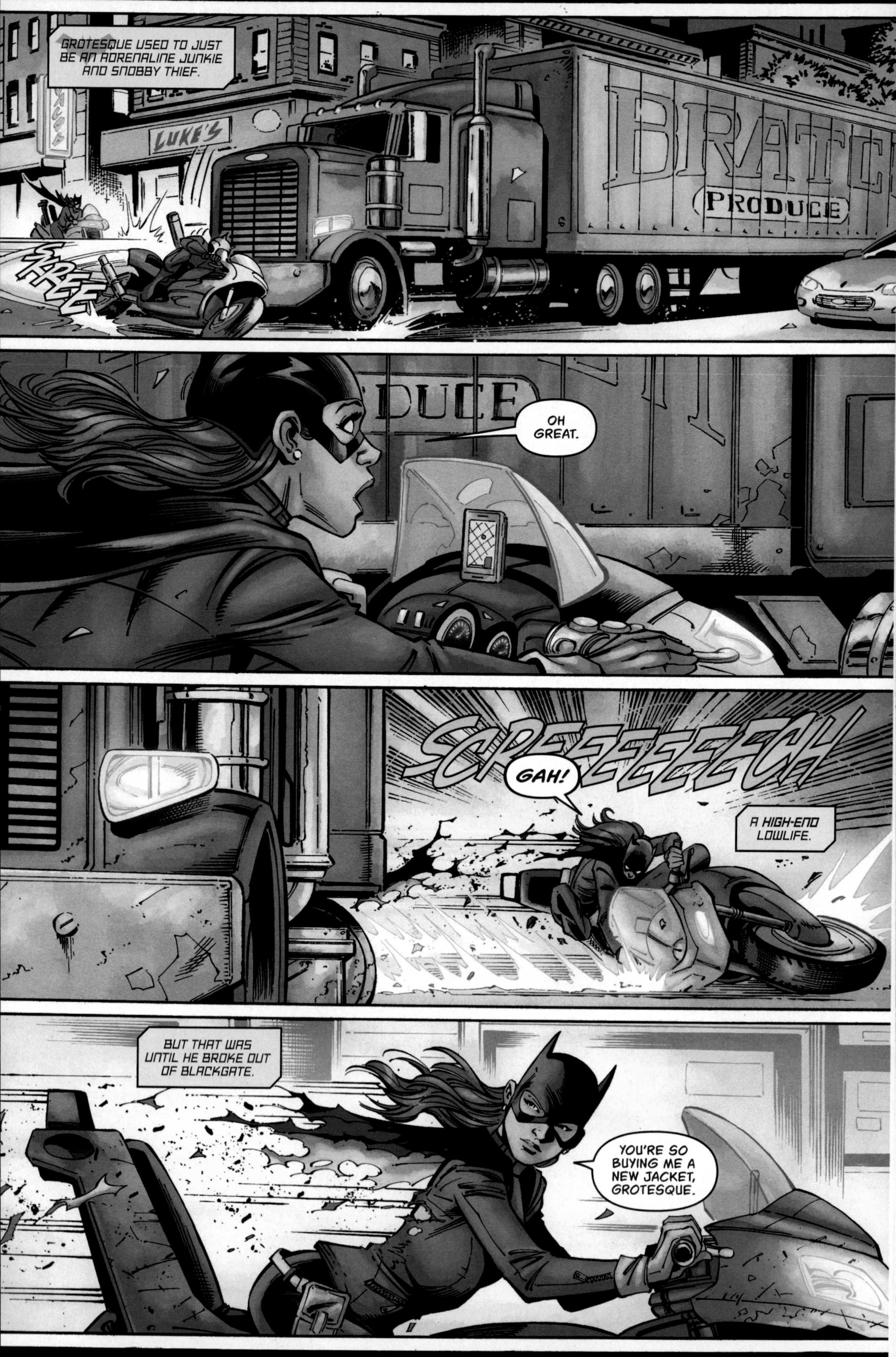
GROTESQUE USED TO JUST BE AN ADRENALINE JUNKIE AND SNOBBY THIEF.
LUKE'S
BRATC
PRODUCE
SKREE
DUCE
OH GREAT.
SCREEEEEECH
GAH!
A HIGH-END LOWLIFE.
BUT THAT WAS UNTIL HE BROKE OUT OF BLACKGATE.
YOU'RE SO BUYING ME A NEW JACKET, GROTESQUE.

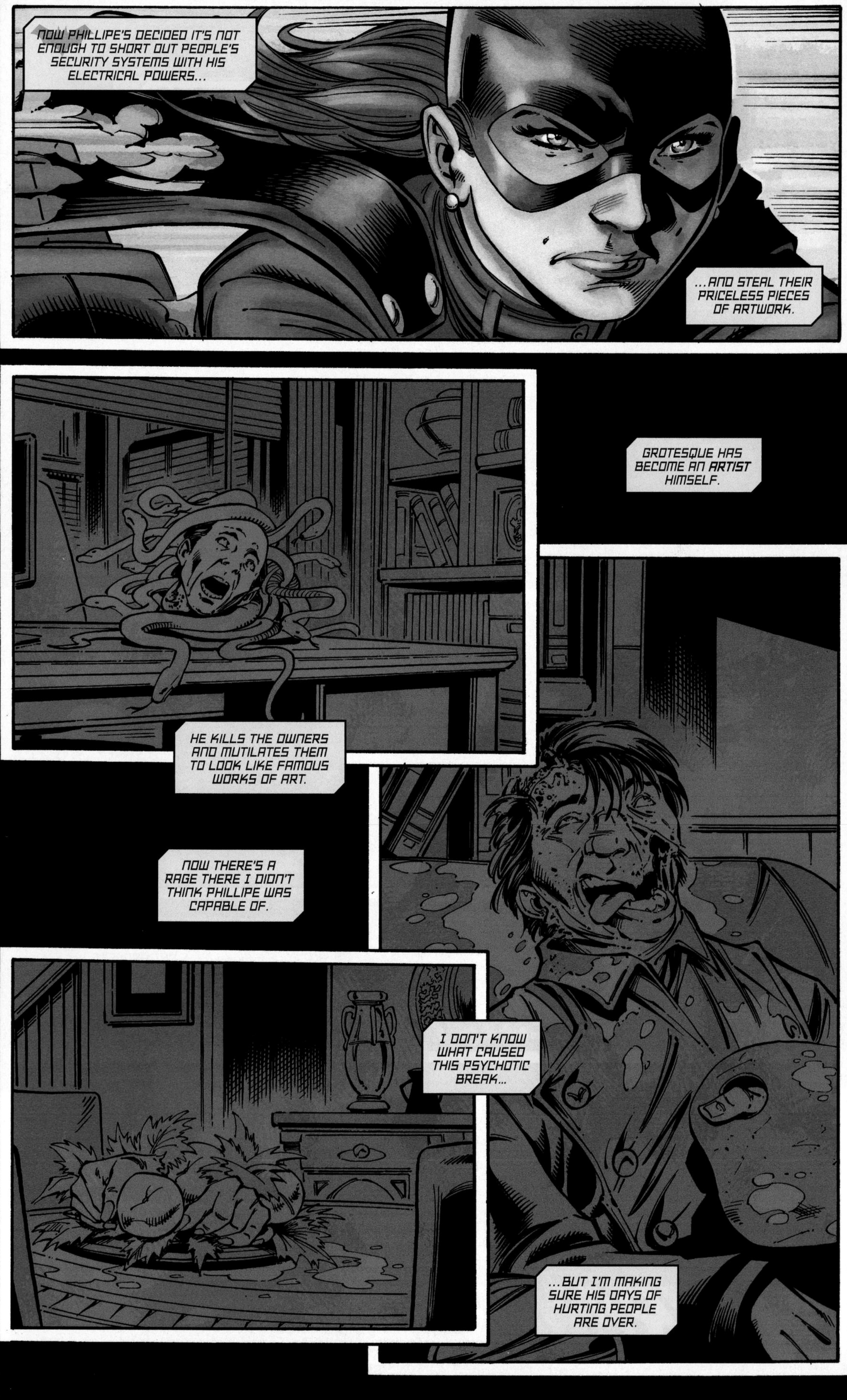
NOW PHILLIPE'S DECIDED IT'S NOT ENOUGH TO SHORT OUT PEOPLE'S SECURITY SYSTEMS WITH HIS ELECTRICAL POWERS...
...AND STEAL THEIR PRICELESS PIECES OF ARTWORK.
GROTESQUE HAS BECOME AN ARTIST HIMSELF.
HE KILLS THE OWNERS AND MUTILATES THEM TO LOOK LIKE FAMOUS WORKS OF ART.
NOW THERE'S A RAGE THERE I DIDN'T THINK PHILLIPE WAS CAPABLE OF.
I DON'T KNOW WHAT CAUSED THIS PSYCHOTIC BREAK...
...BUT I'M MAKING SURE HIS DAYS OF HURTING PEOPLE ARE OVER.

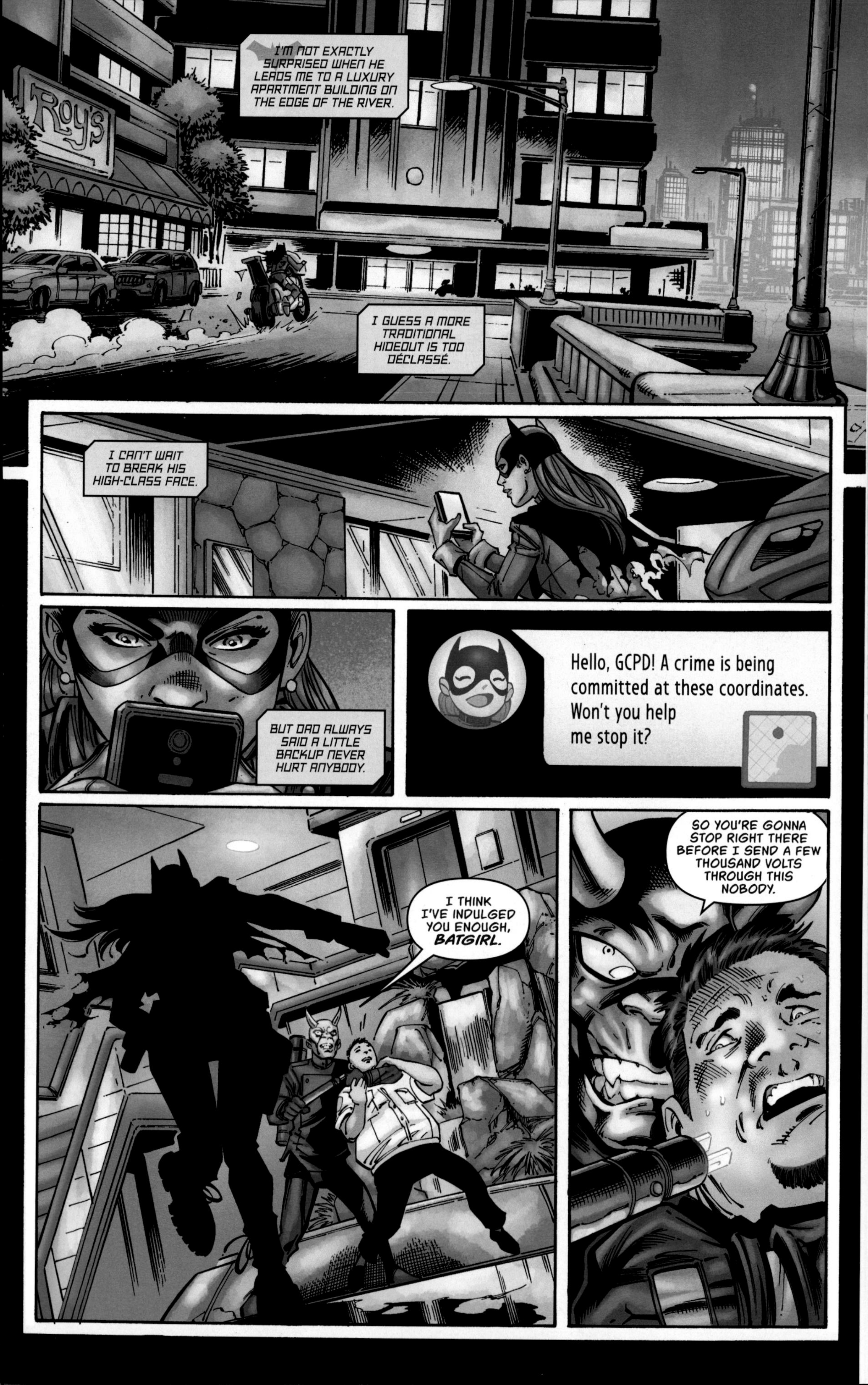
I'M NOT EXACTLY SURPRISED WHEN HE LEADS ME TO A LUXURY APARTMENT BUILDING ON THE EDGE OF THE RIVER.
Roy's
I GUESS A MORE TRADITIONAL HIDEOUT IS TOO DÉCLASSÉ.
I CAN'T WAIT TO BREAK HIS HIGH-CLASS FACE.
BUT DAD ALWAYS SAID A LITTLE BACKUP NEVER HURT ANYBODY.
Hello, GCPD! A crime is being committed at these coordinates. Won't you help me stop it?
I THINK I'VE INDULGED YOU ENOUGH, BATGIRL.
SO YOU'RE GONNA STOP RIGHT THERE BEFORE I SEND A FEW THOUSAND VOLTS THROUGH THIS NOBODY.

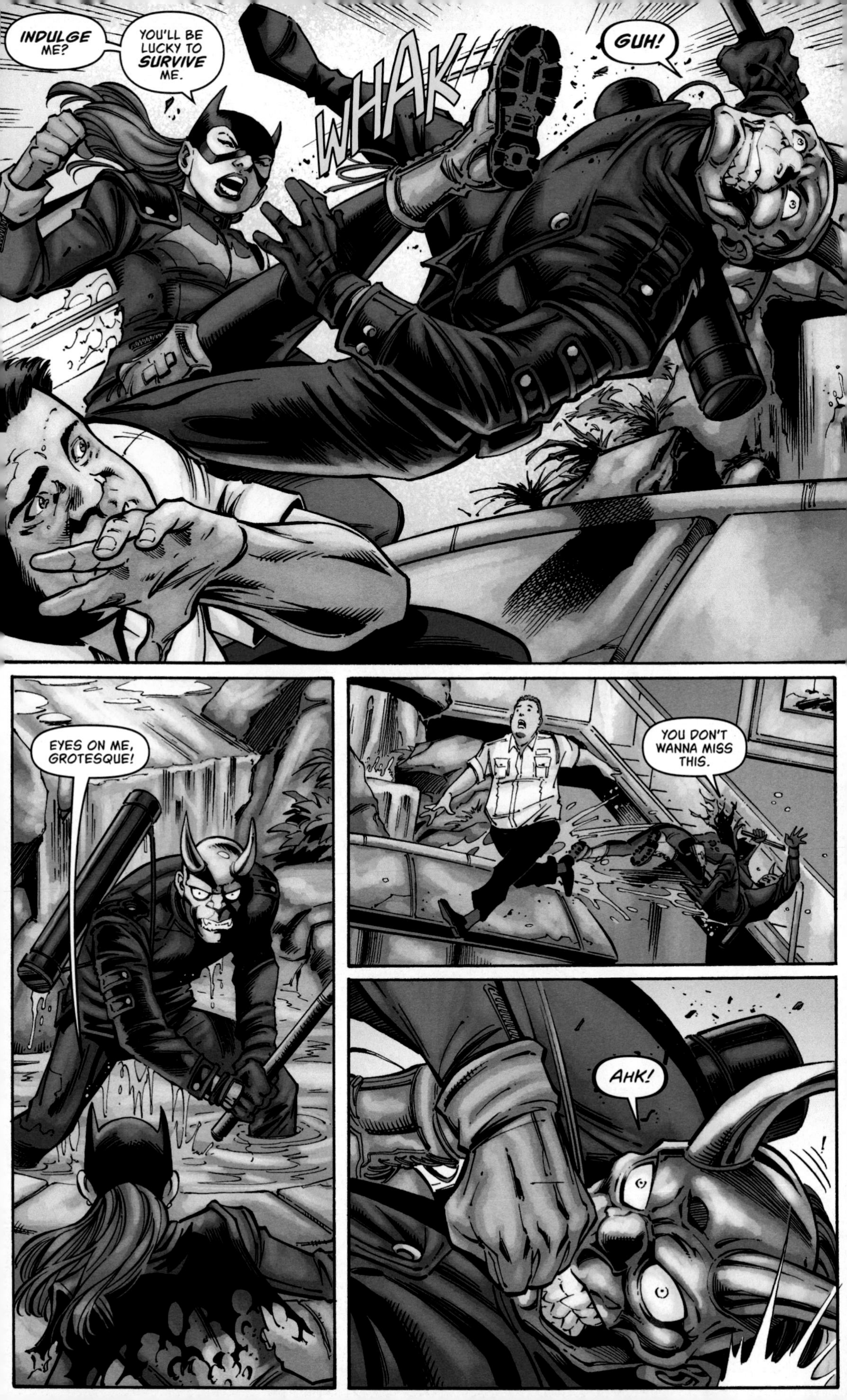
INDULGE ME?
YOU'LL BE LUCKY TO SURVIVE ME.
WHAK
GUH!
EYES ON ME, GROTESQUE!
YOU DON'T WANNA MISS THIS.
AHK!
!

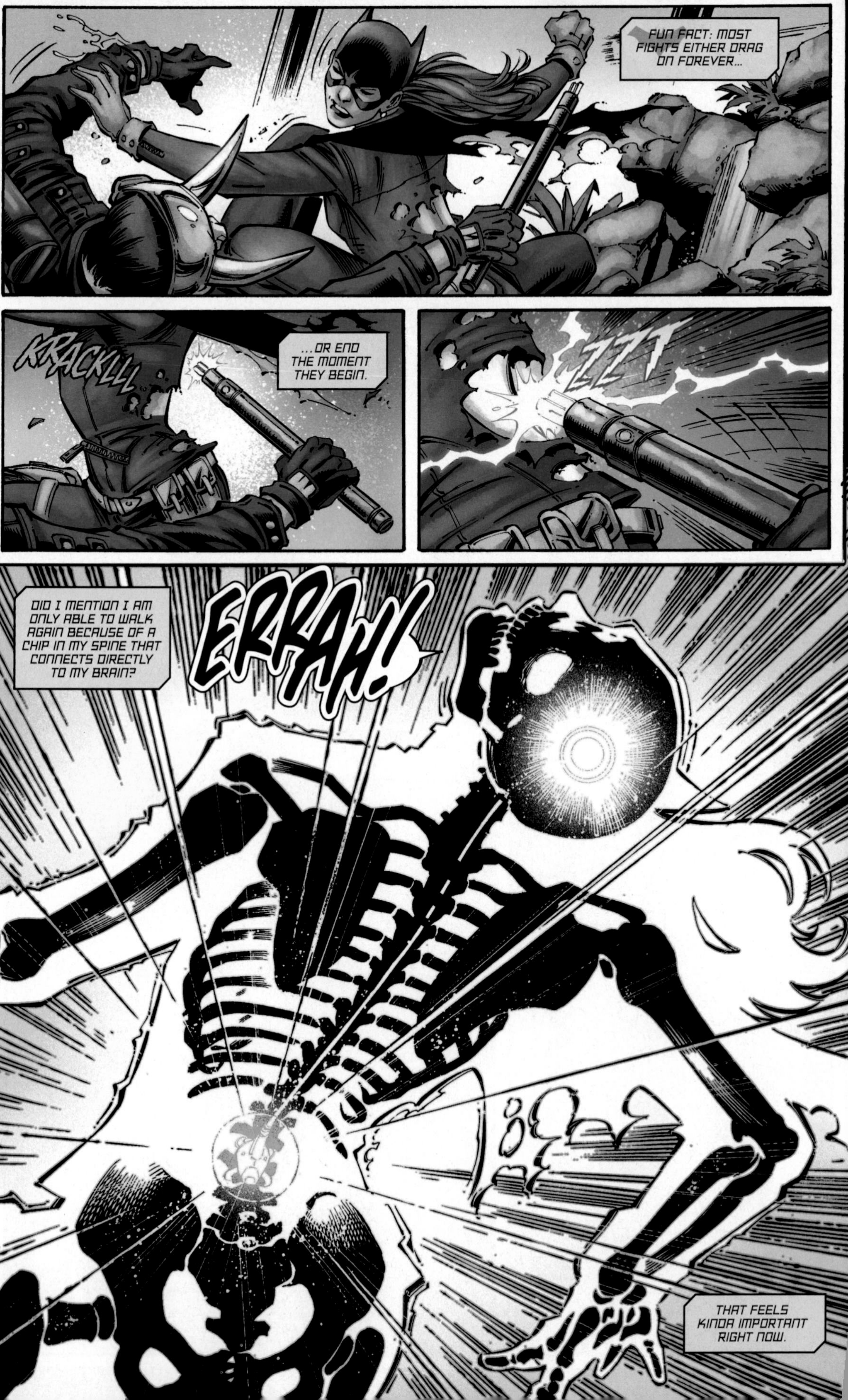

FUN FACT: MOST FIGHTS EITHER DRAG ON FOREVER...
KRACKLLL
...OR END THE MOMENT THEY BEGIN.
ZZZT
DID I MENTION I AM ONLY ABLE TO WALK AGAIN BECAUSE OF A CHIP IN MY SPINE THAT CONNECTS DIRECTLY TO MY BRAIN?
ERRAH!
THAT FEELS KINDA IMPORTANT RIGHT NOW.

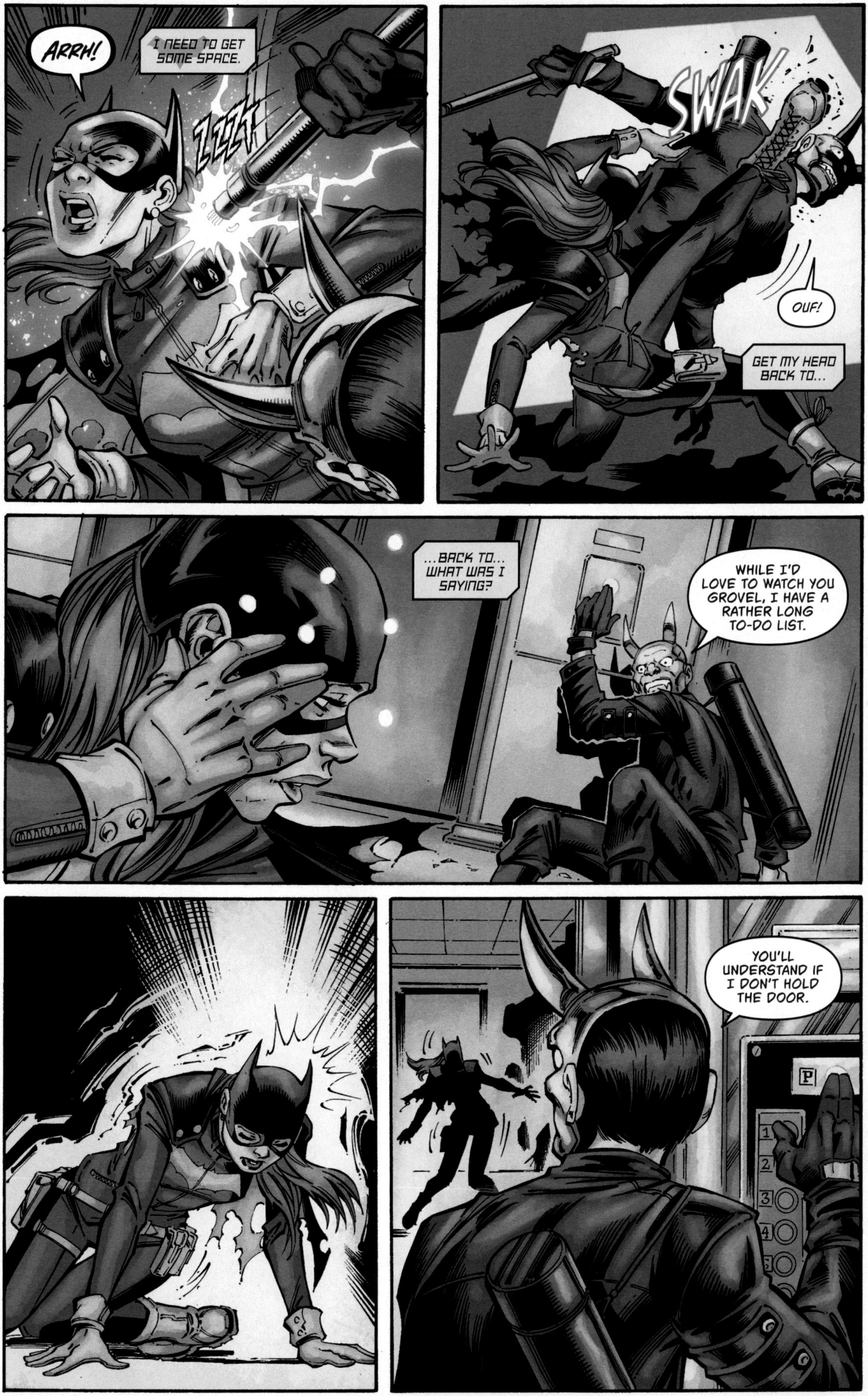
ARRH!
I NEED TO GET SOME SPACE.
ZZZT
SWAK
OUF!
GET MY HEAD BACK TO...
...BACK TO... WHAT WAS I SAYING?
WHILE I'D LOVE TO WATCH YOU GROVEL, I HAVE A RATHER LONG TO-DO LIST.
YOU'LL UNDERSTAND IF I DON'T HOLD THE DOOR.
P
1
2
3
4

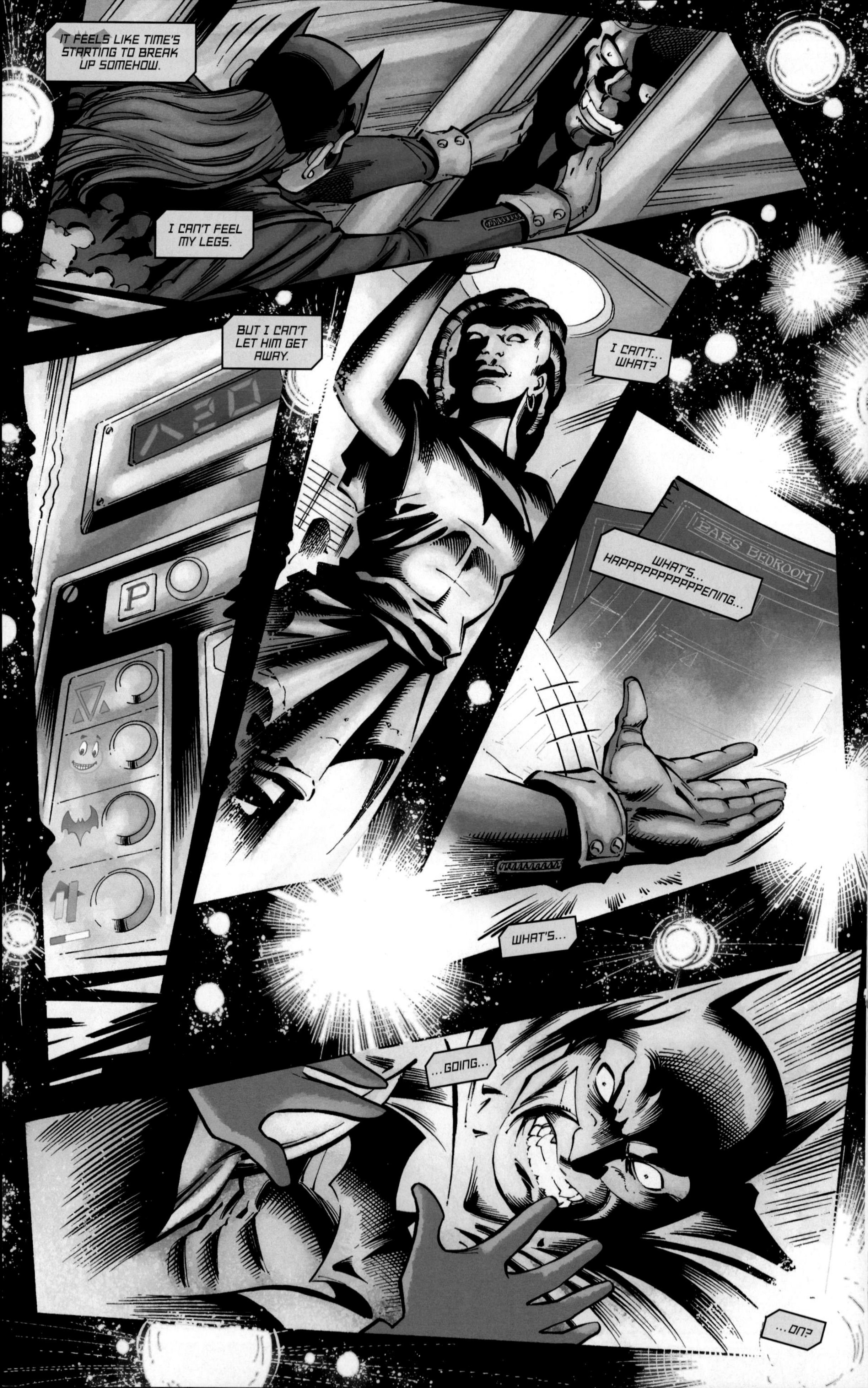
IT FEELS LIKE TIME'S STARTING TO BREAK UP SOMEHOW.
I CAN'T FEEL MY LEGS.
BUT I CAN'T LET HIM GET AWAY.
I CAN'T... WHAT?
BABS BEDROOM
WHAT'S... HAPPPPPPPPPPPPENING...
WHAT'S...
...GOING...
...ON?

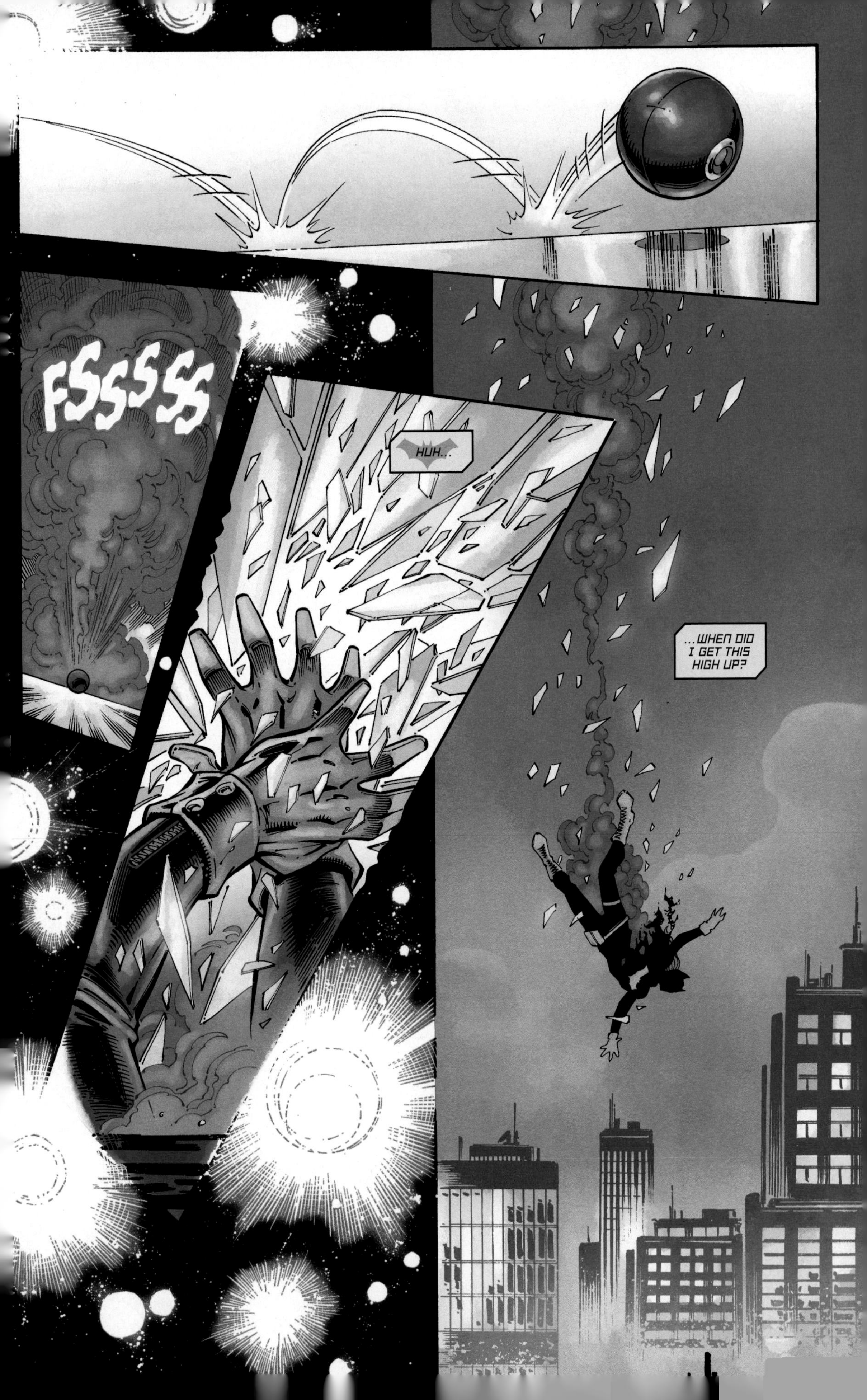
FSSSSS
HUH...
...WHEN DID I GET THIS HIGH UP?

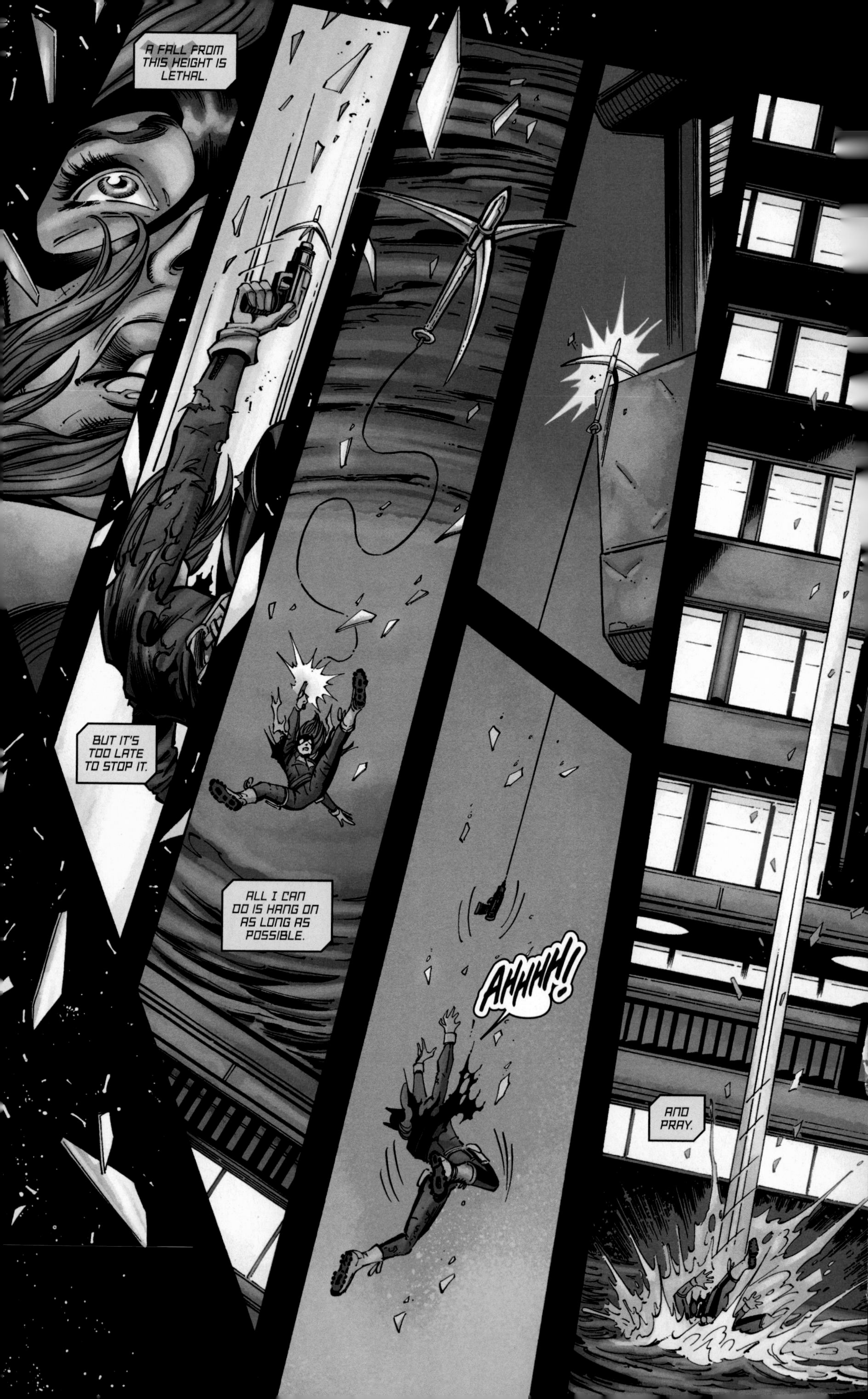
A FALL FROM THIS HEIGHT IS LETHAL.
BUT IT'S TOO LATE TO STOP IT.
ALL I CAN DO IS HANG ON AS LONG AS POSSIBLE.
AHHHH!!
AND PRAY.

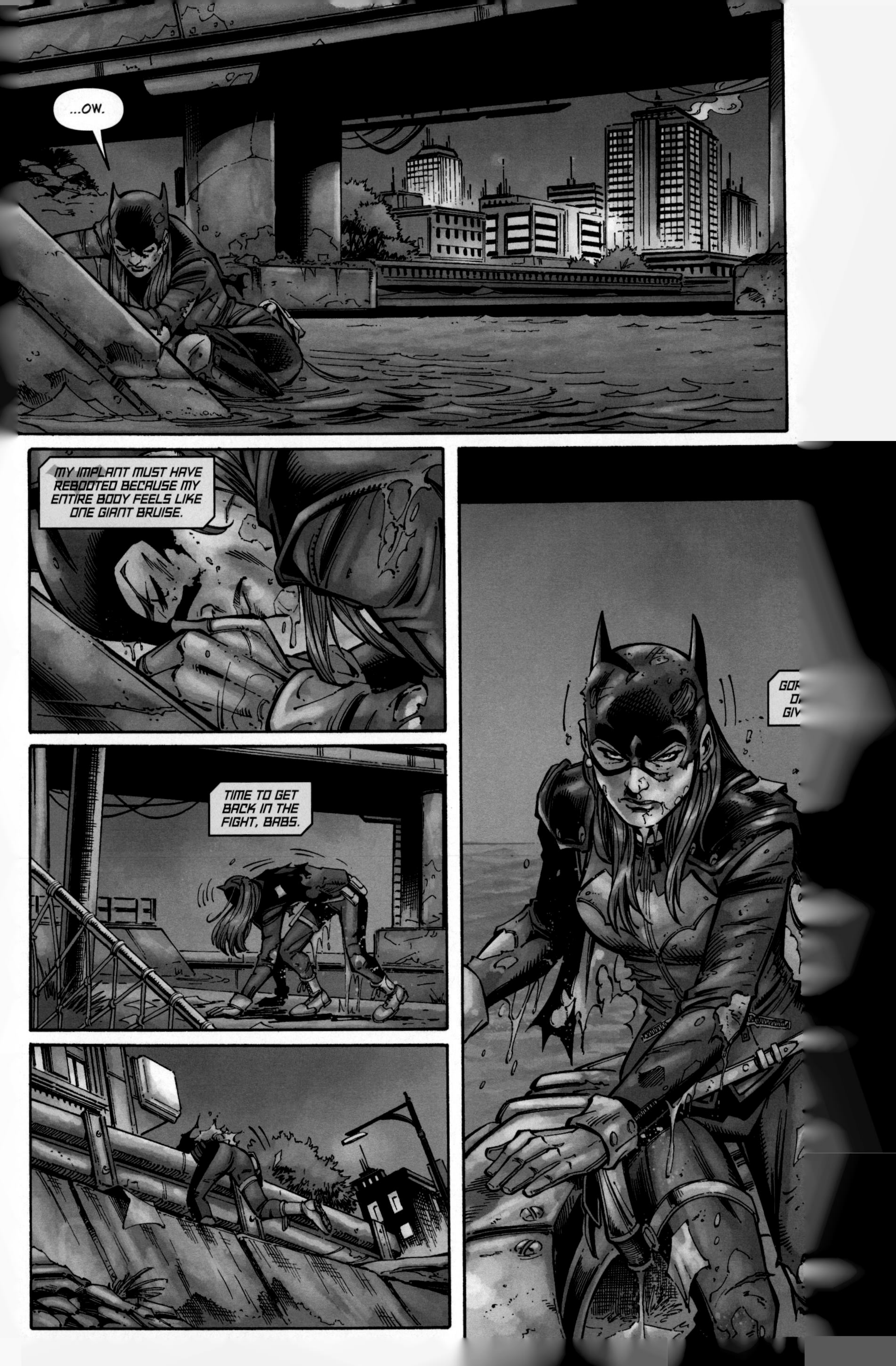
...OW.
MY IMPLANT MUST HAVE REBOOTED BECAUSE MY ENTIRE BODY FEELS LIKE ONE GIANT BRUISE.
TIME TO GET BACK IN THE FIGHT, BABS.

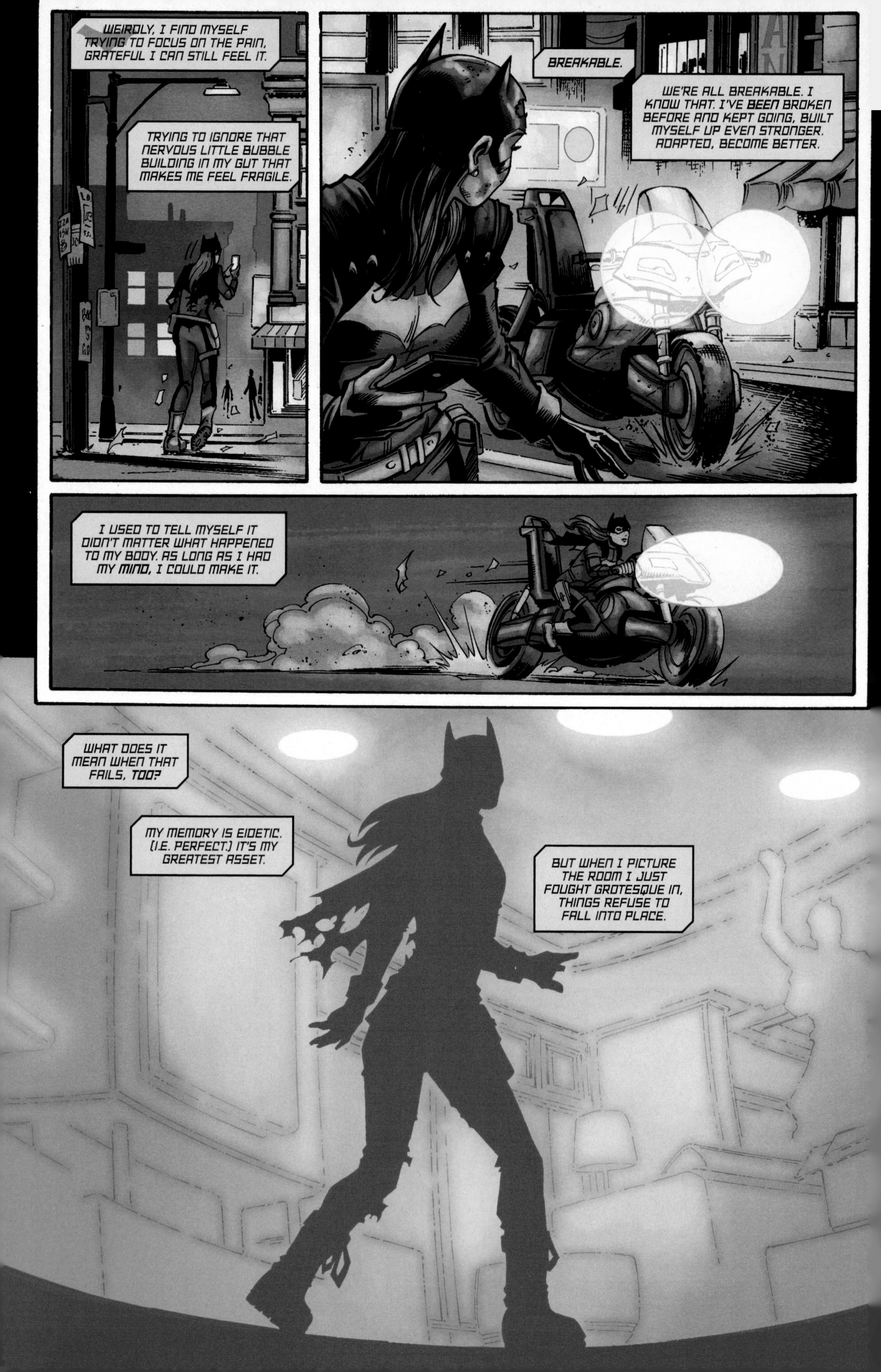
WEIRDLY, I FIND MYSELF TRYING TO FOCUS ON THE PAIN, GRATEFUL I CAN STILL FEEL IT.
TRYING TO IGNORE THAT NERVOUS LITTLE BUBBLE BUILDING IN MY GUT THAT MAKES ME FEEL FRAGILE.
BREAKABLE.
WE'RE ALL BREAKABLE. I KNOW THAT. I'VE BEEN BROKEN BEFORE AND KEPT GOING, BUILT MYSELF UP EVEN STRONGER. ADAPTED, BECOME BETTER.
I USED TO TELL MYSELF IT DIDN'T MATTER WHAT HAPPENED TO MY BODY. AS LONG AS I HAD MY MIND, I COULD MAKE IT.
WHAT DOES IT MEAN WHEN THAT FAILS, TOO?
MY MEMORY IS EIDETIC. (I.E. PERFECT.) IT'S MY GREATEST ASSET.
BUT WHEN I PICTURE THE ROOM I JUST FOUGHT GROTESQUE IN, THINGS REFUSE TO FALL INTO PLACE.

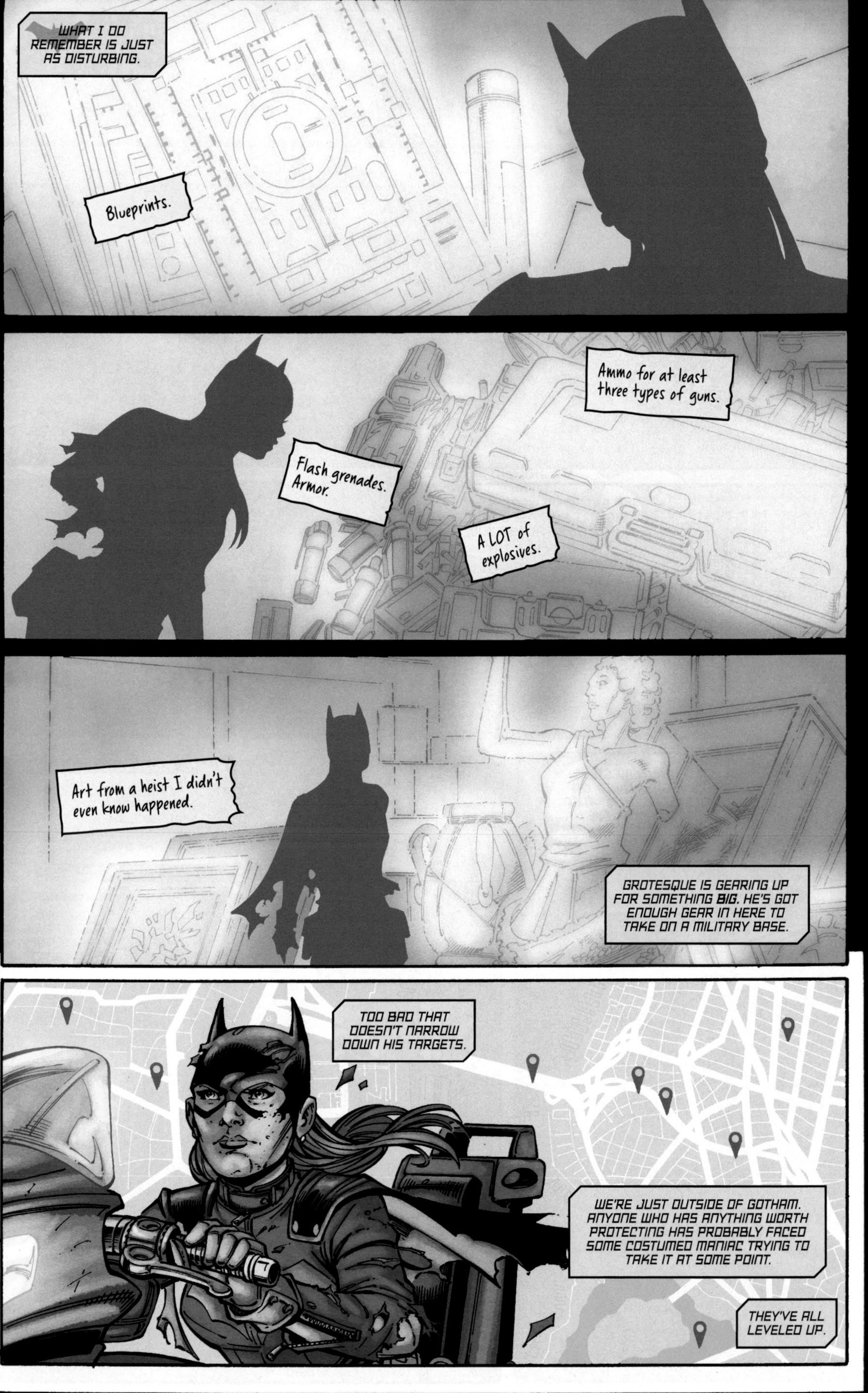
WHAT I DO REMEMBER IS JUST AS DISTURBING.
Blueprints.
Ammo for at least three types of guns.
Flash grenades. Armor.
A LOT of explosives.
Art from a heist I didn't even know happened.
GROTESQUE IS GEARING UP FOR SOMETHING BIG. HE'S GOT ENOUGH GEAR IN HERE TO TAKE ON A MILITARY BASE.
TOO BAD THAT DOESN'T NARROW DOWN HIS TARGETS.
WE'RE JUST OUTSIDE OF GOTHAM. ANYONE WHO HAS ANYTHING WORTH PROTECTING HAS PROBABLY FACED SOME COSTUMED MANIAC TRYING TO TAKE IT AT SOME POINT.
THEY'VE ALL LEVELED UP.

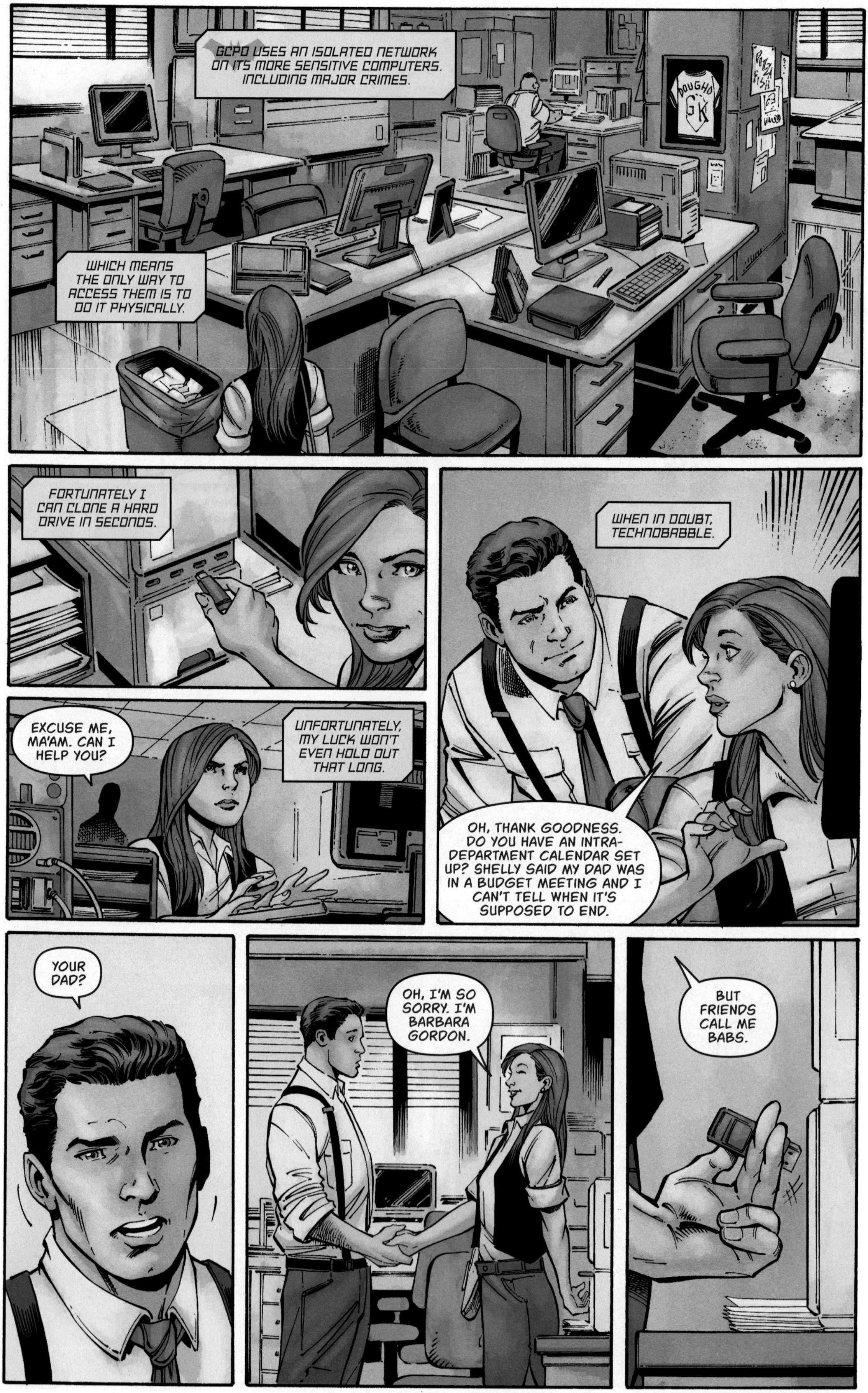
GCPD USES AN ISOLATED NETWORK ON ITS MORE SENSITIVE COMPUTERS. INCLUDING MAJOR CRIMES.
WHICH MEANS THE ONLY WAY TO ACCESS THEM IS TO DO IT PHYSICALLY.
FORTUNATELY I CAN CLONE A HARD DRIVE IN SECONDS.
WHEN IN DOUBT, TECHNOBABBLE.
EXCUSE ME, MA'AM. CAN I HELP YOU?
UNFORTUNATELY, MY LUCK WON'T EVEN HOLD OUT THAT LONG.
OH, THANK GOODNESS. DO YOU HAVE AN INTRA-DEPARTMENT CALENDAR SET UP? SHELLY SAID MY DAD WAS IN A BUDGET MEETING AND I CAN'T TELL WHEN IT'S SUPPOSED TO END.
YOUR DAD?
OH, I'M SO SORRY. I'M BARBARA GORDON.
BUT FRIENDS CALL ME BABS.

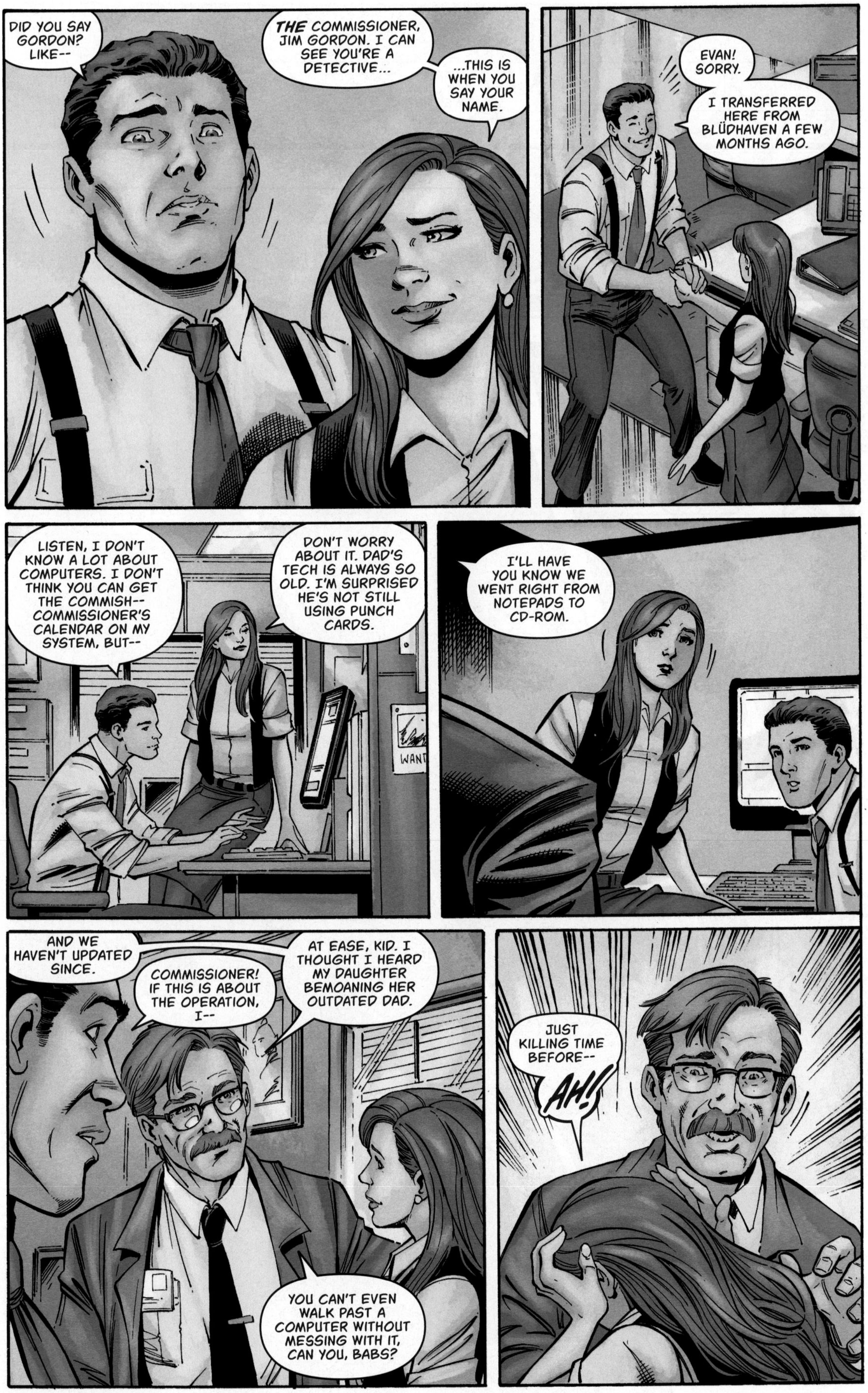
DID YOU SAY GORDON? LIKE--
*THE* COMMISSIONER, JIM GORDON. I CAN SEE YOU'RE A DETECTIVE...
...THIS IS WHEN YOU SAY YOUR NAME.
EVAN! SORRY.
I TRANSFERRED HERE FROM BLÜDHAVEN A FEW MONTHS AGO.
LISTEN, I DON'T KNOW A LOT ABOUT COMPUTERS. I DON'T THINK YOU CAN GET THE COMMISH-- COMMISSIONER'S CALENDAR ON MY SYSTEM, BUT--
DON'T WORRY ABOUT IT. DAD'S TECH IS ALWAYS SO OLD. I'M SURPRISED HE'S NOT STILL USING PUNCH CARDS.
WANT
I'LL HAVE YOU KNOW WE WENT RIGHT FROM NOTEPADS TO CD-ROM.
AND WE HAVEN'T UPDATED SINCE.
COMMISSIONER! IF THIS IS ABOUT THE OPERATION, I--
AT EASE, KID. I THOUGHT I HEARD MY DAUGHTER BEMOANING HER OUTDATED DAD.
YOU CAN'T EVEN WALK PAST A COMPUTER WITHOUT MESSING WITH IT, CAN YOU, BABS?
JUST KILLING TIME BEFORE--
AH!

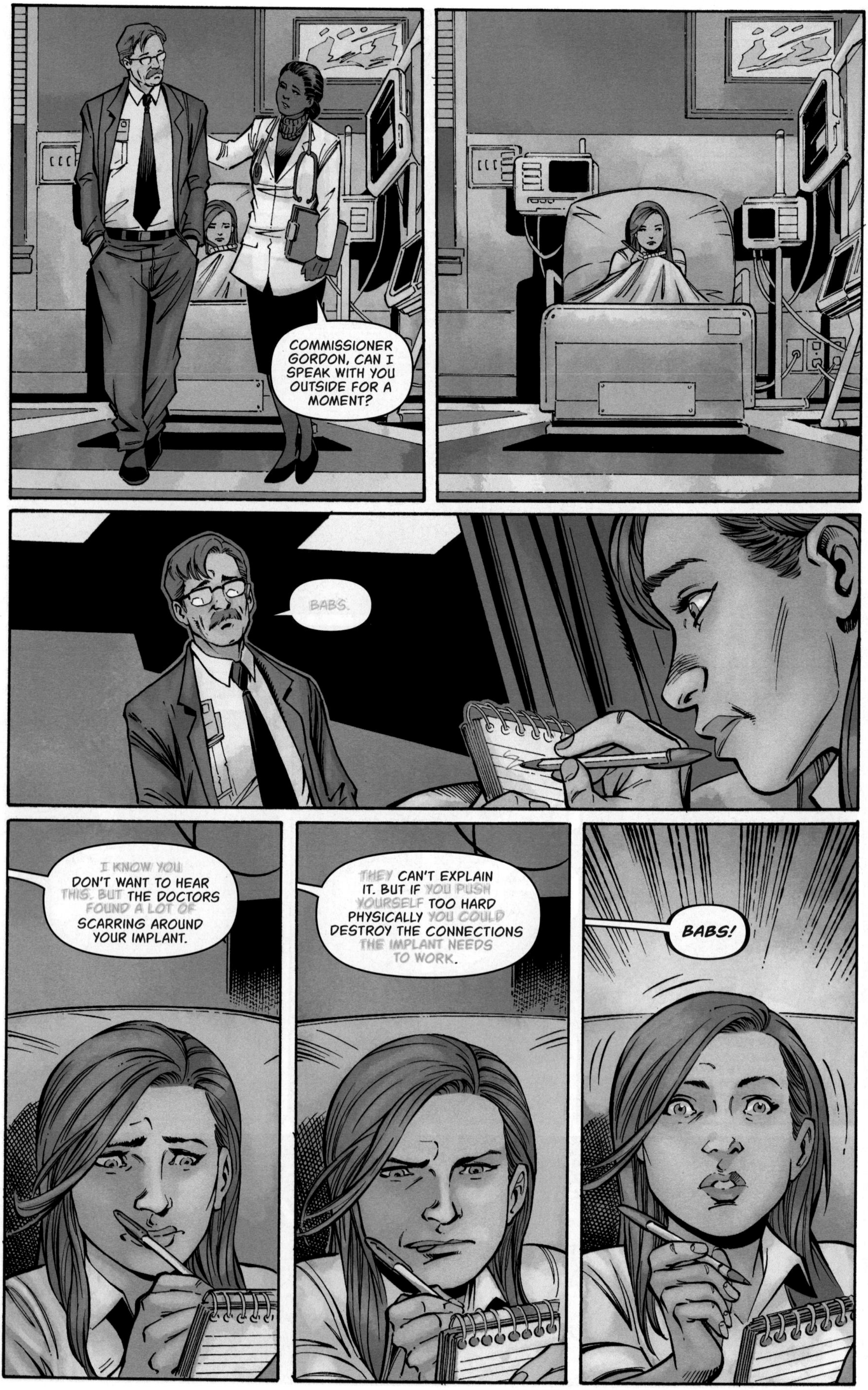
COMMISSIONER GORDON, CAN I SPEAK WITH YOU OUTSIDE FOR A MOMENT?
BABS.
I KNOW YOU DON'T WANT TO HEAR THIS, BUT THE DOCTORS FOUND A LOT OF SCARRING AROUND YOUR IMPLANT.
THEY CAN'T EXPLAIN IT. BUT IF YOU PUSH YOURSELF TOO HARD PHYSICALLY YOU COULD DESTROY THE CONNECTIONS THE IMPLANT NEEDS TO WORK.
BABS!

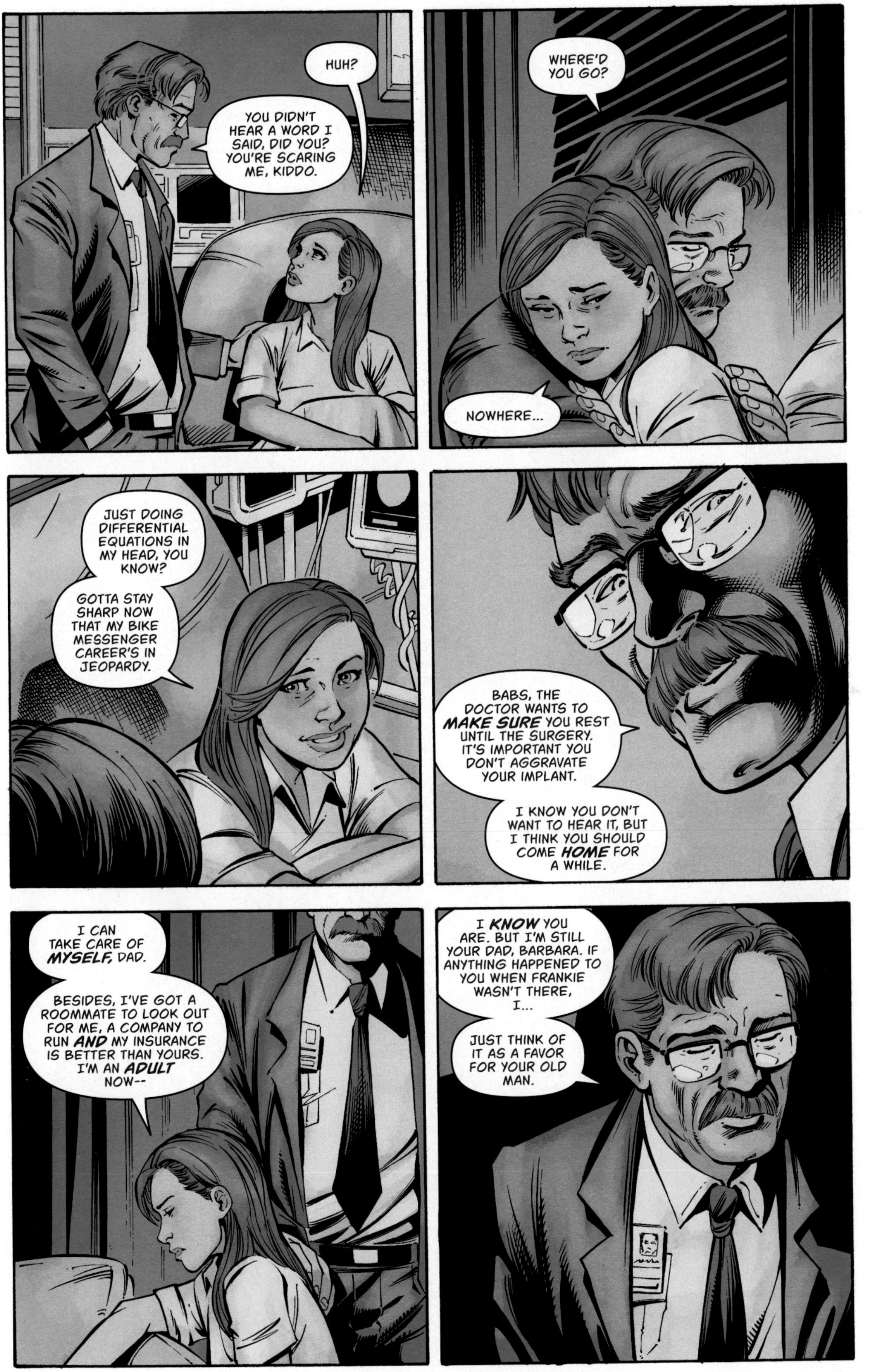
HUH?
YOU DIDN'T HEAR A WORD I SAID, DID YOU? YOU'RE SCARING ME, KIDDO.
WHERE'D YOU GO?
NOWHERE...
JUST DOING DIFFERENTIAL EQUATIONS IN MY HEAD, YOU KNOW?
GOTTA STAY SHARP NOW THAT MY BIKE MESSENGER CAREER'S IN JEOPARDY.
BABS, THE DOCTOR WANTS TO MAKE SURE YOU REST UNTIL THE SURGERY. IT'S IMPORTANT YOU DON'T AGGRAVATE YOUR IMPLANT.
I KNOW YOU DON'T WANT TO HEAR IT, BUT I THINK YOU SHOULD COME HOME FOR A WHILE.
I CAN TAKE CARE OF MYSELF, DAD.
BESIDES, I'VE GOT A ROOMMATE TO LOOK OUT FOR ME, A COMPANY TO RUN AND MY INSURANCE IS BETTER THAN YOURS. I'M AN ADULT NOW--
I KNOW YOU ARE. BUT I'M STILL YOUR DAD, BARBARA. IF ANYTHING HAPPENED TO YOU WHEN FRANKIE WASN'T THERE, I...
JUST THINK OF IT AS A FAVOR FOR YOUR OLD MAN.

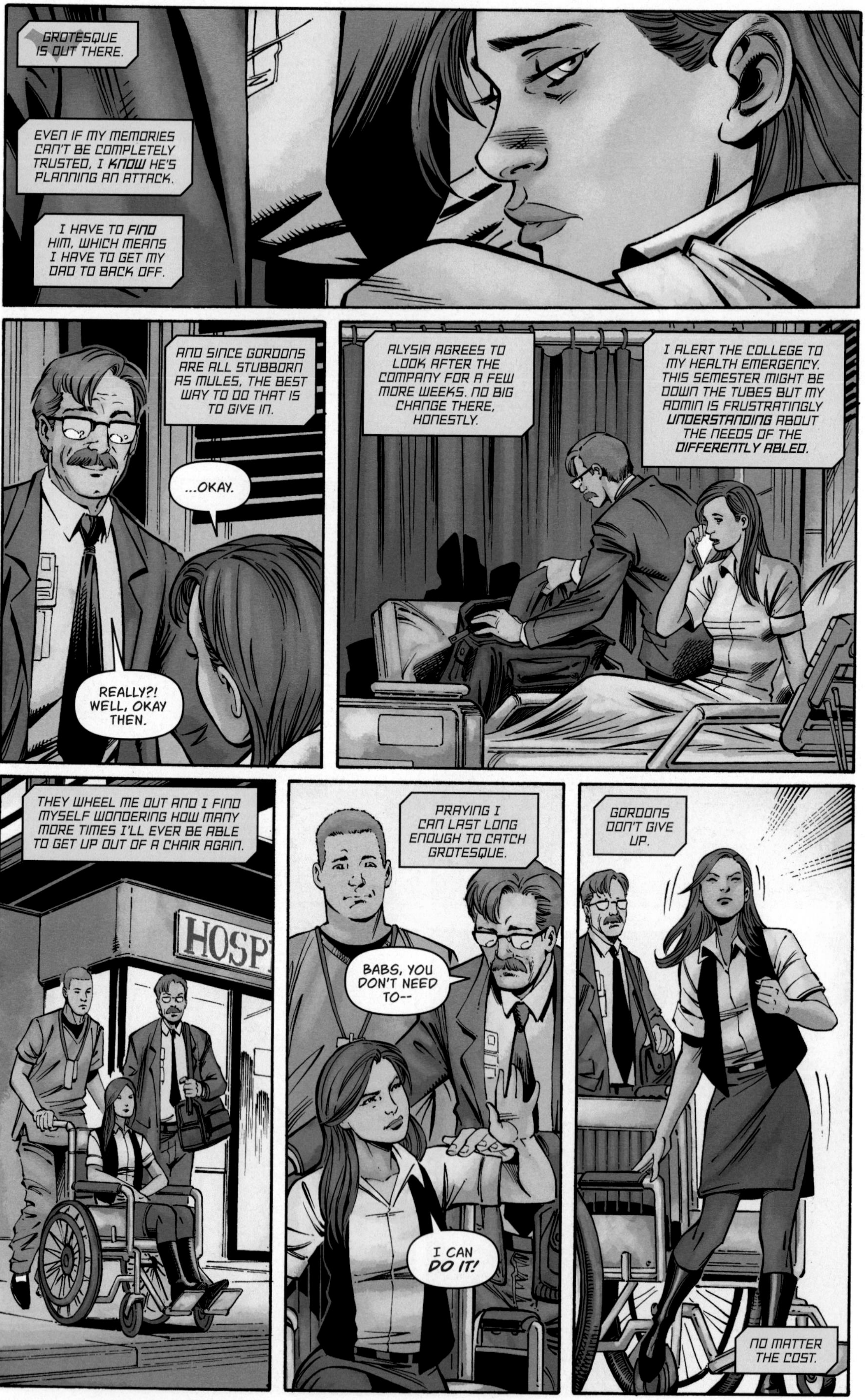
GROTESQUE IS OUT THERE.
EVEN IF MY MEMORIES CAN'T BE COMPLETELY TRUSTED, I KNOW HE'S PLANNING AN ATTACK.
I HAVE TO FIND HIM, WHICH MEANS I HAVE TO GET MY DAD TO BACK OFF.
AND SINCE GORDONS ARE ALL STUBBORN AS MULES, THE BEST WAY TO DO THAT IS TO GIVE IN.
...OKAY.
REALLY?! WELL, OKAY THEN.
ALYSIA AGREES TO LOOK AFTER THE COMPANY FOR A FEW MORE WEEKS. NO BIG CHANGE THERE, HONESTLY.
I ALERT THE COLLEGE TO MY HEALTH EMERGENCY. THIS SEMESTER MIGHT BE DOWN THE TUBES BUT MY ADMIN IS FRUSTRATINGLY UNDERSTANDING ABOUT THE NEEDS OF THE DIFFERENTLY ABLED.
THEY WHEEL ME OUT AND I FIND MYSELF WONDERING HOW MANY MORE TIMES I'LL EVER BE ABLE TO GET UP OUT OF A CHAIR AGAIN.
HOSP
PRAYING I CAN LAST LONG ENOUGH TO CATCH GROTESQUE.
BABS, YOU DON'T NEED TO--
I CAN DO IT!
GORDONS DON'T GIVE UP.
NO MATTER THE COST.

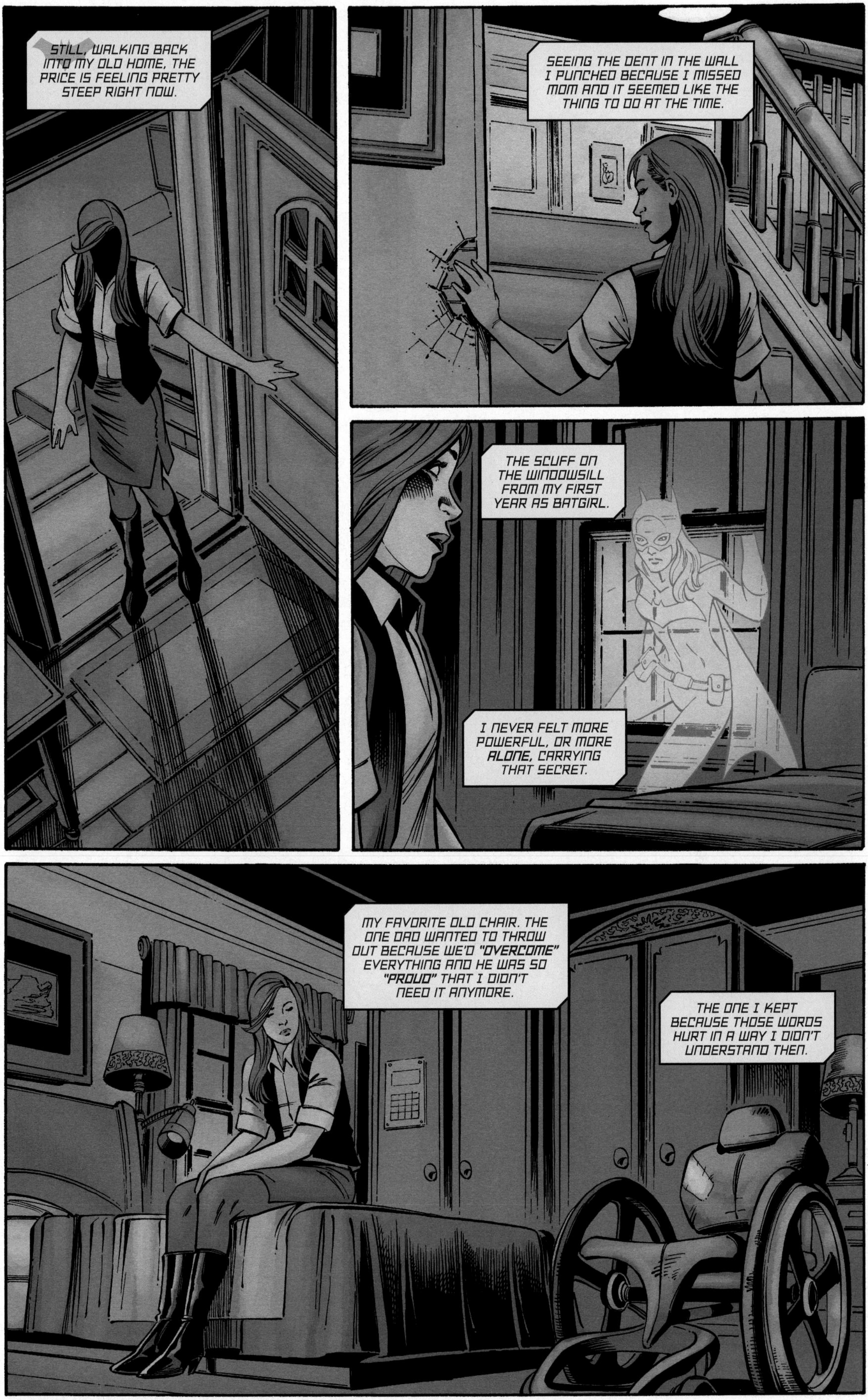
STILL, WALKING BACK INTO MY OLD HOME, THE PRICE IS FEELING PRETTY STEEP RIGHT NOW.
SEEING THE DENT IN THE WALL I PUNCHED BECAUSE I MISSED MOM AND IT SEEMED LIKE THE THING TO DO AT THE TIME.
THE SCUFF ON THE WINDOWSILL FROM MY FIRST YEAR AS BATGIRL.
I NEVER FELT MORE POWERFUL, OR MORE ALONE, CARRYING THAT SECRET.
MY FAVORITE OLD CHAIR. THE ONE DAD WANTED TO THROW OUT BECAUSE WE'D "OVERCOME" EVERYTHING AND HE WAS SO "PROUD" THAT I DIDN'T NEED IT ANYMORE.
THE ONE I KEPT BECAUSE THOSE WORDS HURT IN A WAY I DIDN'T UNDERSTAND THEN.

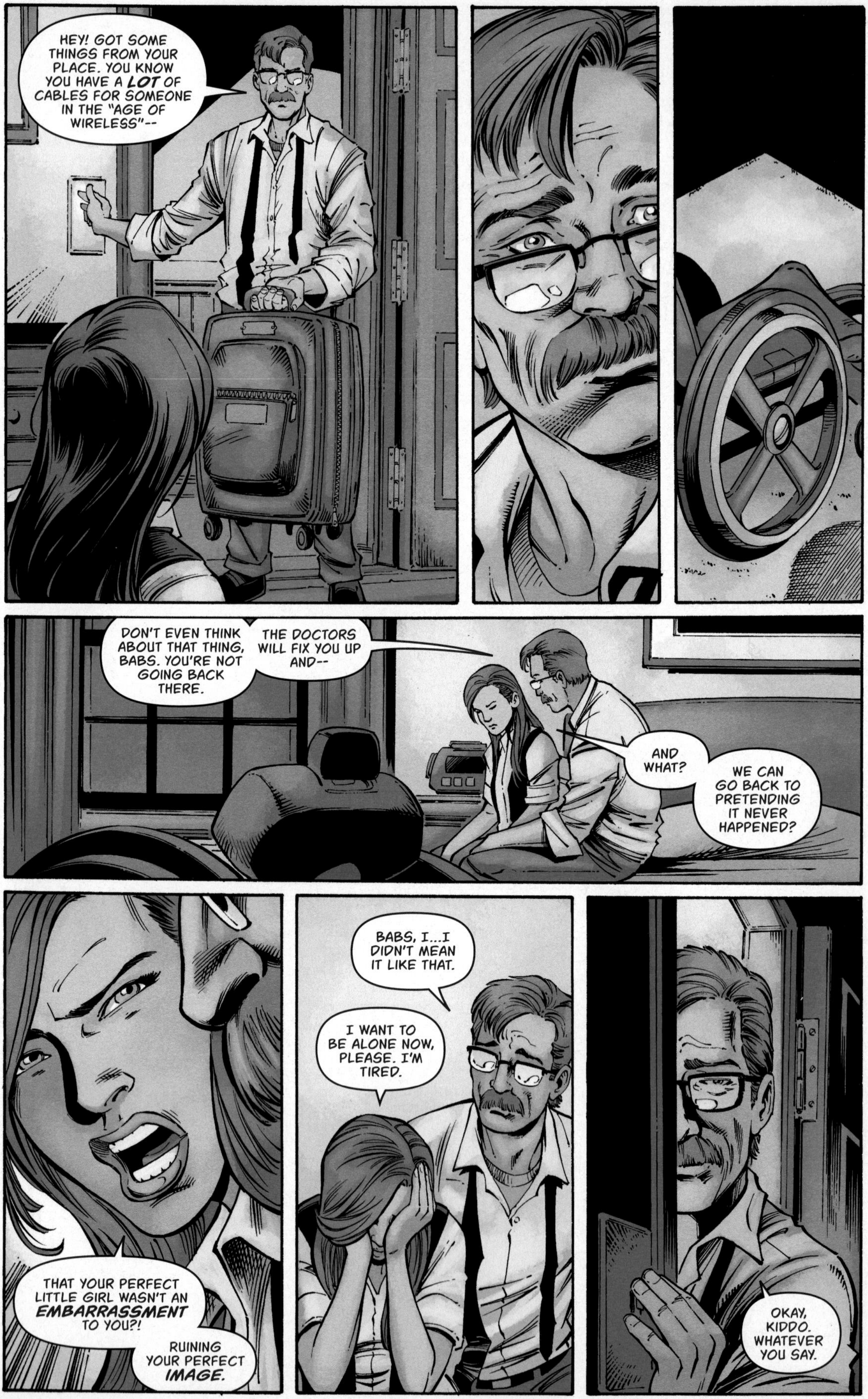
HEY! GOT SOME THINGS FROM YOUR PLACE. YOU KNOW YOU HAVE A **LOT** OF CABLES FOR SOMEONE IN THE "AGE OF WIRELESS"--
DON'T EVEN THINK ABOUT THAT THING, BABS. YOU'RE NOT GOING BACK THERE.
THE DOCTORS WILL FIX YOU UP AND--
AND WHAT?
WE CAN GO BACK TO PRETENDING IT NEVER HAPPENED?
THAT YOUR PERFECT LITTLE GIRL WASN'T AN **EMBARRASSMENT** TO YOU?!
RUINING YOUR PERFECT **IMAGE**.
BABS, I...I DIDN'T MEAN IT LIKE THAT.
I WANT TO BE ALONE NOW, PLEASE. I'M TIRED.
OKAY, KIDDO. WHATEVER YOU SAY.

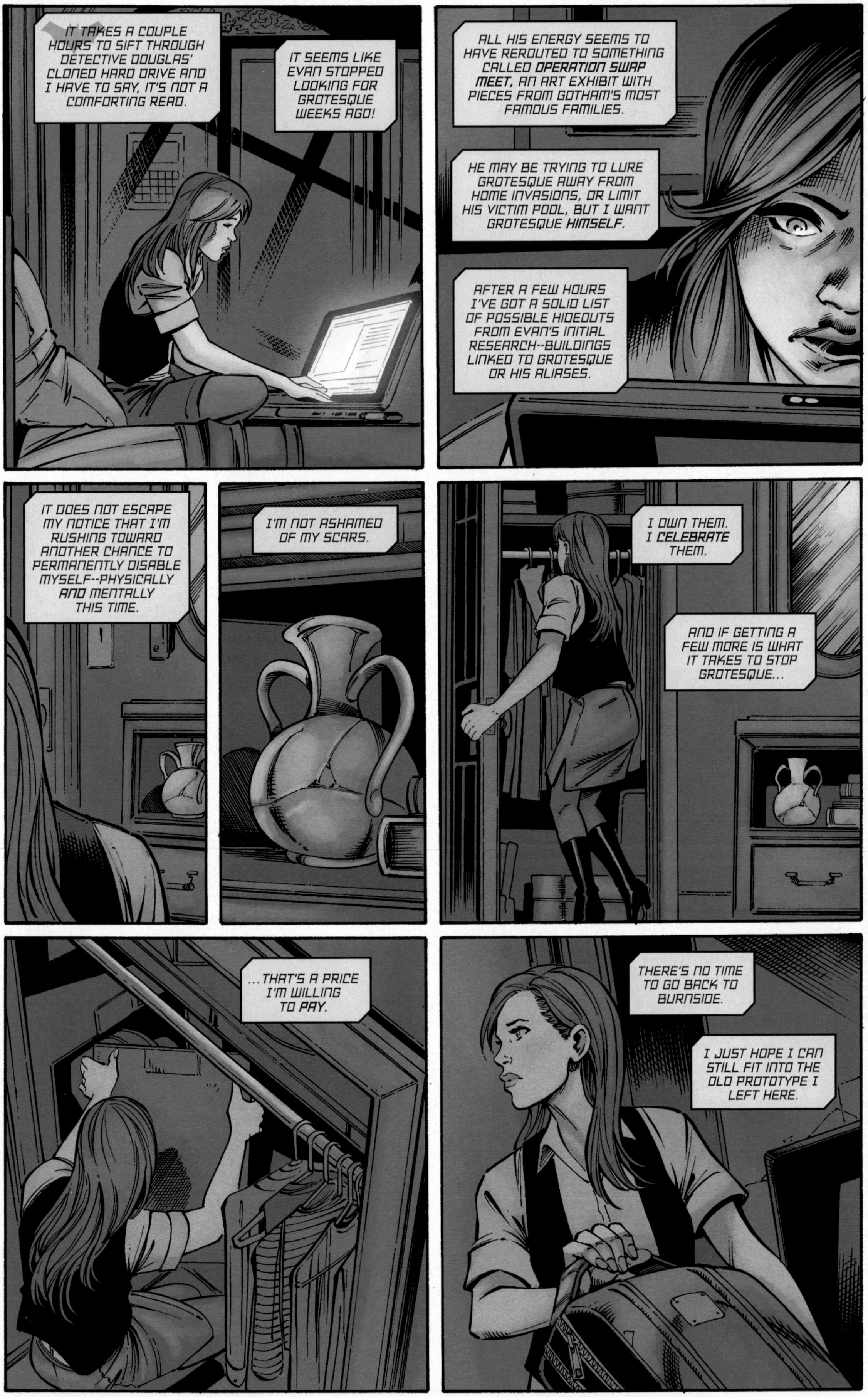
IT TAKES A COUPLE HOURS TO SIFT THROUGH DETECTIVE DOUGLAS' CLONED HARD DRIVE AND I HAVE TO SAY, IT'S NOT A COMFORTING READ.
IT SEEMS LIKE EVAN STOPPED LOOKING FOR GROTESQUE WEEKS AGO!
ALL HIS ENERGY SEEMS TO HAVE REROUTED TO SOMETHING CALLED OPERATION SWAP MEET, AN ART EXHIBIT WITH PIECES FROM GOTHAM'S MOST FAMOUS FAMILIES.
HE MAY BE TRYING TO LURE GROTESQUE AWAY FROM HOME INVASIONS, OR LIMIT HIS VICTIM POOL, BUT I WANT GROTESQUE HIMSELF.
AFTER A FEW HOURS I'VE GOT A SOLID LIST OF POSSIBLE HIDEOUTS FROM EVAN'S INITIAL RESEARCH--BUILDINGS LINKED TO GROTESQUE OR HIS ALIASES.
IT DOES NOT ESCAPE MY NOTICE THAT I'M RUSHING TOWARD ANOTHER CHANCE TO PERMANENTLY DISABLE MYSELF--PHYSICALLY AND MENTALLY THIS TIME.
I'M NOT ASHAMED OF MY SCARS.
I OWN THEM. I CELEBRATE THEM.
AND IF GETTING A FEW MORE IS WHAT IT TAKES TO STOP GROTESQUE...
...THAT'S A PRICE I'M WILLING TO PAY.
THERE'S NO TIME TO GO BACK TO BURNSIDE.
I JUST HOPE I CAN STILL FIT INTO THE OLD PROTOTYPE I LEFT HERE.

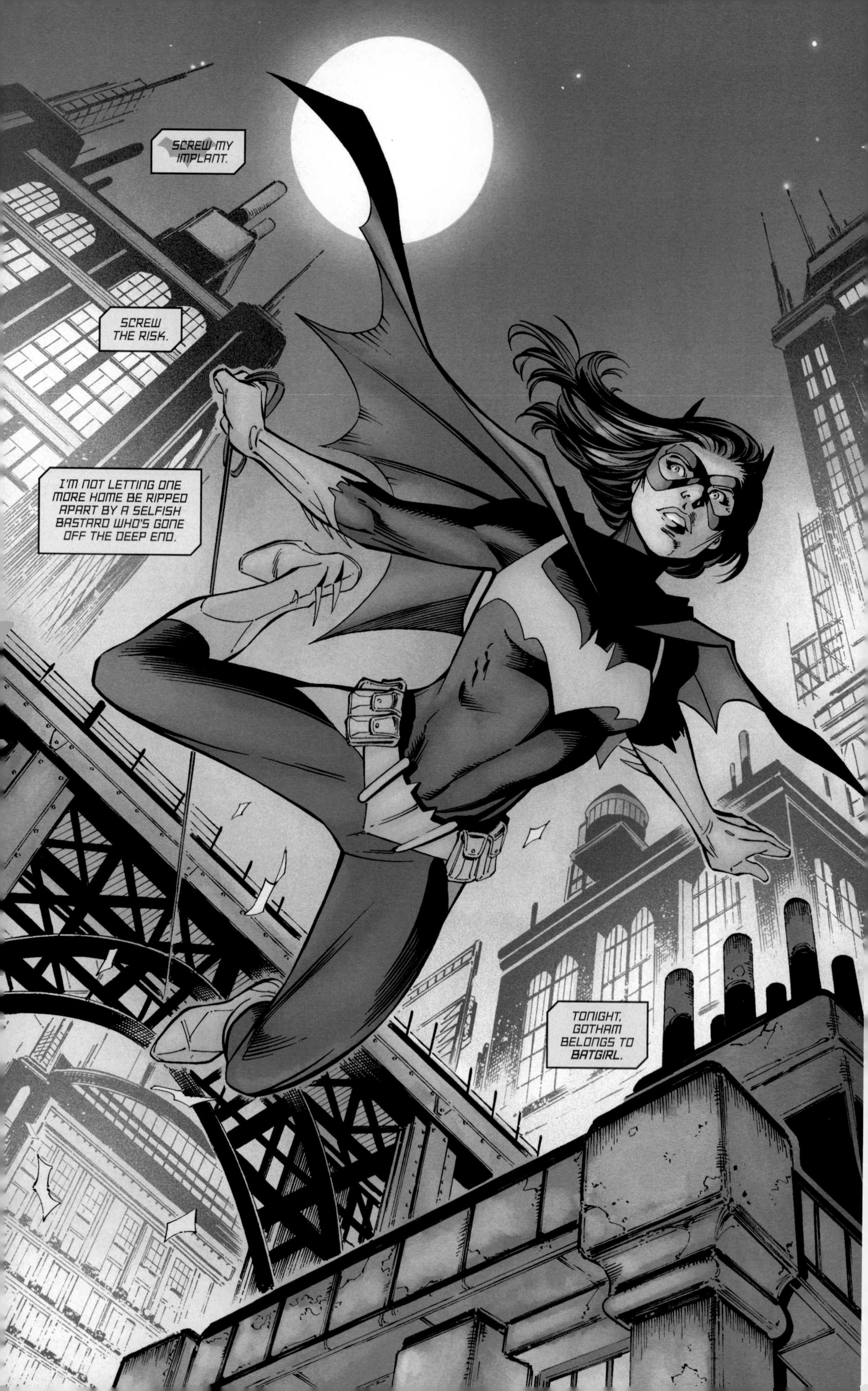
SCREW MY IMPLANT.
SCREW THE RISK.
I'M NOT LETTING ONE MORE HOME BE RIPPED APART BY A SELFISH BASTARD WHO'S GONE OFF THE DEEP END.
TONIGHT, GOTHAM BELONGS TO BATGIRL.

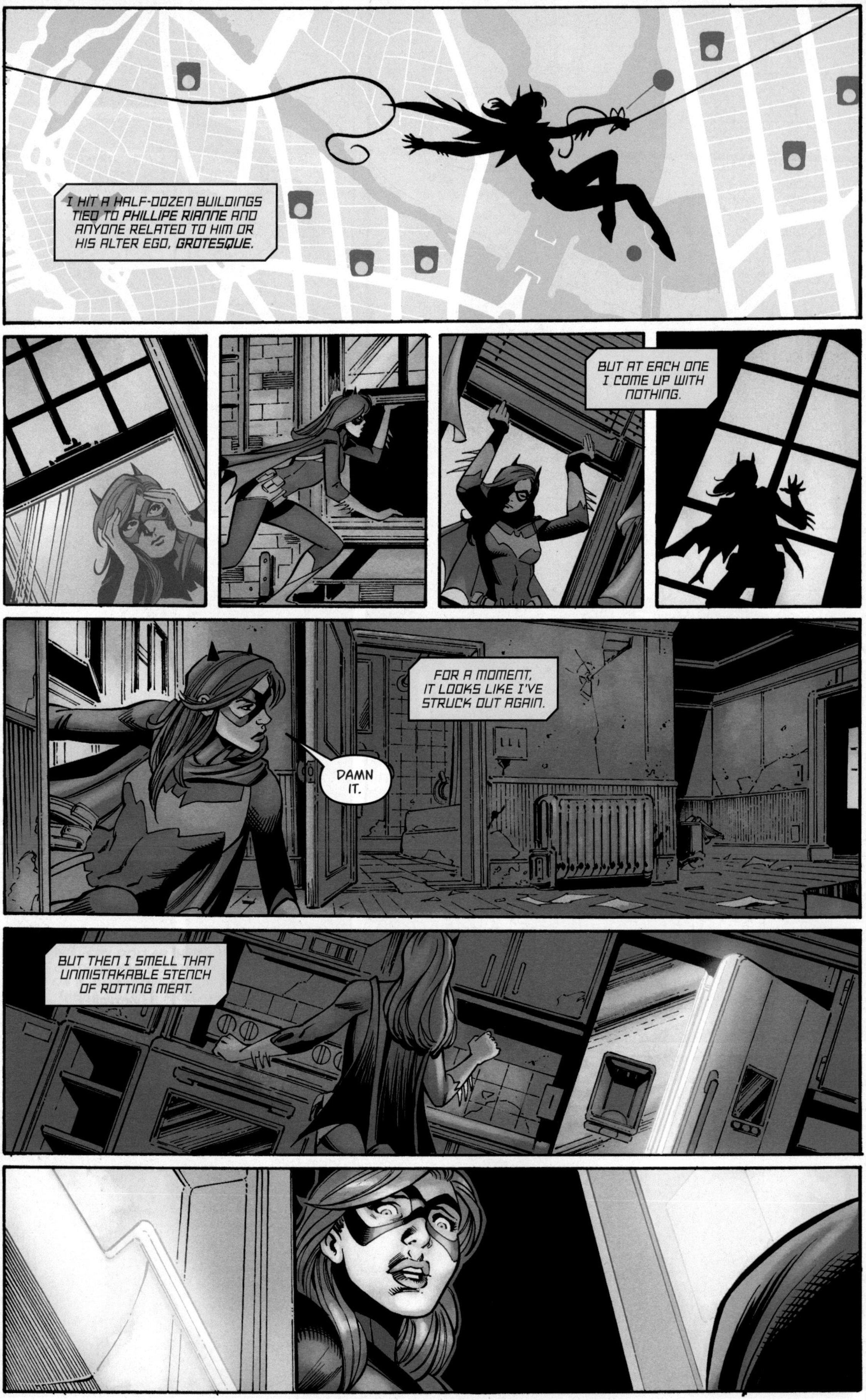
I HIT A HALF-DOZEN BUILDINGS TIED TO PHILLIPE RIANNE AND ANYONE RELATED TO HIM OR HIS ALTER EGO, GROTESQUE.
BUT AT EACH ONE I COME UP WITH NOTHING.
FOR A MOMENT, IT LOOKS LIKE I'VE STRUCK OUT AGAIN.
DAMN IT.
BUT THEN I SMELL THAT UNMISTAKABLE STENCH OF ROTTING MEAT.

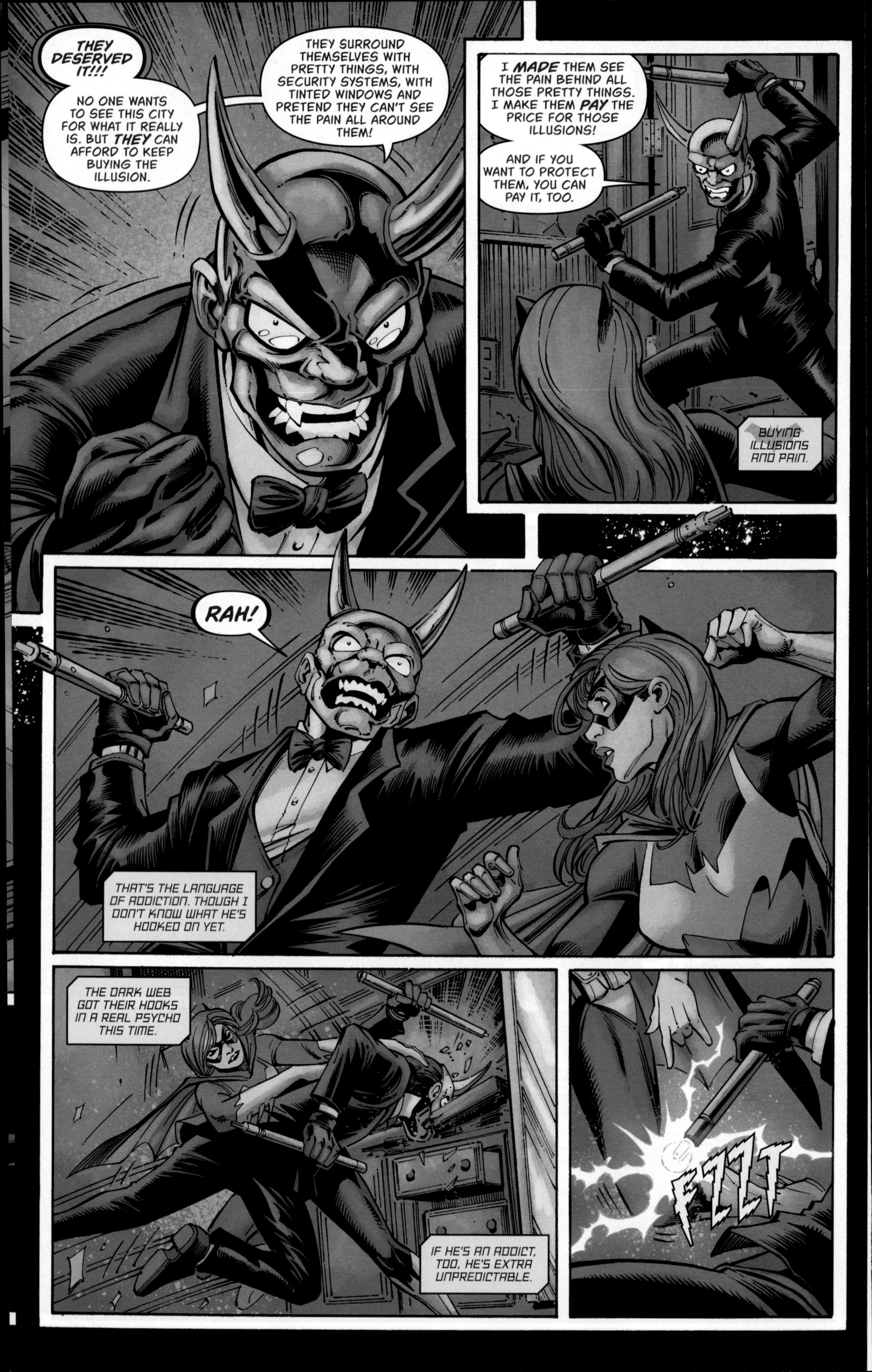
THEY DESERVED IT!!!
NO ONE WANTS TO SEE THIS CITY FOR WHAT IT REALLY IS. BUT THEY CAN AFFORD TO KEEP BUYING THE ILLUSION.
THEY SURROUND THEMSELVES WITH PRETTY THINGS, WITH SECURITY SYSTEMS, WITH TINTED WINDOWS AND PRETEND THEY CAN'T SEE THE PAIN ALL AROUND THEM!
I MADE THEM SEE THE PAIN BEHIND ALL THOSE PRETTY THINGS. I MAKE THEM PAY THE PRICE FOR THOSE ILLUSIONS!
AND IF YOU WANT TO PROTECT THEM, YOU CAN PAY IT, TOO.
BUYING ILLUSIONS AND PAIN.
RAH!
THAT'S THE LANGUAGE OF ADDICTION. THOUGH I DON'T KNOW WHAT HE'S HOOKED ON YET.
THE DARK WEB GOT THEIR HOOKS IN A REAL PSYCHO THIS TIME.
IF HE'S AN ADDICT, TOO, HE'S EXTRA UNPREDICTABLE.
FZZT

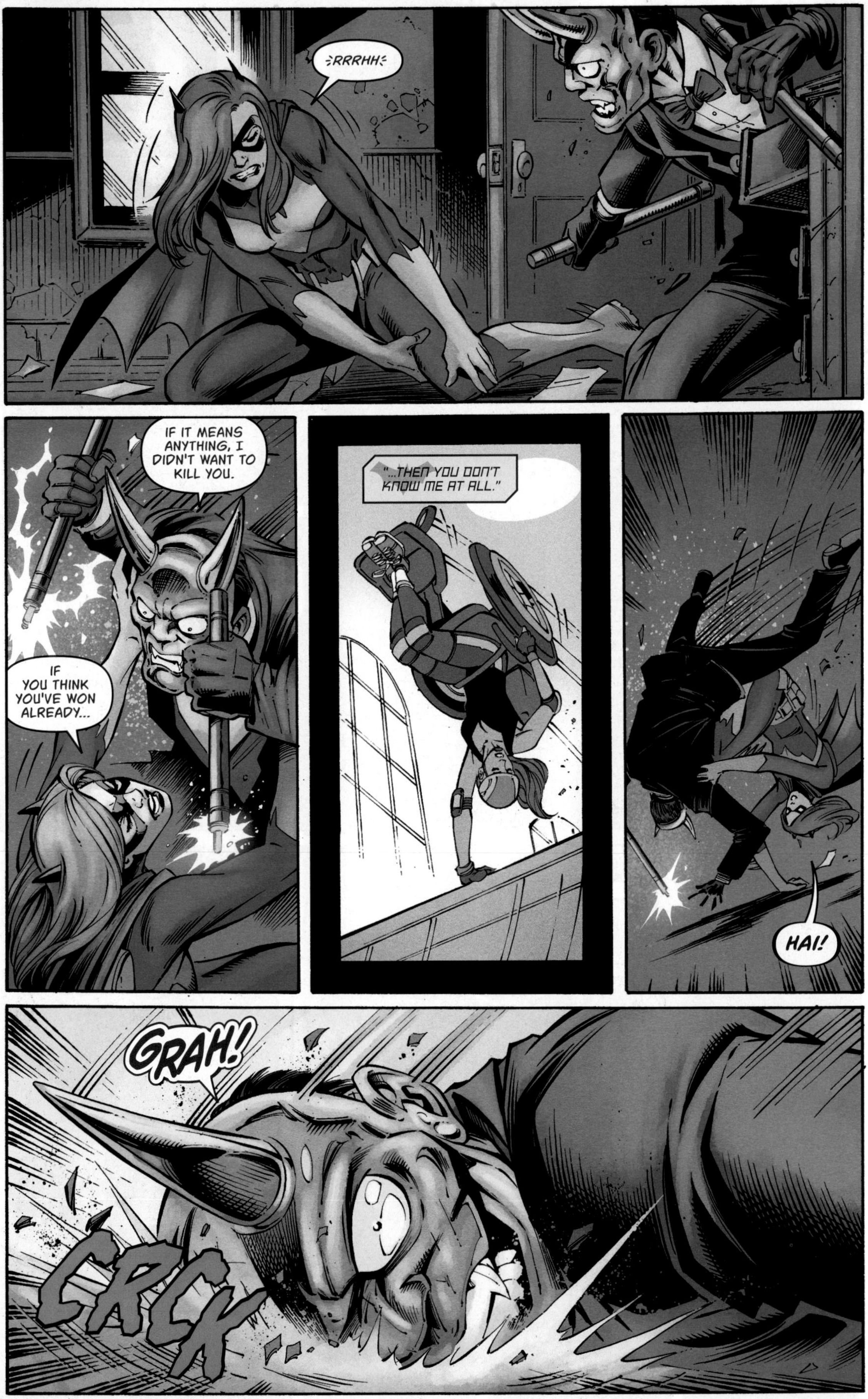
RRRHH
IF IT MEANS ANYTHING, I DIDN'T WANT TO KILL YOU.
IF YOU THINK YOU'VE WON ALREADY...
"...THEN YOU DON'T KNOW ME AT ALL."
HAI!
GRAH!
CRCK

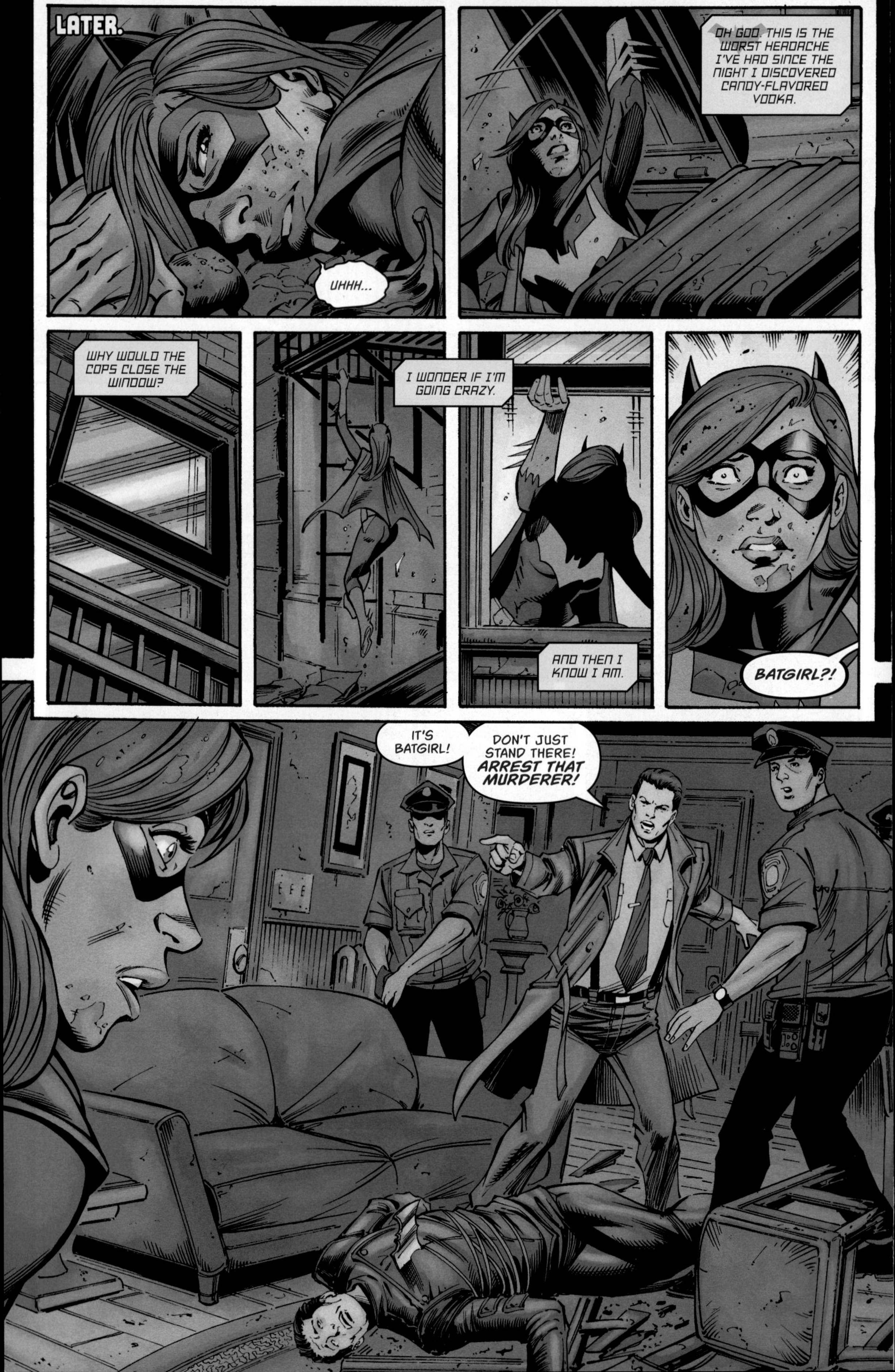
LATER.
UHHH...
OH GOD. THIS IS THE WORST HEADACHE I'VE HAD SINCE THE NIGHT I DISCOVERED CANDY-FLAVORED VODKA.
WHY WOULD THE COPS CLOSE THE WINDOW?
I WONDER IF I'M GOING CRAZY.
AND THEN I KNOW I AM.
BATGIRL?!
IT'S BATGIRL!
DON'T JUST STAND THERE! ARREST THAT MURDERER!

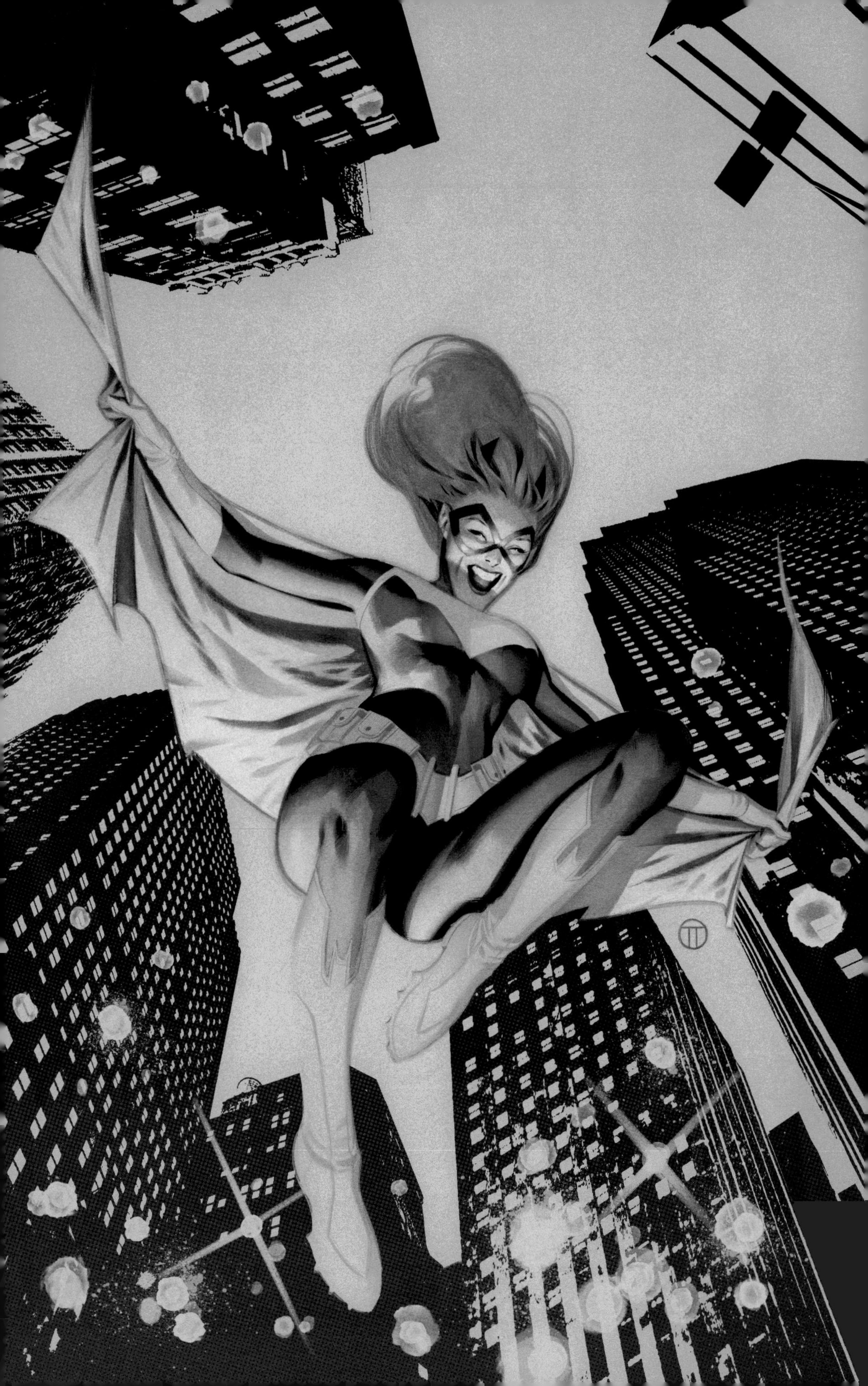

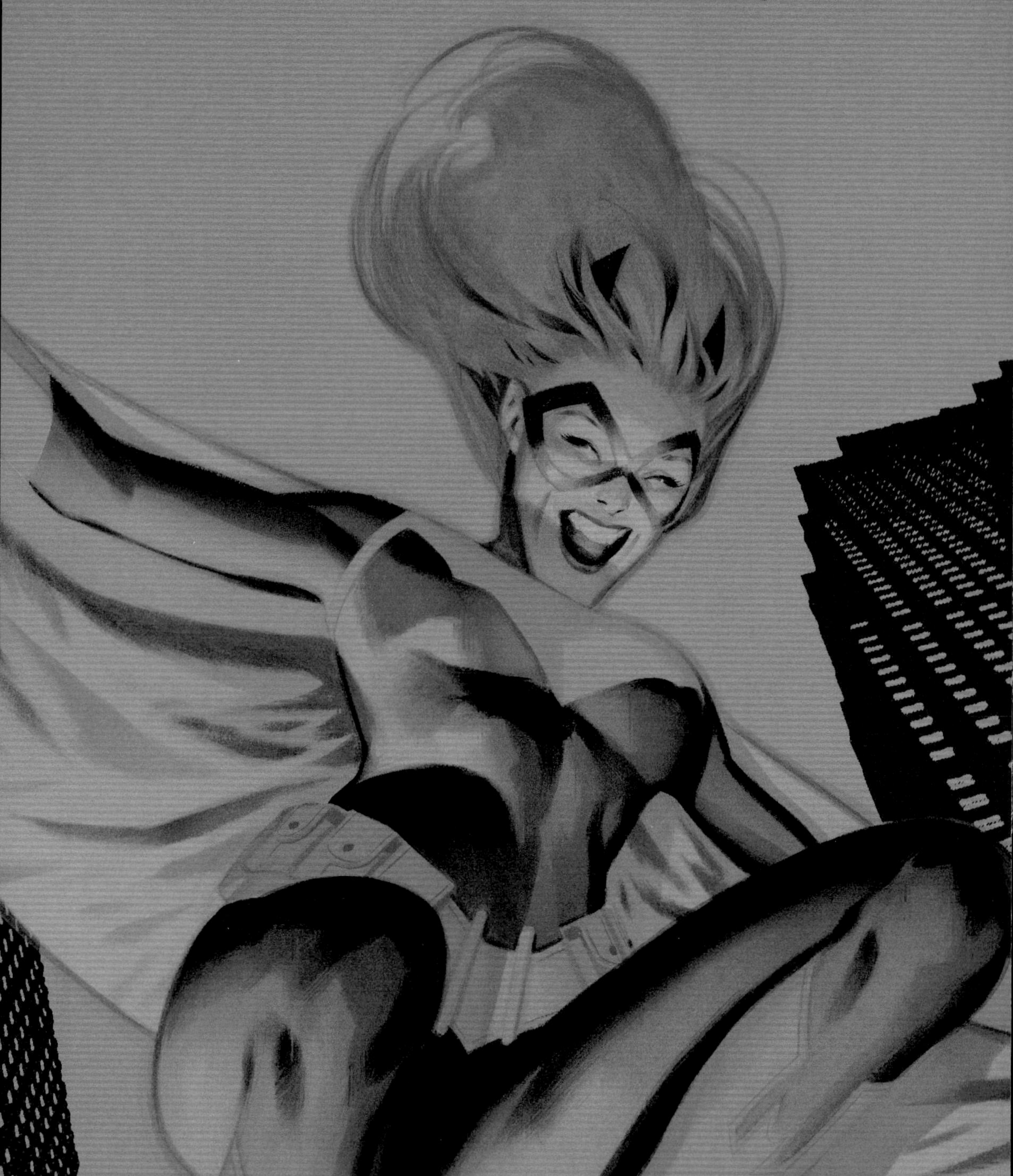

# BATGIRL
#28

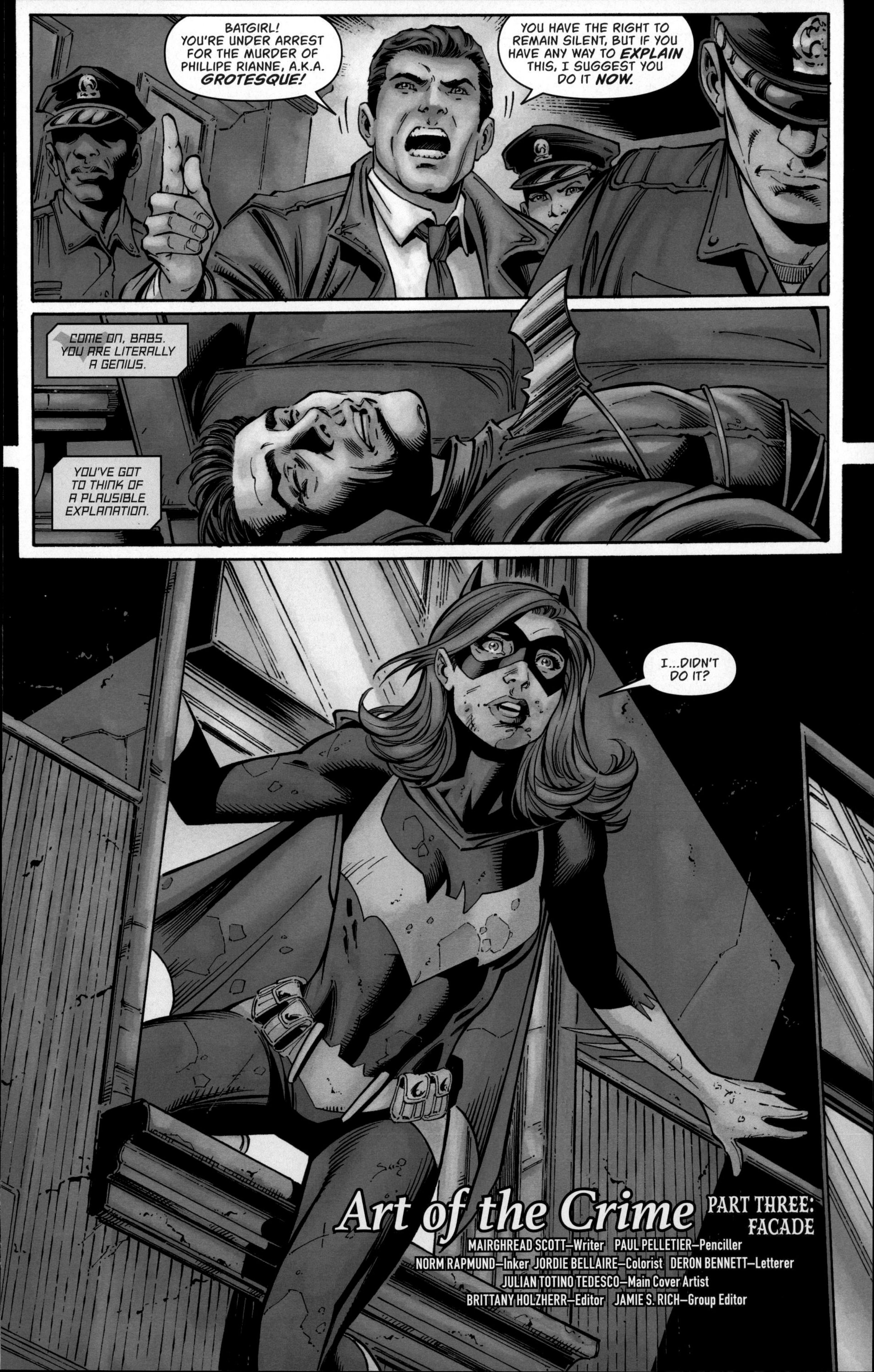
BATGIRL! YOU'RE UNDER ARREST FOR THE MURDER OF PHILLIPE RIANNE, A.K.A. GROTESQUE!
YOU HAVE THE RIGHT TO REMAIN SILENT, BUT IF YOU HAVE ANY WAY TO EXPLAIN THIS, I SUGGEST YOU DO IT NOW.
COME ON, BABS. YOU ARE LITERALLY A GENIUS.
YOU'VE GOT TO THINK OF A PLAUSIBLE EXPLANATION.
I...DIDN'T DO IT?
Art of the Crime PART THREE: FACADE
MAIRGHREAD SCOTT—Writer PAUL PELLETIER—Penciller
NORM RAPMUND—Inker JORDIE BELLAIRE—Colorist DERON BENNETT—Letterer
JULIAN TOTINO TEDESCO—Main Cover Artist
BRITTANY HOLZHERR—Editor JAMIE S. RICH—Group Editor

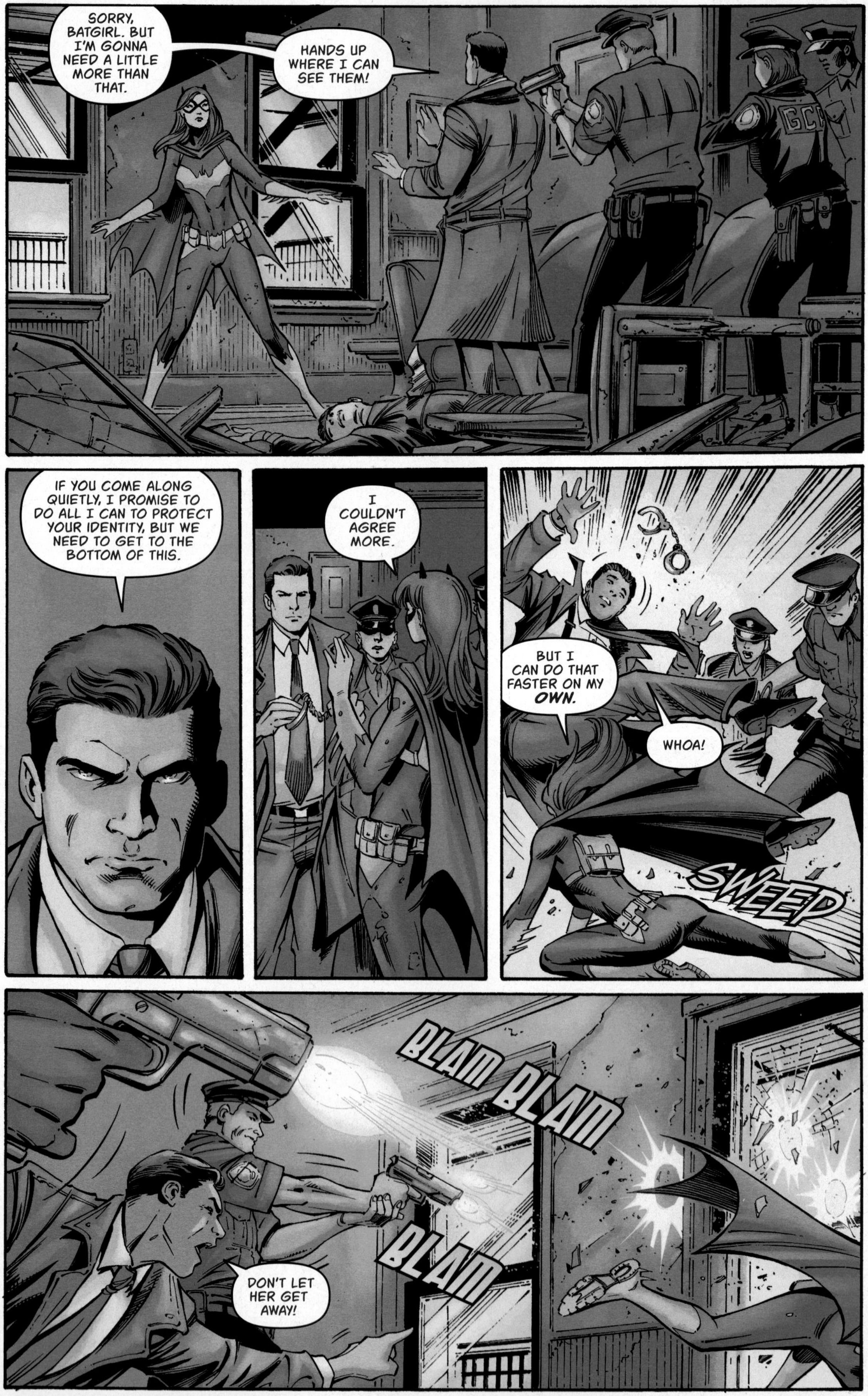
SORRY, BATGIRL. BUT I'M GONNA NEED A LITTLE MORE THAN THAT.
HANDS UP WHERE I CAN SEE THEM!
GCP
IF YOU COME ALONG QUIETLY, I PROMISE TO DO ALL I CAN TO PROTECT YOUR IDENTITY, BUT WE NEED TO GET TO THE BOTTOM OF THIS.
I COULDN'T AGREE MORE.
BUT I CAN DO THAT FASTER ON MY OWN.
WHOA!
SWEEP
BLAM BLAM
BLAM
DON'T LET HER GET AWAY!

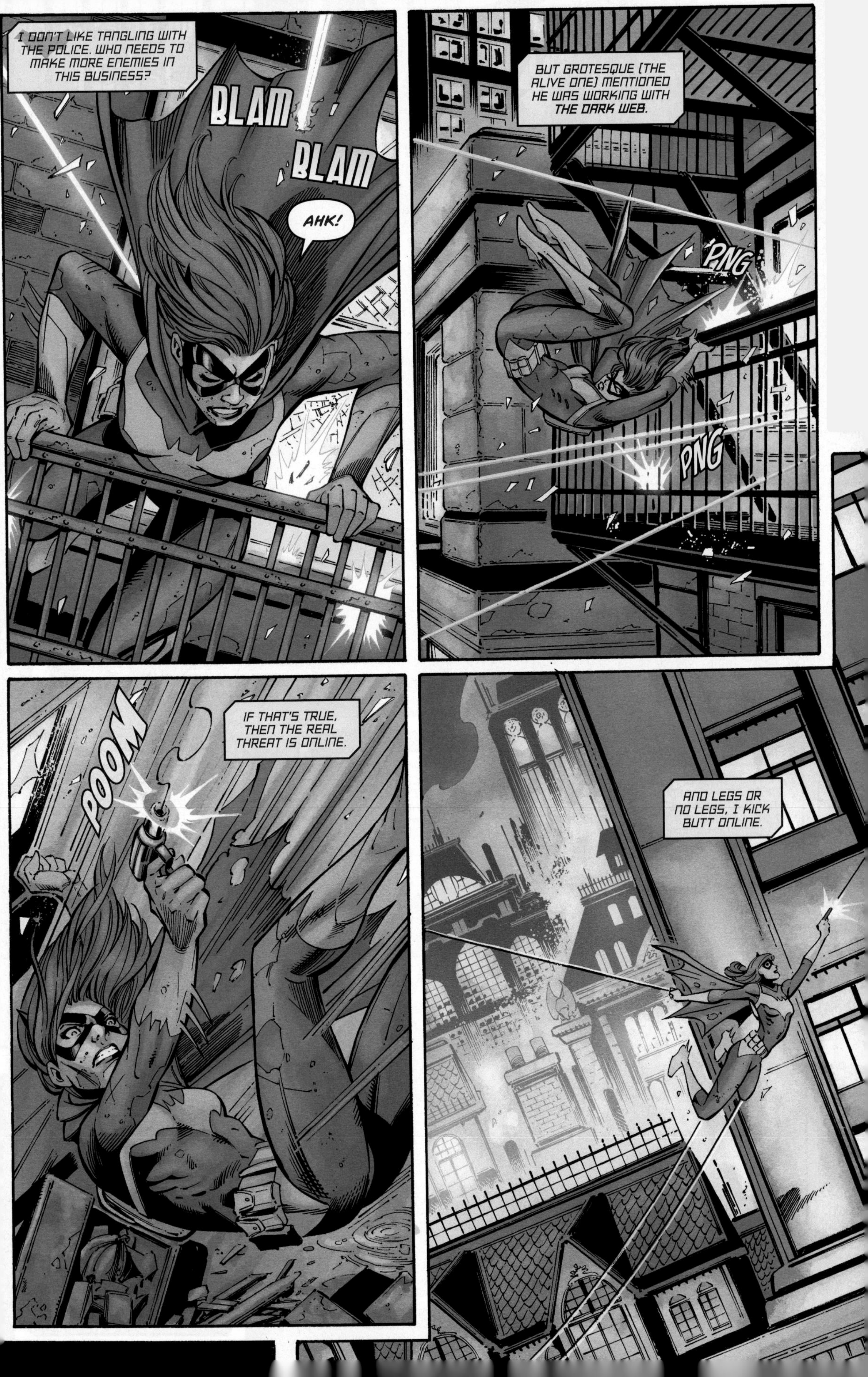

I DON'T LIKE TANGLING WITH THE POLICE. WHO NEEDS TO MAKE MORE ENEMIES IN THIS BUSINESS?
BLAM
BLAM
AHK!
BUT GROTESQUE (THE ALIVE ONE) MENTIONED HE WAS WORKING WITH THE DARK WEB.
PNG
PNG
IF THAT'S TRUE, THEN THE REAL THREAT IS ONLINE.
POOM
AND LEGS OR NO LEGS, I KICK BUTT ONLINE.

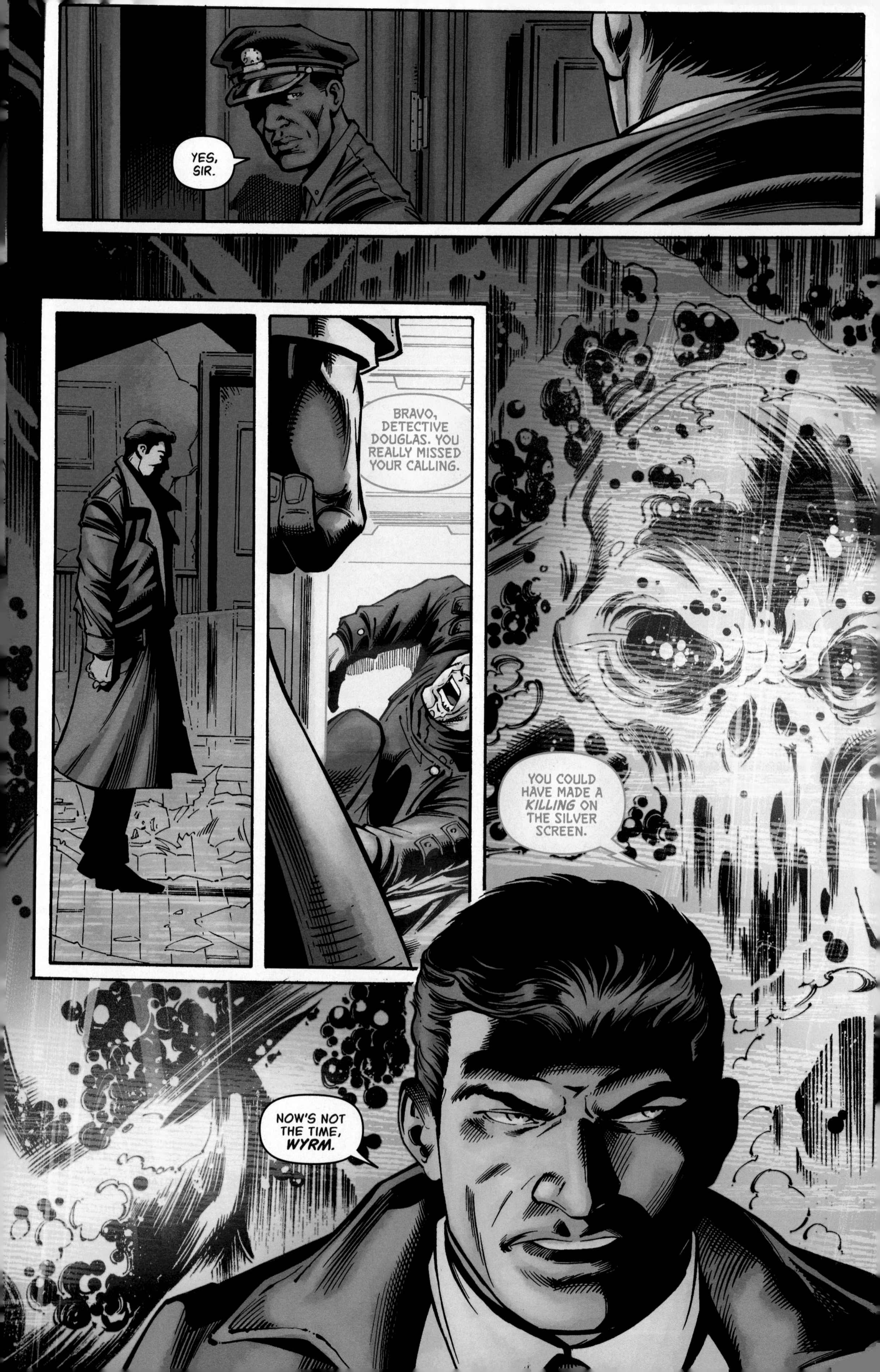
YES, SIR.
BRAVO, DETECTIVE DOUGLAS. YOU REALLY MISSED YOUR CALLING.
YOU COULD HAVE MADE A *KILLING* ON THE SILVER SCREEN.
NOW'S NOT THE TIME, ***WYRM.***

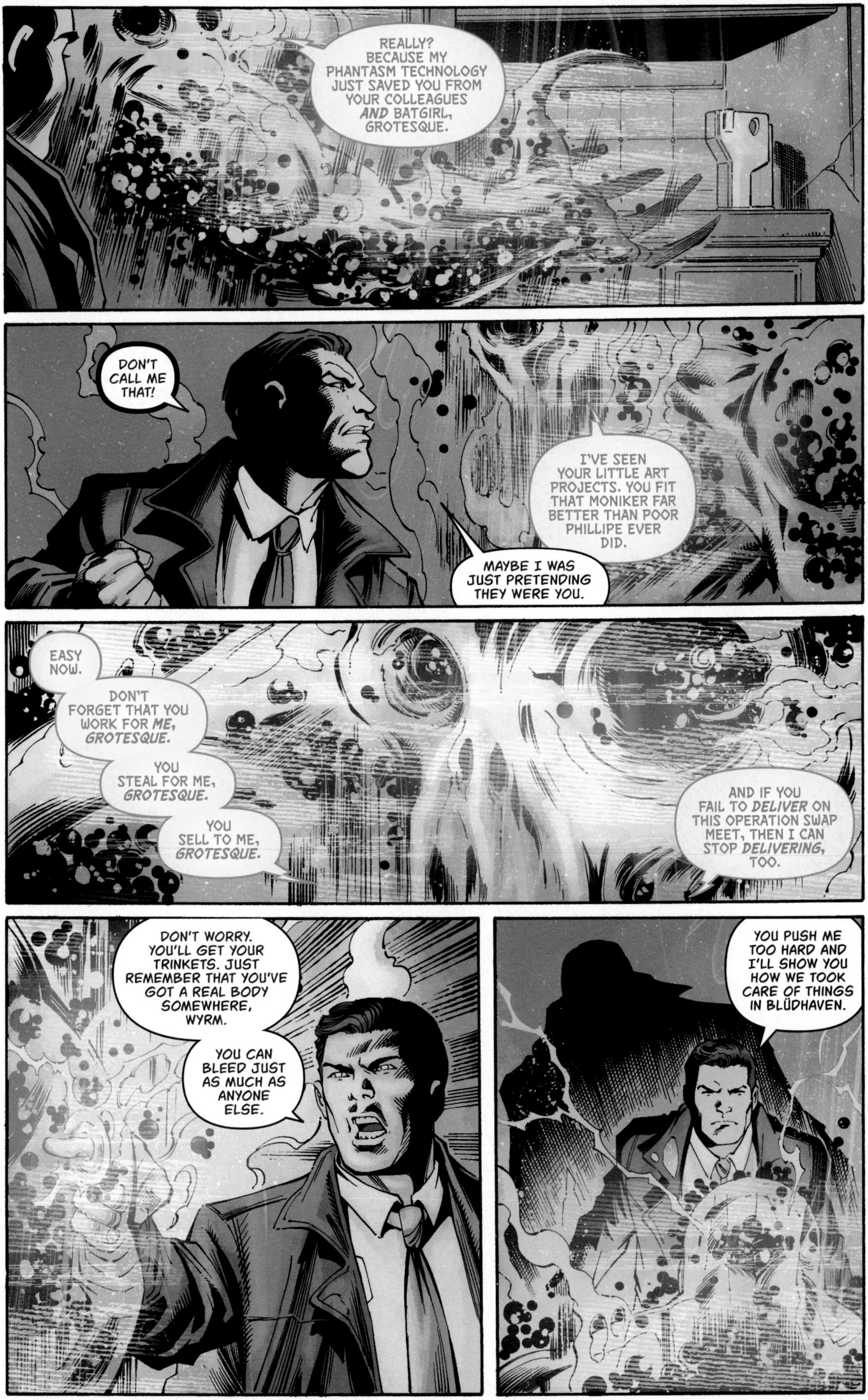
REALLY? BECAUSE MY PHANTASM TECHNOLOGY JUST SAVED YOU FROM YOUR COLLEAGUES *AND* BATGIRL, GROTESQUE.
DON'T CALL ME THAT!
I'VE SEEN YOUR LITTLE ART PROJECTS. YOU FIT THAT MONIKER FAR BETTER THAN POOR PHILLIPE EVER DID.
MAYBE I WAS JUST PRETENDING THEY WERE YOU.
EASY NOW.
DON'T FORGET THAT YOU WORK FOR *ME, GROTESQUE.*
YOU STEAL FOR ME, *GROTESQUE.*
YOU SELL TO ME, *GROTESQUE.*
AND IF YOU FAIL TO *DELIVER* ON THIS OPERATION SWAP MEET, THEN I CAN STOP *DELIVERING,* TOO.
DON'T WORRY. YOU'LL GET YOUR TRINKETS. JUST REMEMBER THAT YOU'VE GOT A REAL BODY SOMEWHERE, WYRM.
YOU CAN BLEED JUST AS MUCH AS ANYONE ELSE.
YOU PUSH ME TOO HARD AND I'LL SHOW YOU HOW WE TOOK CARE OF THINGS IN BLÜDHAVEN.

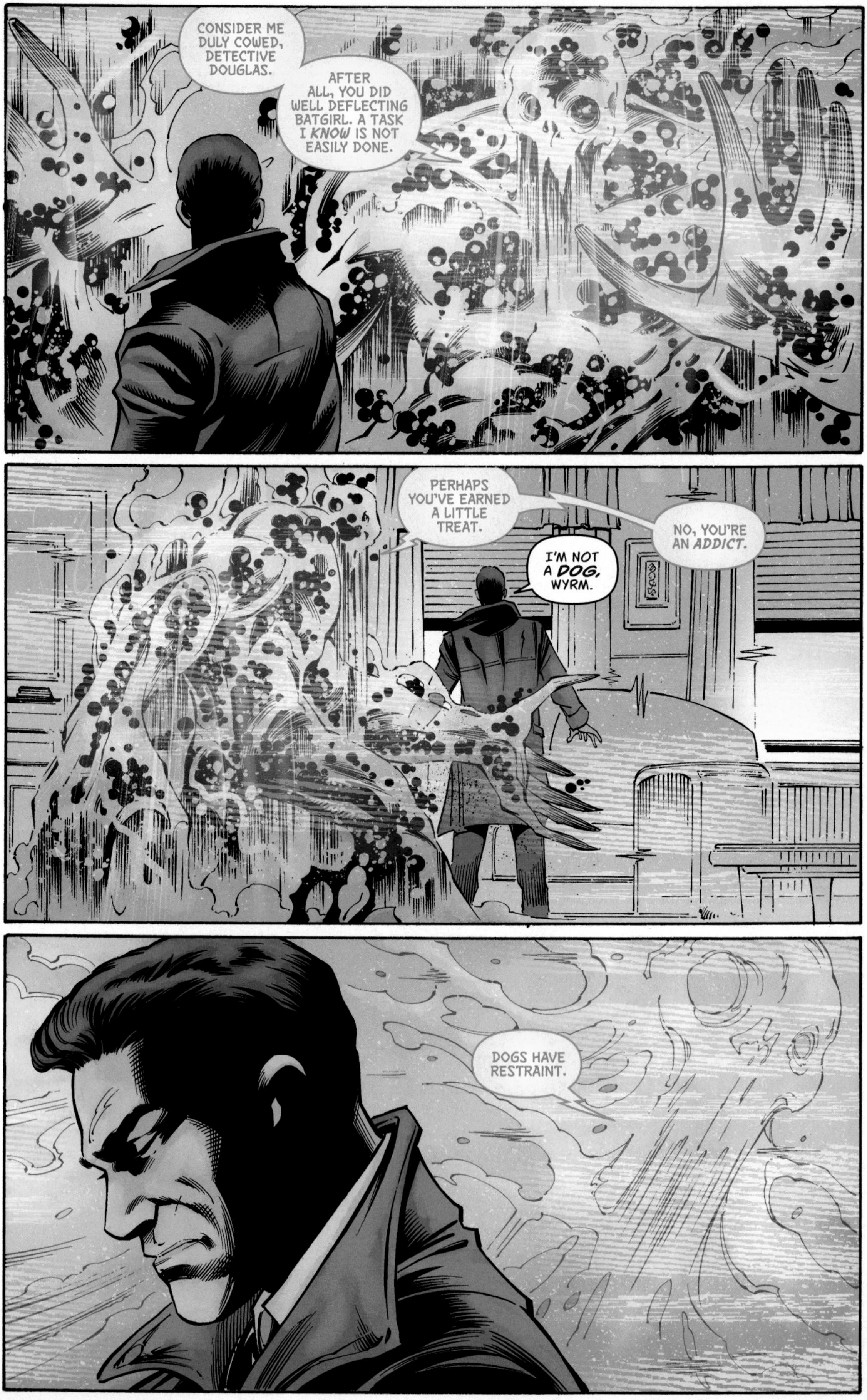
CONSIDER ME DULY COWED, DETECTIVE DOUGLAS.
AFTER ALL, YOU DID WELL DEFLECTING BATGIRL. A TASK I *KNOW* IS NOT EASILY DONE.
PERHAPS YOU'VE EARNED A LITTLE TREAT.
I'M NOT A ***DOG,*** WYRM.
NO, YOU'RE AN *ADDICT*.
DOGS HAVE RESTRAINT.

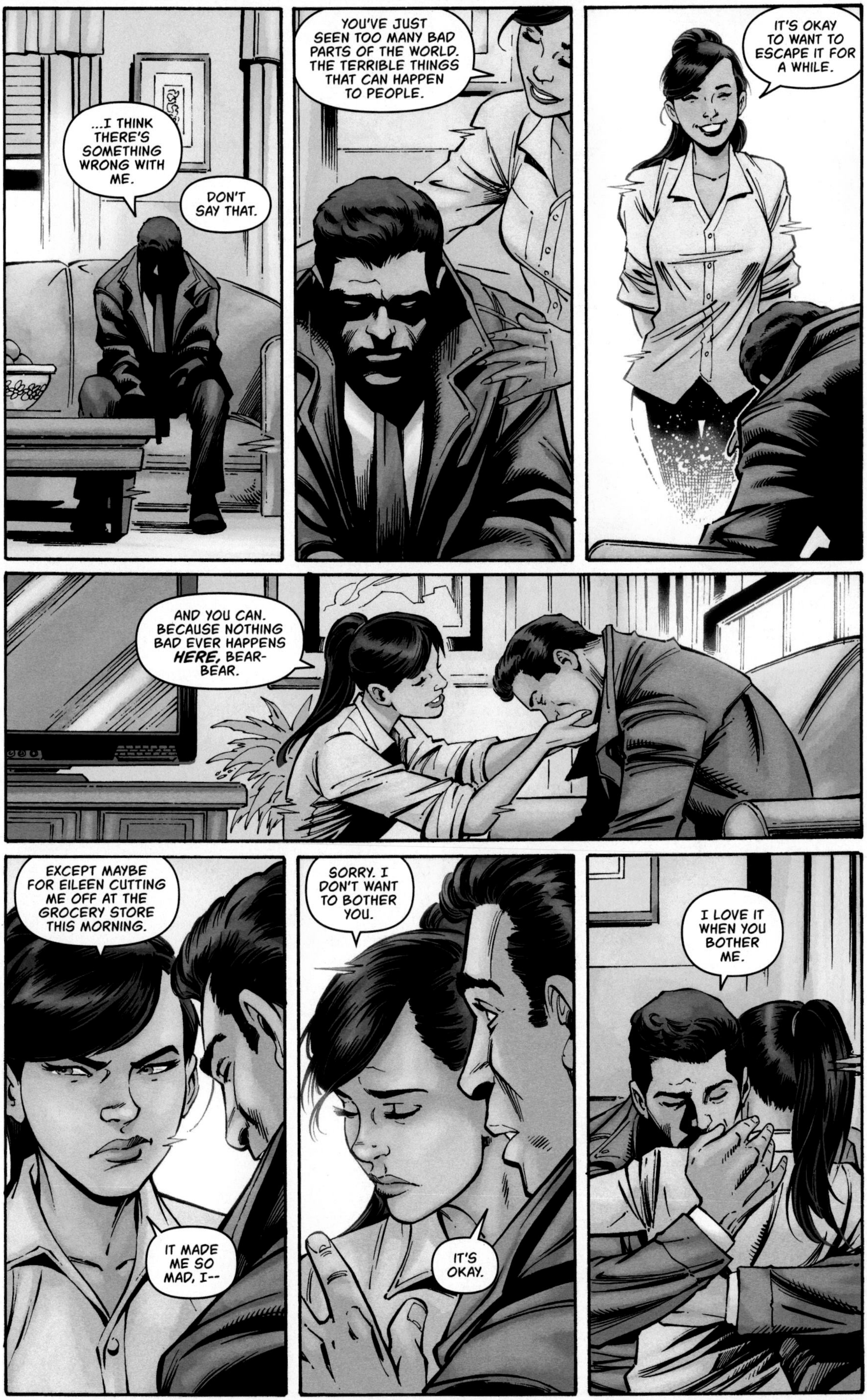
...I THINK THERE'S SOMETHING WRONG WITH ME.
DON'T SAY THAT.
YOU'VE JUST SEEN TOO MANY BAD PARTS OF THE WORLD. THE TERRIBLE THINGS THAT CAN HAPPEN TO PEOPLE.
IT'S OKAY TO WANT TO ESCAPE IT FOR A WHILE.
AND YOU CAN. BECAUSE NOTHING BAD EVER HAPPENS *HERE,* BEAR-BEAR.
EXCEPT MAYBE FOR EILEEN CUTTING ME OFF AT THE GROCERY STORE THIS MORNING.
IT MADE ME SO MAD, I--
SORRY. I DON'T WANT TO BOTHER YOU.
IT'S OKAY.
I LOVE IT WHEN YOU BOTHER ME.

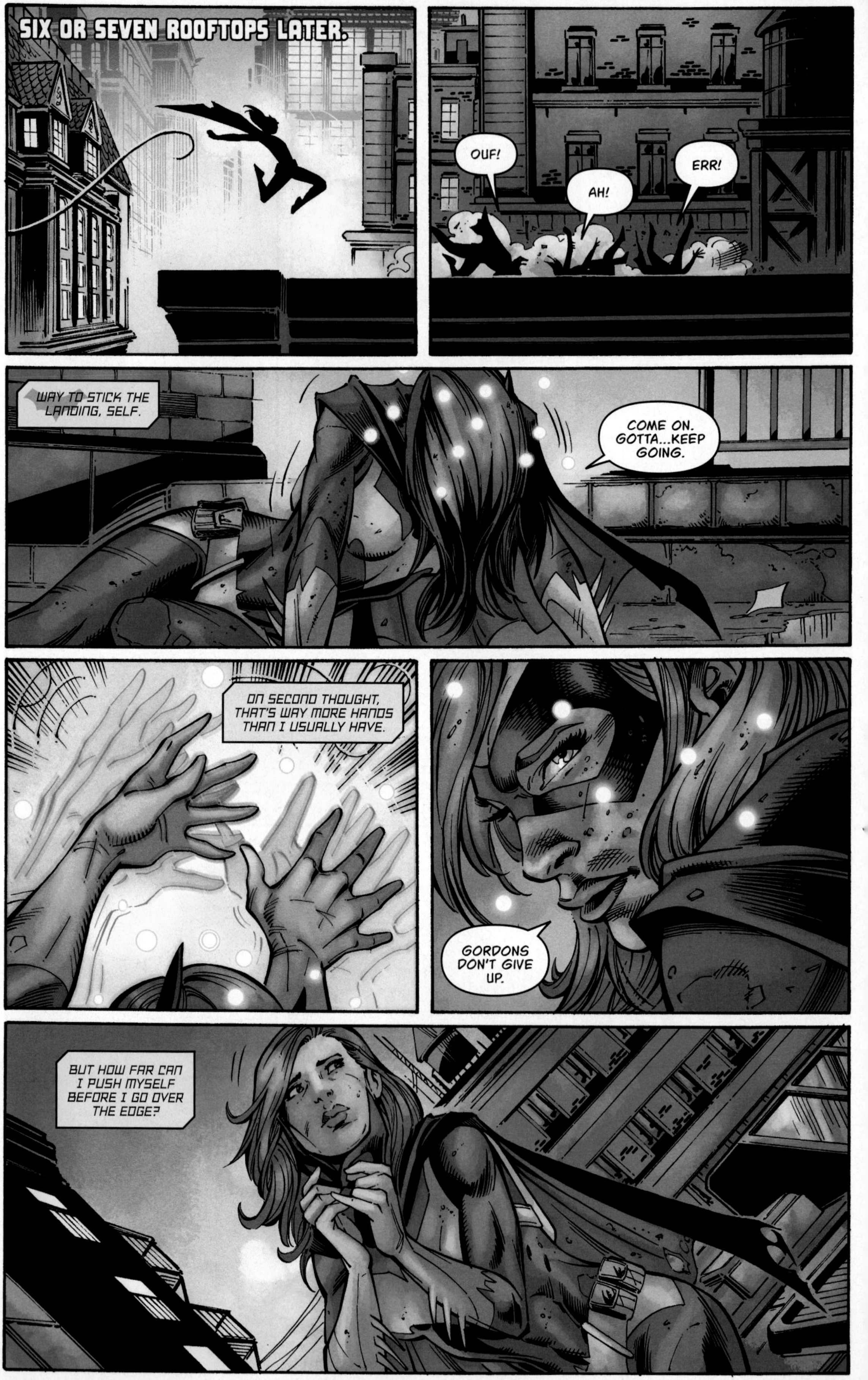
SIX OR SEVEN ROOFTOPS LATER.
OUF!
AH!
ERR!
WAY TO STICK THE LANDING, SELF.
COME ON. GOTTA...KEEP GOING.
ON SECOND THOUGHT, THAT'S WAY MORE HANDS THAN I USUALLY HAVE.
GORDONS DON'T GIVE UP.
BUT HOW FAR CAN I PUSH MYSELF BEFORE I GO OVER THE EDGE?

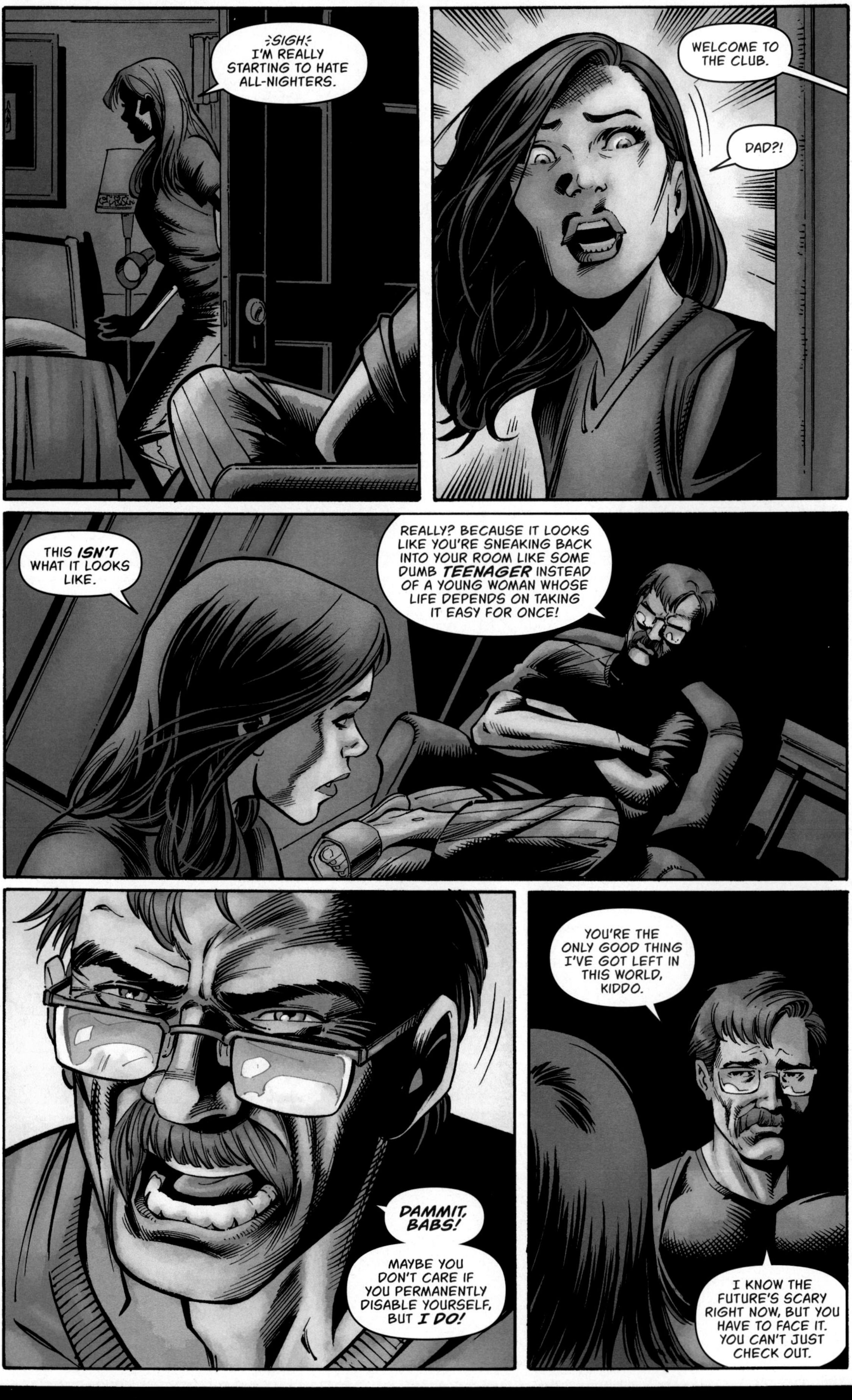

SIGH
I'M REALLY STARTING TO HATE ALL-NIGHTERS.
WELCOME TO THE CLUB.
DAD?!
THIS ISN'T WHAT IT LOOKS LIKE.
REALLY? BECAUSE IT LOOKS LIKE YOU'RE SNEAKING BACK INTO YOUR ROOM LIKE SOME DUMB TEENAGER INSTEAD OF A YOUNG WOMAN WHOSE LIFE DEPENDS ON TAKING IT EASY FOR ONCE!
DAMMIT, BABS!
MAYBE YOU DON'T CARE IF YOU PERMANENTLY DISABLE YOURSELF, BUT I DO!
YOU'RE THE ONLY GOOD THING I'VE GOT LEFT IN THIS WORLD, KIDDO.
I KNOW THE FUTURE'S SCARY RIGHT NOW, BUT YOU HAVE TO FACE IT. YOU CAN'T JUST CHECK OUT.

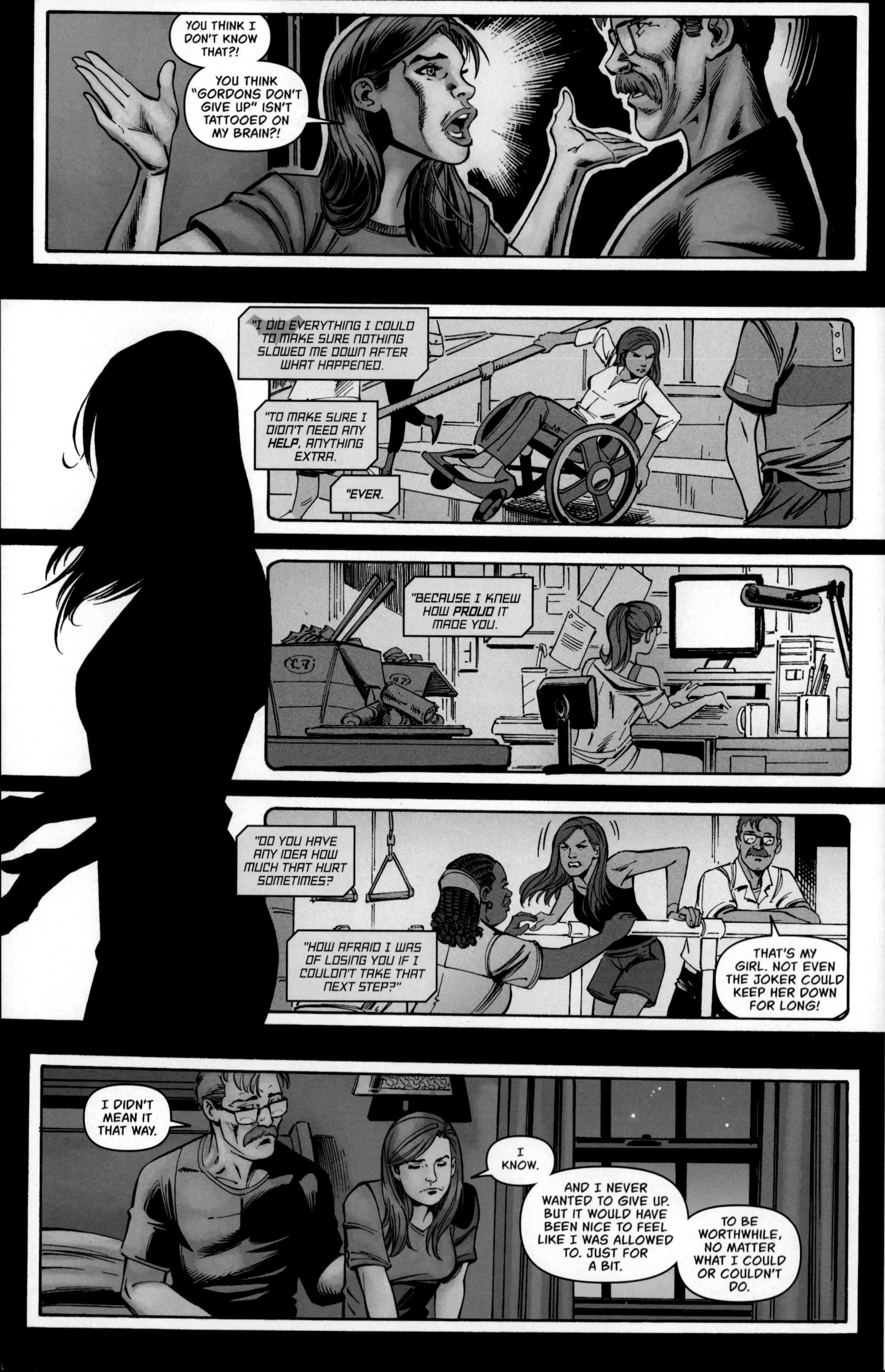
YOU THINK I DON'T KNOW THAT?!
YOU THINK "GORDONS DON'T GIVE UP" ISN'T TATTOOED ON MY BRAIN?!
"I DID EVERYTHING I COULD TO MAKE SURE NOTHING SLOWED ME DOWN AFTER WHAT HAPPENED.
"TO MAKE SURE I DIDN'T NEED ANY HELP, ANYTHING EXTRA.
"EVER.
"BECAUSE I KNEW HOW PROUD IT MADE YOU.
"DO YOU HAVE ANY IDEA HOW MUCH THAT HURT SOMETIMES?
"HOW AFRAID I WAS OF LOSING YOU IF I COULDN'T TAKE THAT NEXT STEP?"
THAT'S MY GIRL. NOT EVEN THE JOKER COULD KEEP HER DOWN FOR LONG!
I DIDN'T MEAN IT THAT WAY.
I KNOW.
AND I NEVER WANTED TO GIVE UP. BUT IT WOULD HAVE BEEN NICE TO FEEL LIKE I WAS ALLOWED TO. JUST FOR A BIT.
TO BE WORTHWHILE, NO MATTER WHAT I COULD OR COULDN'T DO.

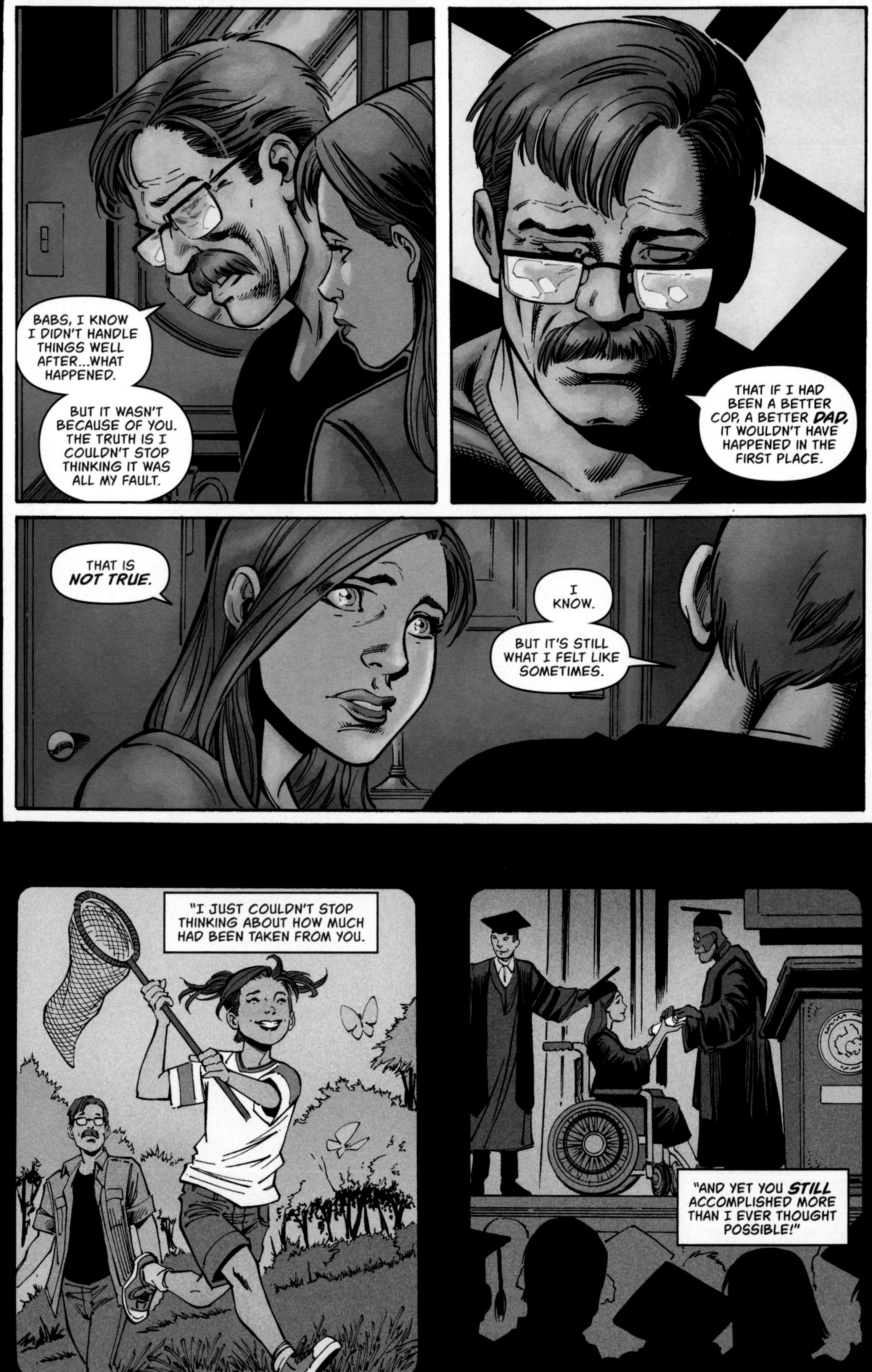
BABS, I KNOW I DIDN'T HANDLE THINGS WELL AFTER...WHAT HAPPENED.
BUT IT WASN'T BECAUSE OF YOU. THE TRUTH IS I COULDN'T STOP THINKING IT WAS ALL MY FAULT.
THAT IF I HAD BEEN A BETTER COP, A BETTER **DAD,** IT WOULDN'T HAVE HAPPENED IN THE FIRST PLACE.
THAT IS **NOT TRUE.**
I KNOW.
BUT IT'S STILL WHAT I FELT LIKE SOMETIMES.
"I JUST COULDN'T STOP THINKING ABOUT HOW MUCH HAD BEEN TAKEN FROM YOU.
"AND YET YOU **STILL** ACCOMPLISHED MORE THAN I EVER THOUGHT POSSIBLE!"

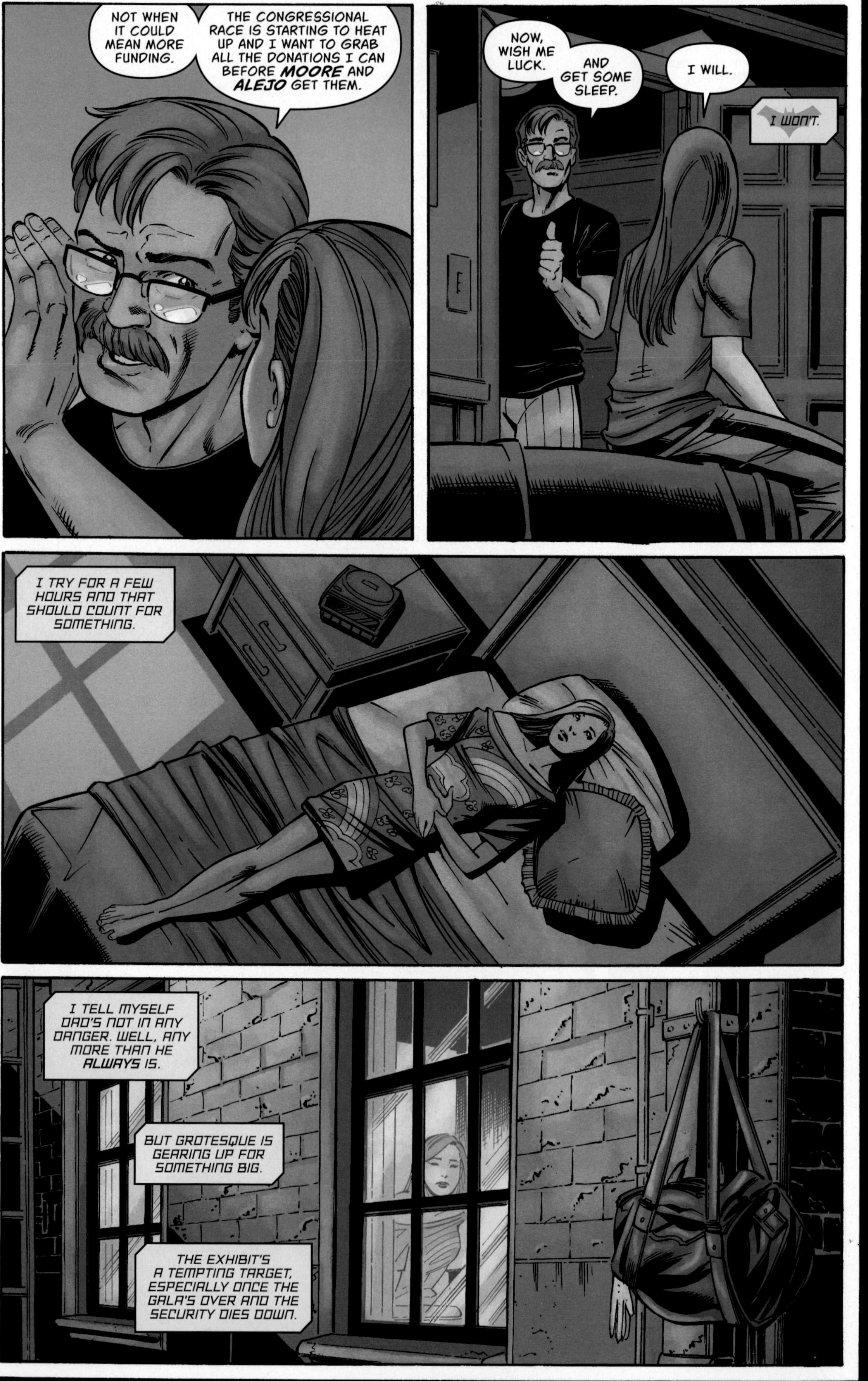
NOT WHEN IT COULD MEAN MORE FUNDING.
THE CONGRESSIONAL RACE IS STARTING TO HEAT UP AND I WANT TO GRAB ALL THE DONATIONS I CAN BEFORE MOORE AND ALEJO GET THEM.
NOW, WISH ME LUCK.
AND GET SOME SLEEP.
I WILL.
I WON'T.
I TRY FOR A FEW HOURS AND THAT SHOULD COUNT FOR SOMETHING.
I TELL MYSELF DAD'S NOT IN ANY DANGER. WELL, ANY MORE THAN HE ALWAYS IS.
BUT GROTESQUE IS GEARING UP FOR SOMETHING BIG.
THE EXHIBIT'S A TEMPTING TARGET, ESPECIALLY ONCE THE GALA'S OVER AND THE SECURITY DIES DOWN.

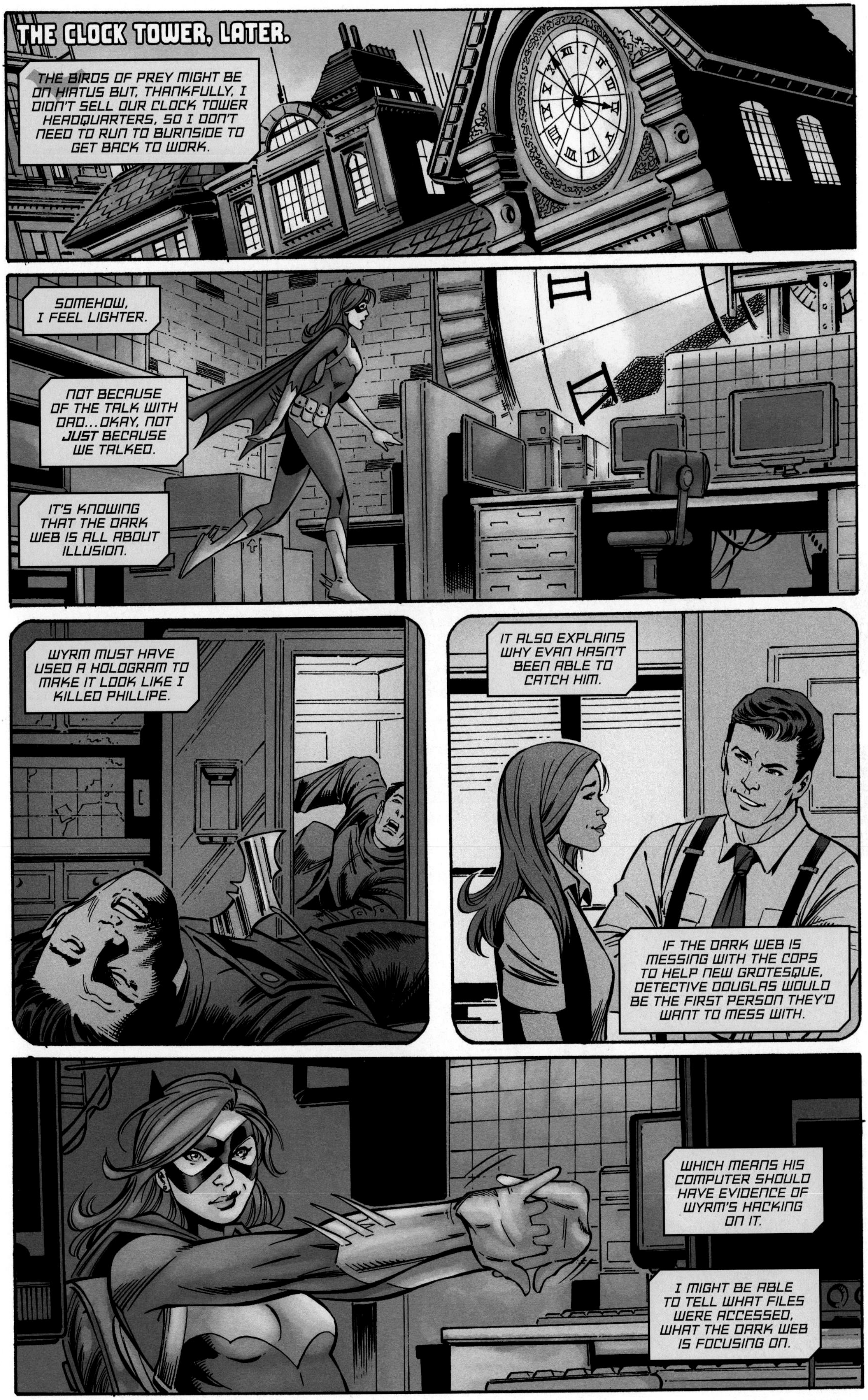
THE CLOCK TOWER, LATER.
THE BIRDS OF PREY MIGHT BE ON HIATUS BUT, THANKFULLY, I DIDN'T SELL OUR CLOCK TOWER HEADQUARTERS, SO I DON'T NEED TO RUN TO BURNSIDE TO GET BACK TO WORK.
SOMEHOW, I FEEL LIGHTER.
NOT BECAUSE OF THE TALK WITH DAD...OKAY, NOT JUST BECAUSE WE TALKED.
IT'S KNOWING THAT THE DARK WEB IS ALL ABOUT ILLUSION.
WYRM MUST HAVE USED A HOLOGRAM TO MAKE IT LOOK LIKE I KILLED PHILLIPE.
IT ALSO EXPLAINS WHY EVAN HASN'T BEEN ABLE TO CATCH HIM.
IF THE DARK WEB IS MESSING WITH THE COPS TO HELP NEW GROTESQUE, DETECTIVE DOUGLAS WOULD BE THE FIRST PERSON THEY'D WANT TO MESS WITH.
WHICH MEANS HIS COMPUTER SHOULD HAVE EVIDENCE OF WYRM'S HACKING ON IT.
I MIGHT BE ABLE TO TELL WHAT FILES WERE ACCESSED, WHAT THE DARK WEB IS FOCUSING ON.

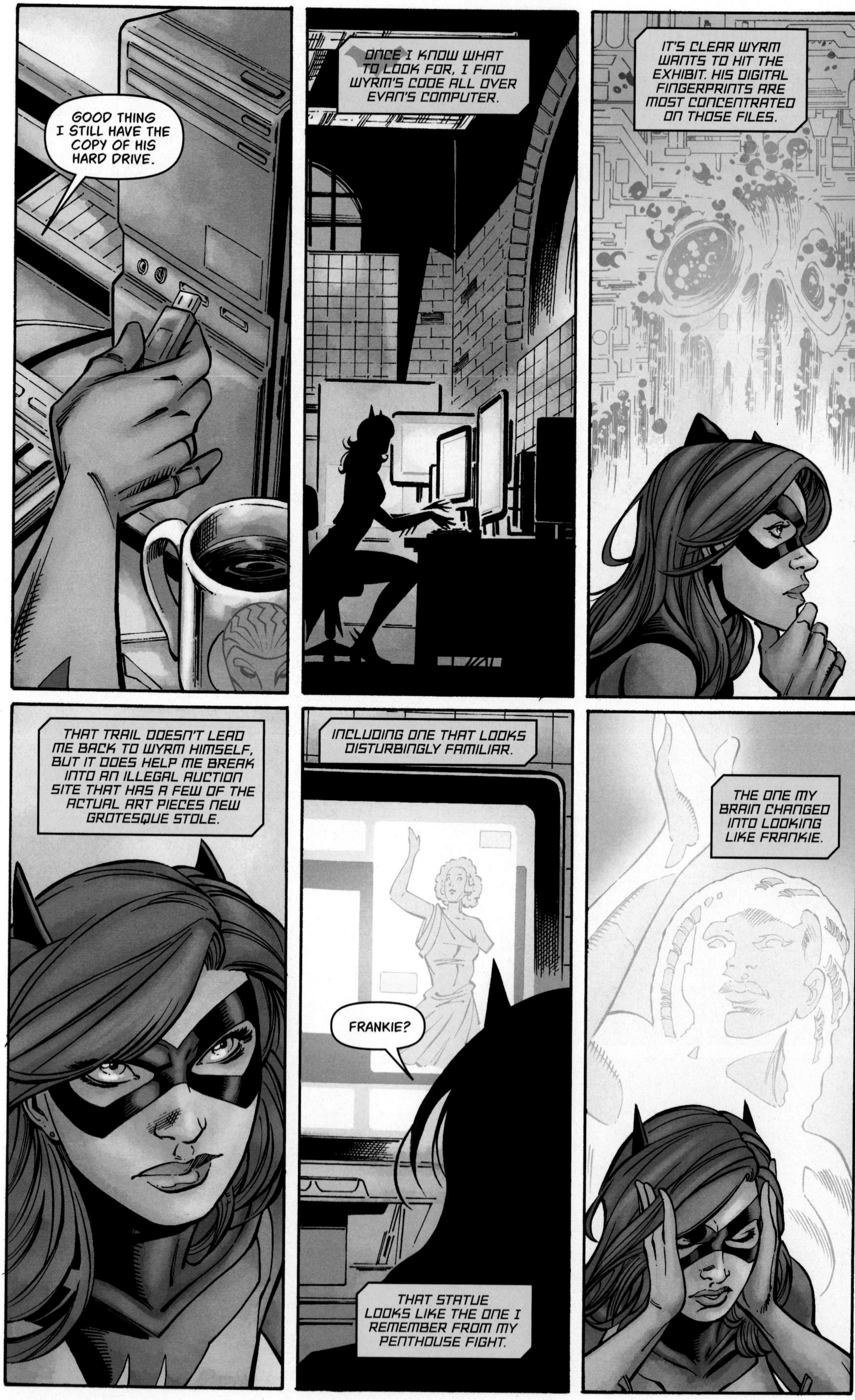
GOOD THING I STILL HAVE THE COPY OF HIS HARD DRIVE.
ONCE I KNOW WHAT TO LOOK FOR, I FIND WYRM'S CODE ALL OVER EVAN'S COMPUTER.
IT'S CLEAR WYRM WANTS TO HIT THE EXHIBIT. HIS DIGITAL FINGERPRINTS ARE MOST CONCENTRATED ON THOSE FILES.
THAT TRAIL DOESN'T LEAD ME BACK TO WYRM HIMSELF, BUT IT DOES HELP ME BREAK INTO AN ILLEGAL AUCTION SITE THAT HAS A FEW OF THE ACTUAL ART PIECES NEW GROTESQUE STOLE.
INCLUDING ONE THAT LOOKS DISTURBINGLY FAMILIAR.
FRANKIE?
THAT STATUE LOOKS LIKE THE ONE I REMEMBER FROM MY PENTHOUSE FIGHT.
THE ONE MY BRAIN CHANGED INTO LOOKING LIKE FRANKIE.

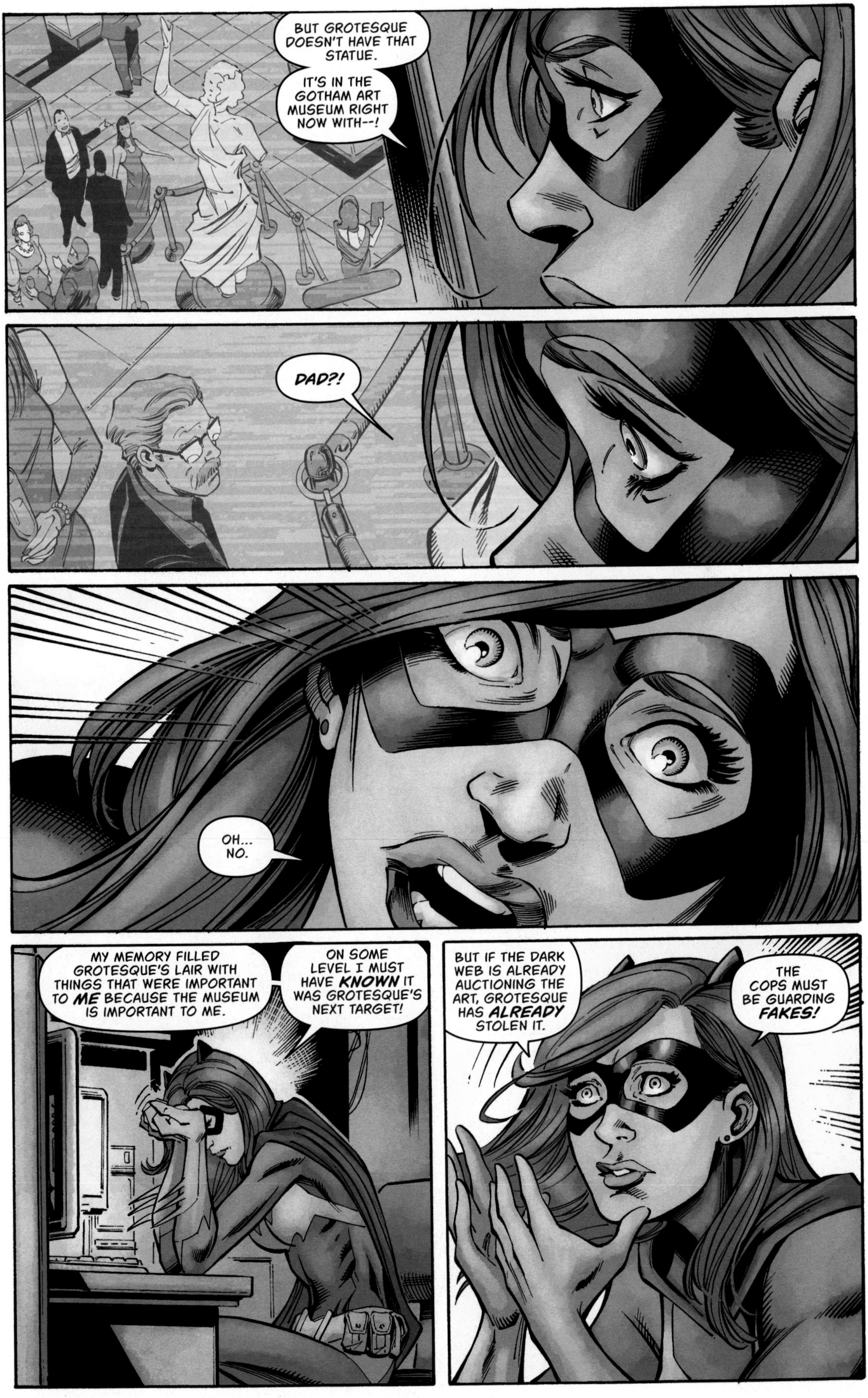
BUT GROTESQUE DOESN'T HAVE THAT STATUE.
IT'S IN THE GOTHAM ART MUSEUM RIGHT NOW WITH--!
DAD?!
OH... NO.
MY MEMORY FILLED GROTESQUE'S LAIR WITH THINGS THAT WERE IMPORTANT TO ME BECAUSE THE MUSEUM IS IMPORTANT TO ME.
ON SOME LEVEL I MUST HAVE KNOWN IT WAS GROTESQUE'S NEXT TARGET!
BUT IF THE DARK WEB IS ALREADY AUCTIONING THE ART, GROTESQUE HAS ALREADY STOLEN IT.
THE COPS MUST BE GUARDING FAKES!

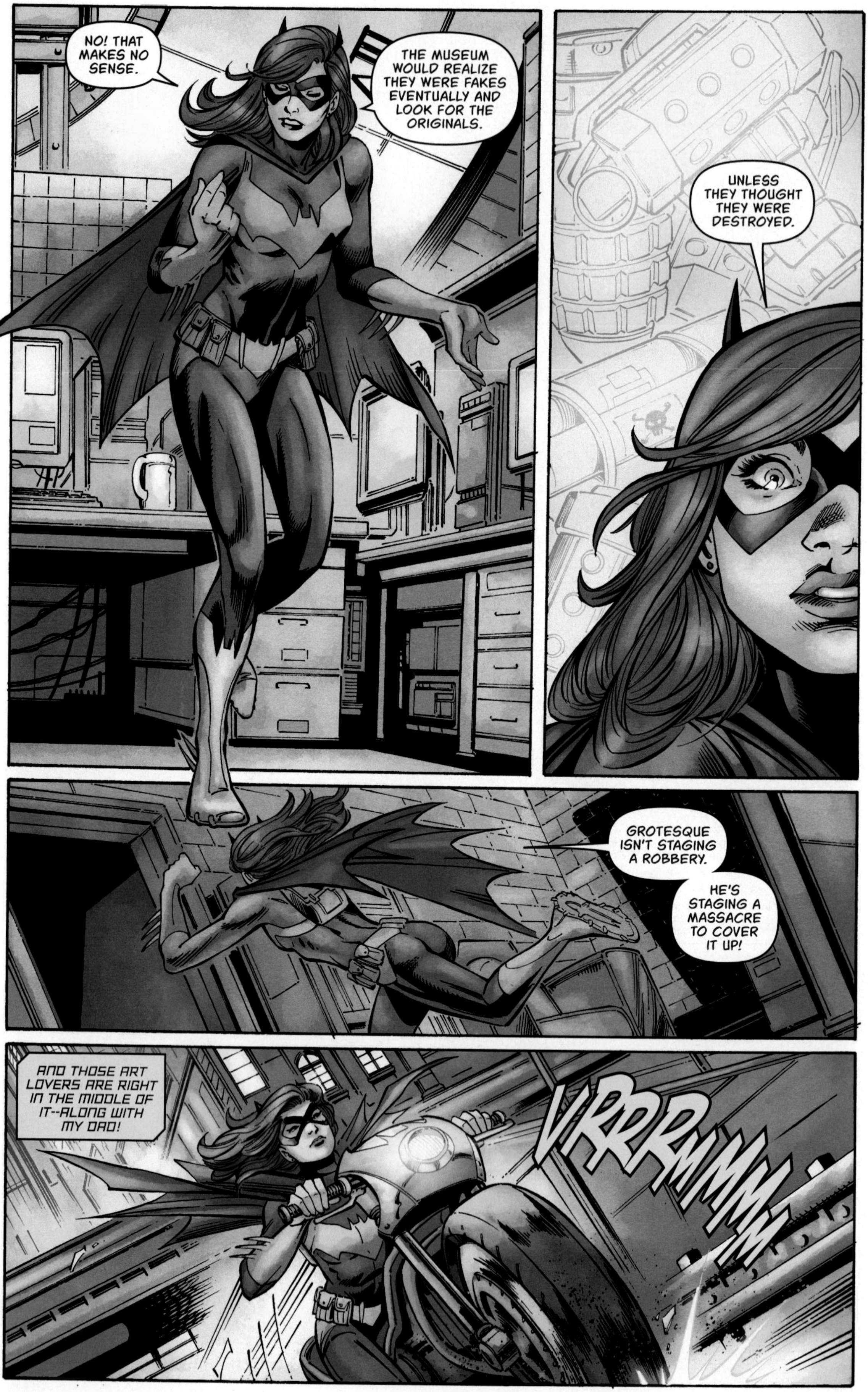
NO! THAT MAKES NO SENSE.
THE MUSEUM WOULD REALIZE THEY WERE FAKES EVENTUALLY AND LOOK FOR THE ORIGINALS.
UNLESS THEY THOUGHT THEY WERE DESTROYED.
GROTESQUE ISN'T STAGING A ROBBERY.
HE'S STAGING A MASSACRE TO COVER IT UP!
AND THOSE ART LOVERS ARE RIGHT IN THE MIDDLE OF IT--ALONG WITH MY DAD!
VRRRMMMM

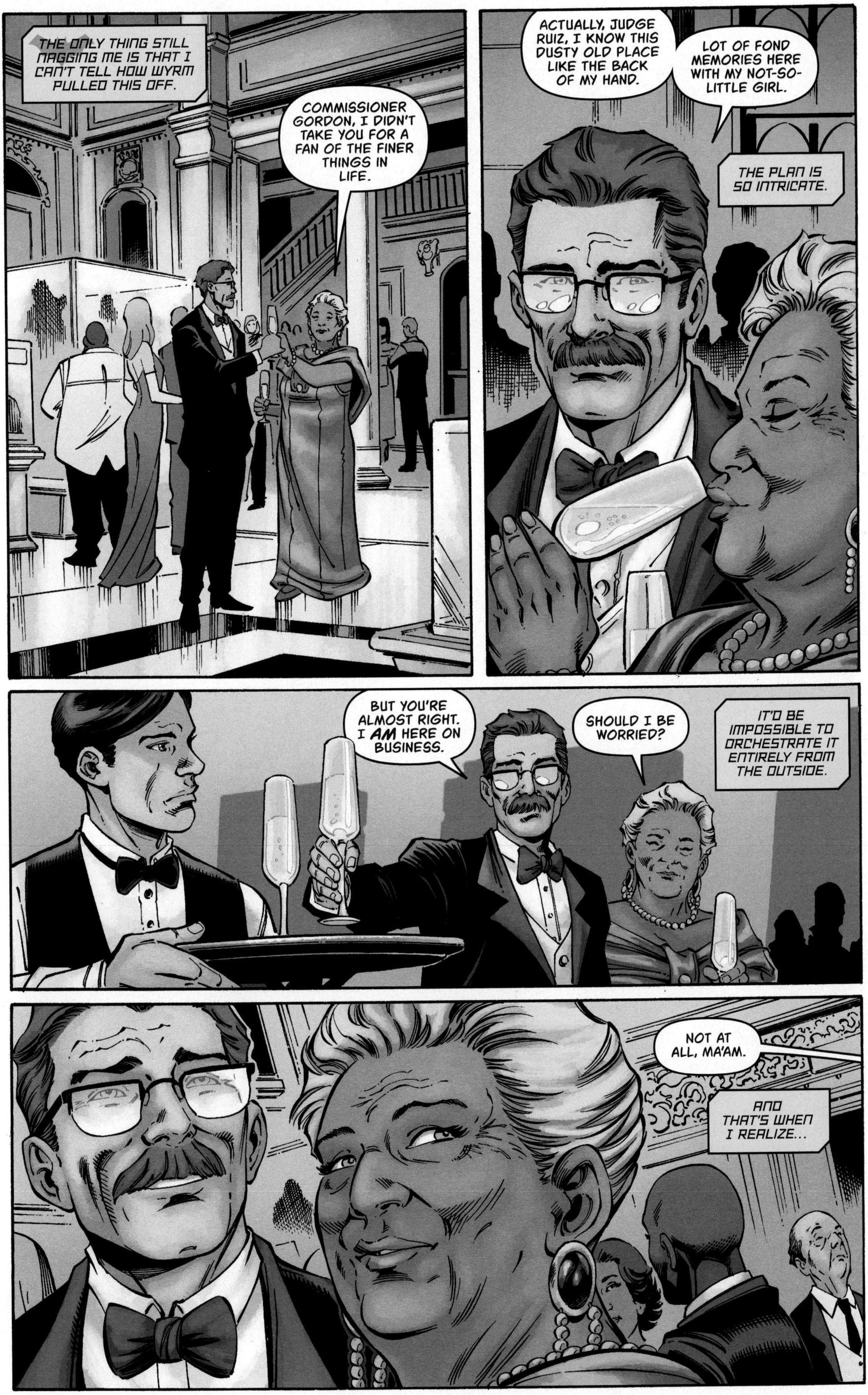
THE ONLY THING STILL NAGGING ME IS THAT I CAN'T TELL HOW WYRM PULLED THIS OFF.
COMMISSIONER GORDON, I DIDN'T TAKE YOU FOR A FAN OF THE FINER THINGS IN LIFE.
ACTUALLY, JUDGE RUIZ, I KNOW THIS DUSTY OLD PLACE LIKE THE BACK OF MY HAND.
LOT OF FOND MEMORIES HERE WITH MY NOT-SO-LITTLE GIRL.
THE PLAN IS SO INTRICATE.
BUT YOU'RE ALMOST RIGHT. I AM HERE ON BUSINESS.
SHOULD I BE WORRIED?
IT'D BE IMPOSSIBLE TO ORCHESTRATE IT ENTIRELY FROM THE OUTSIDE.
NOT AT ALL, MA'AM.
AND THAT'S WHEN I REALIZE...

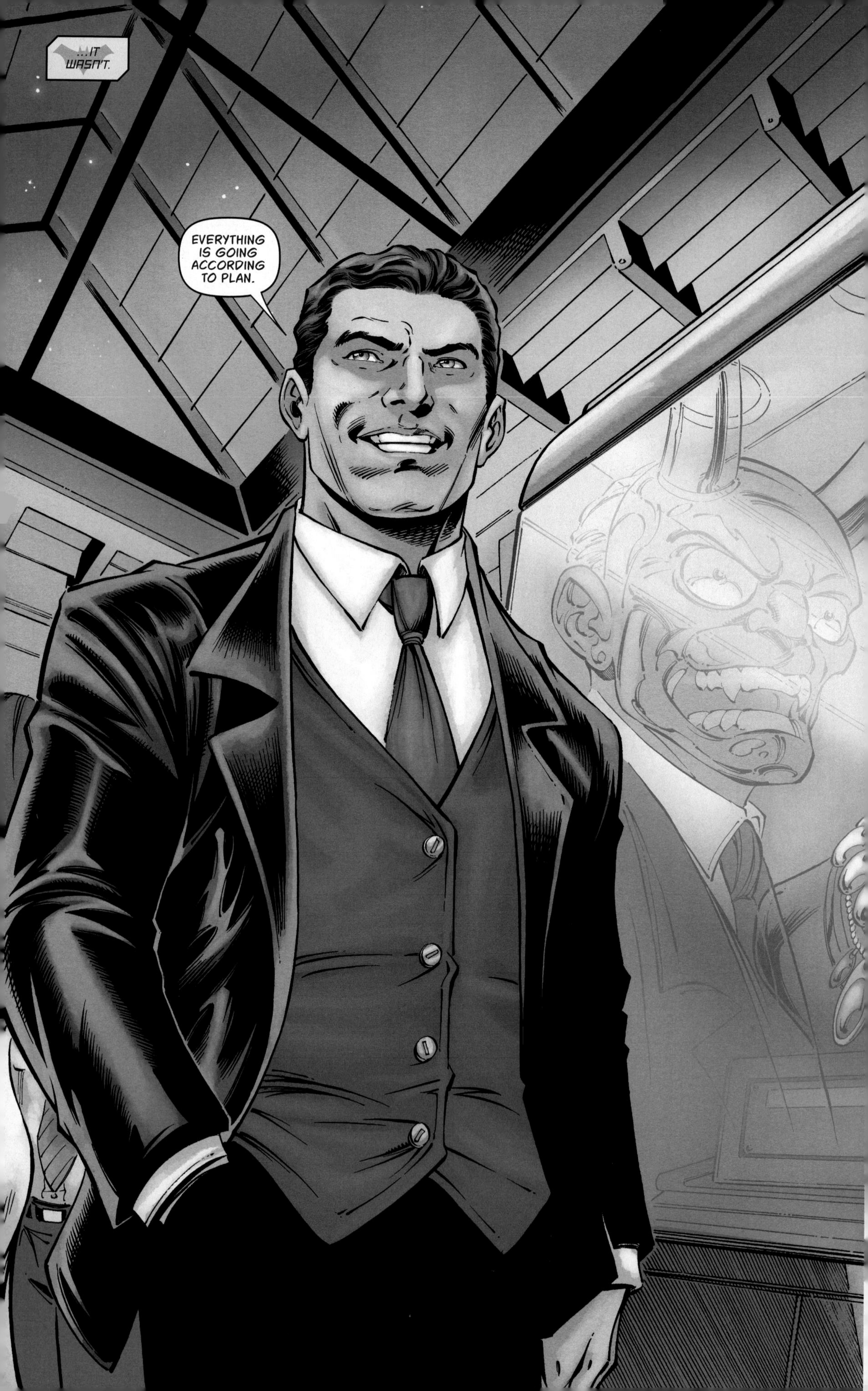
...IT WASN'T.
EVERYTHING IS GOING ACCORDING TO PLAN.

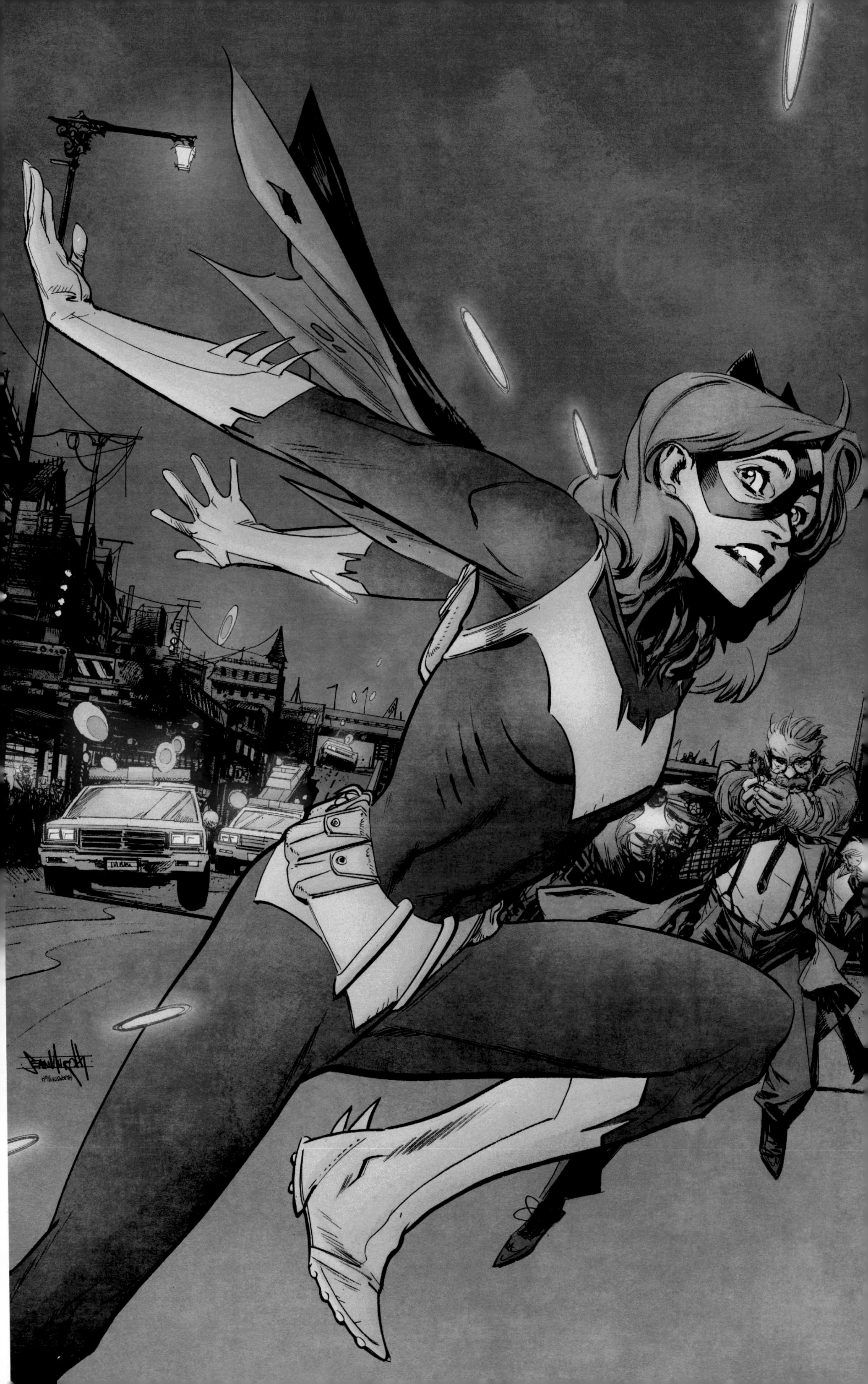

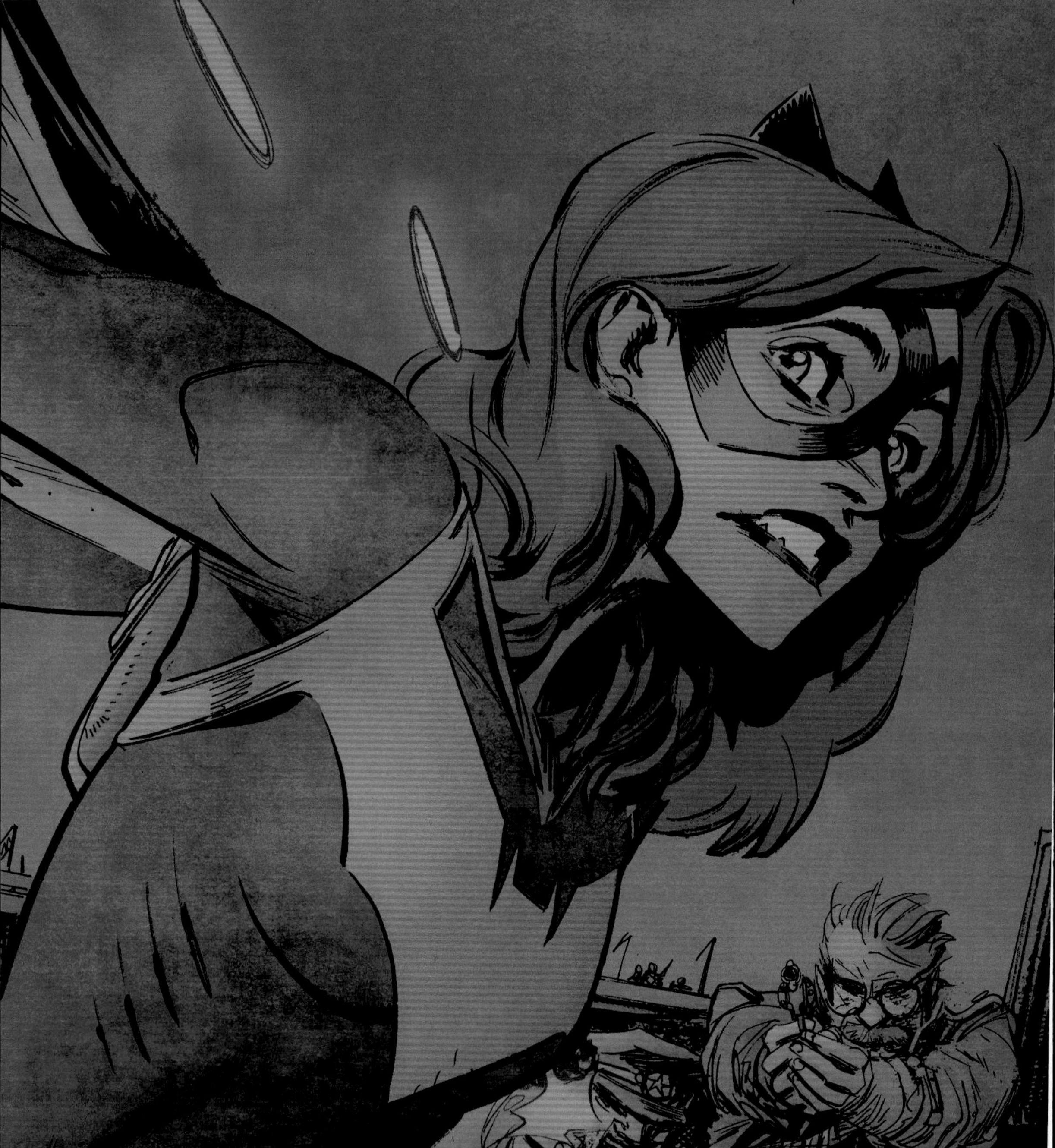

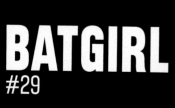

# BATGIRL
#29

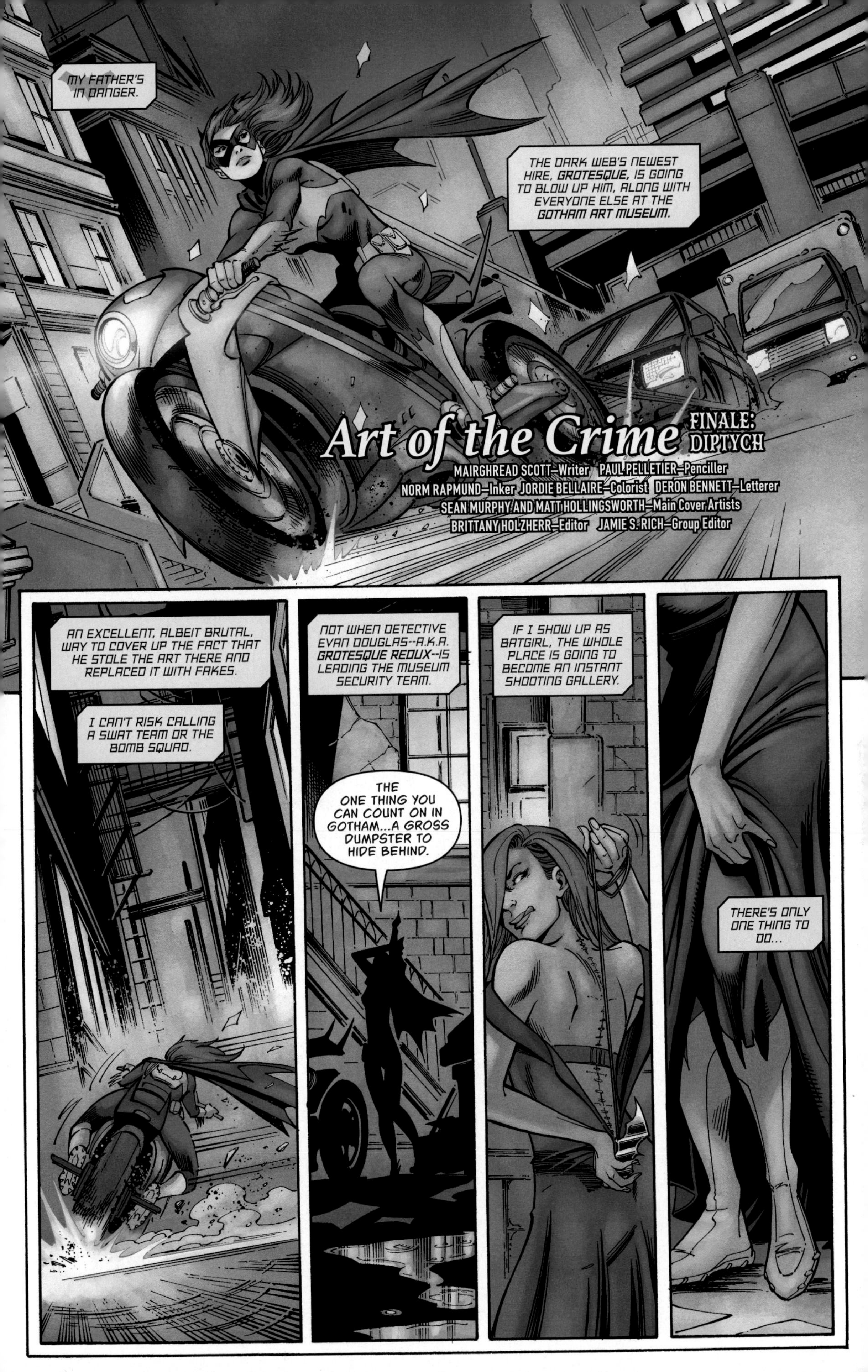
MY FATHER'S IN DANGER.
THE DARK WEB'S NEWEST HIRE, GROTESQUE, IS GOING TO BLOW UP HIM, ALONG WITH EVERYONE ELSE AT THE GOTHAM ART MUSEUM.
Art of the Crime FINALE: DIPTYCH
MAIRGHREAD SCOTT—Writer PAUL PELLETIER—Penciller
NORM RAPMUND—Inker JORDIE BELLAIRE—Colorist DERON BENNETT—Letterer
SEAN MURPHY AND MATT HOLLINGSWORTH—Main Cover Artists
BRITTANY HOLZHERR—Editor JAMIE S. RICH—Group Editor
AN EXCELLENT, ALBEIT BRUTAL, WAY TO COVER UP THE FACT THAT HE STOLE THE ART THERE AND REPLACED IT WITH FAKES.
I CAN'T RISK CALLING A SWAT TEAM OR THE BOMB SQUAD.
NOT WHEN DETECTIVE EVAN DOUGLAS--A.K.A. GROTESQUE REDUX--IS LEADING THE MUSEUM SECURITY TEAM.
THE ONE THING YOU CAN COUNT ON IN GOTHAM...A GROSS DUMPSTER TO HIDE BEHIND.
IF I SHOW UP AS BATGIRL, THE WHOLE PLACE IS GOING TO BECOME AN INSTANT SHOOTING GALLERY.
THERE'S ONLY ONE THING TO DO...

THIS LOOKS LIKE A JOB FOR *BARBARA GORDON.*

COMMISSIONER GORDON. WE HAVE AN UNINVITED GUEST REFUSING TO LET US SEARCH HER BAG.

SAYS SHE'S WITH YOU.

I HAVE A FEELING SHE IS.

LET HER IN.

THIS ISN'T *TAKING IT EASY,* BABS.

WELL, IT WAS THIS OR RUNNING MORE LAPS.

DON'T LET THE PERFECT BE THE ENEMY OF THE GOOD.

YOU COULDN'T LET THEM SEARCH YOUR BAG?

AND LET THEM RUMMAGE THROUGH MY TAMPON STASH?

FAIR ENOUGH. I DON'T RECOGNIZE THE DRESS. IS IT NEW?

"JUST NEW TO YOU.

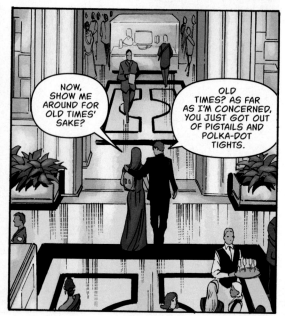

NOW, SHOW ME AROUND FOR OLD TIMES' SAKE?

OLD TIMES? AS FAR AS I'M CONCERNED, YOU JUST GOT OUT OF PIGTAILS AND POLKA-DOT TIGHTS.

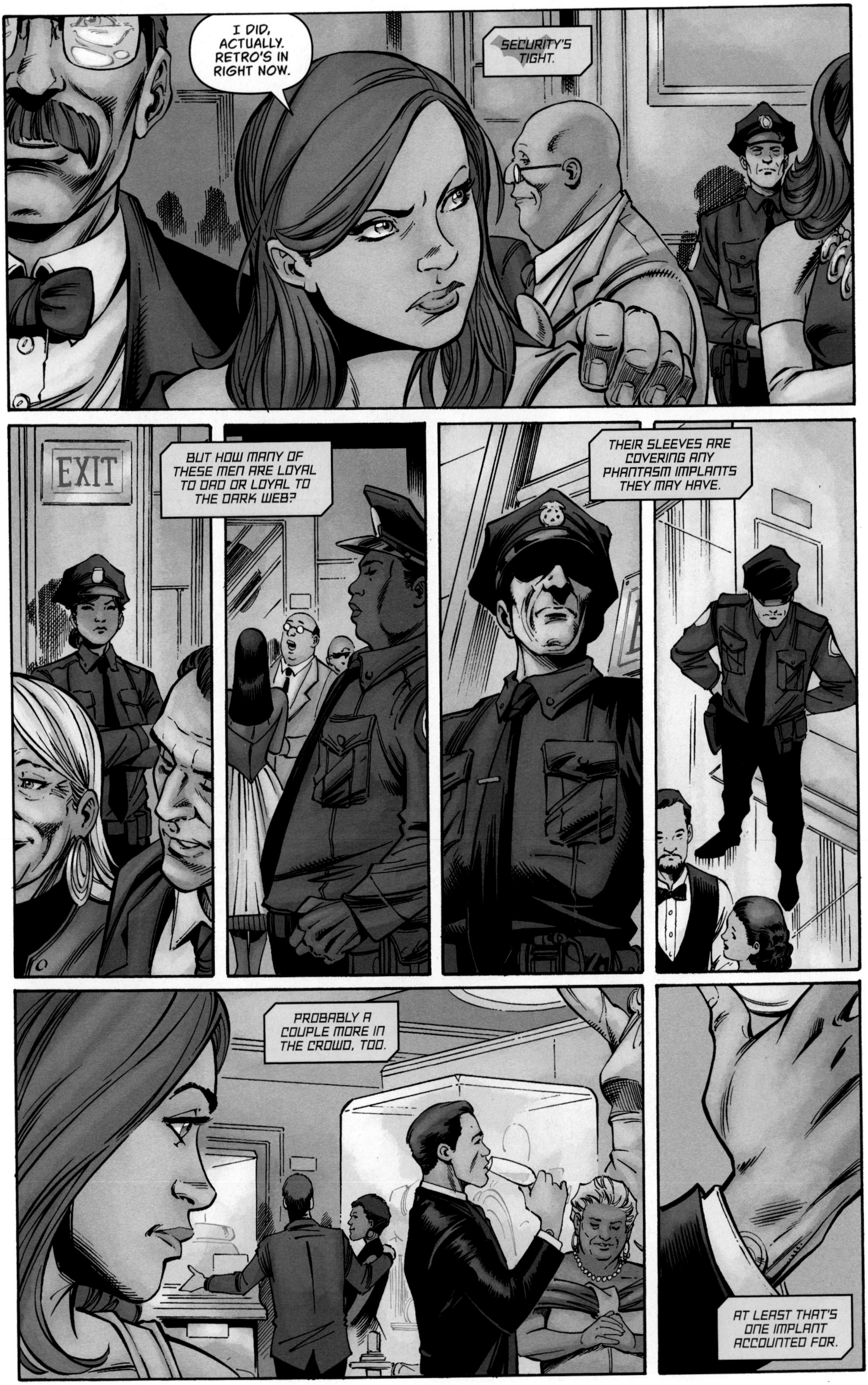
I DID, ACTUALLY. RETRO'S IN RIGHT NOW.
SECURITY'S TIGHT.
EXIT
BUT HOW MANY OF THESE MEN ARE LOYAL TO DAD OR LOYAL TO THE DARK WEB?
THEIR SLEEVES ARE COVERING ANY PHANTASM IMPLANTS THEY MAY HAVE.
PROBABLY A COUPLE MORE IN THE CROWD, TOO.
AT LEAST THAT'S ONE IMPLANT ACCOUNTED FOR.

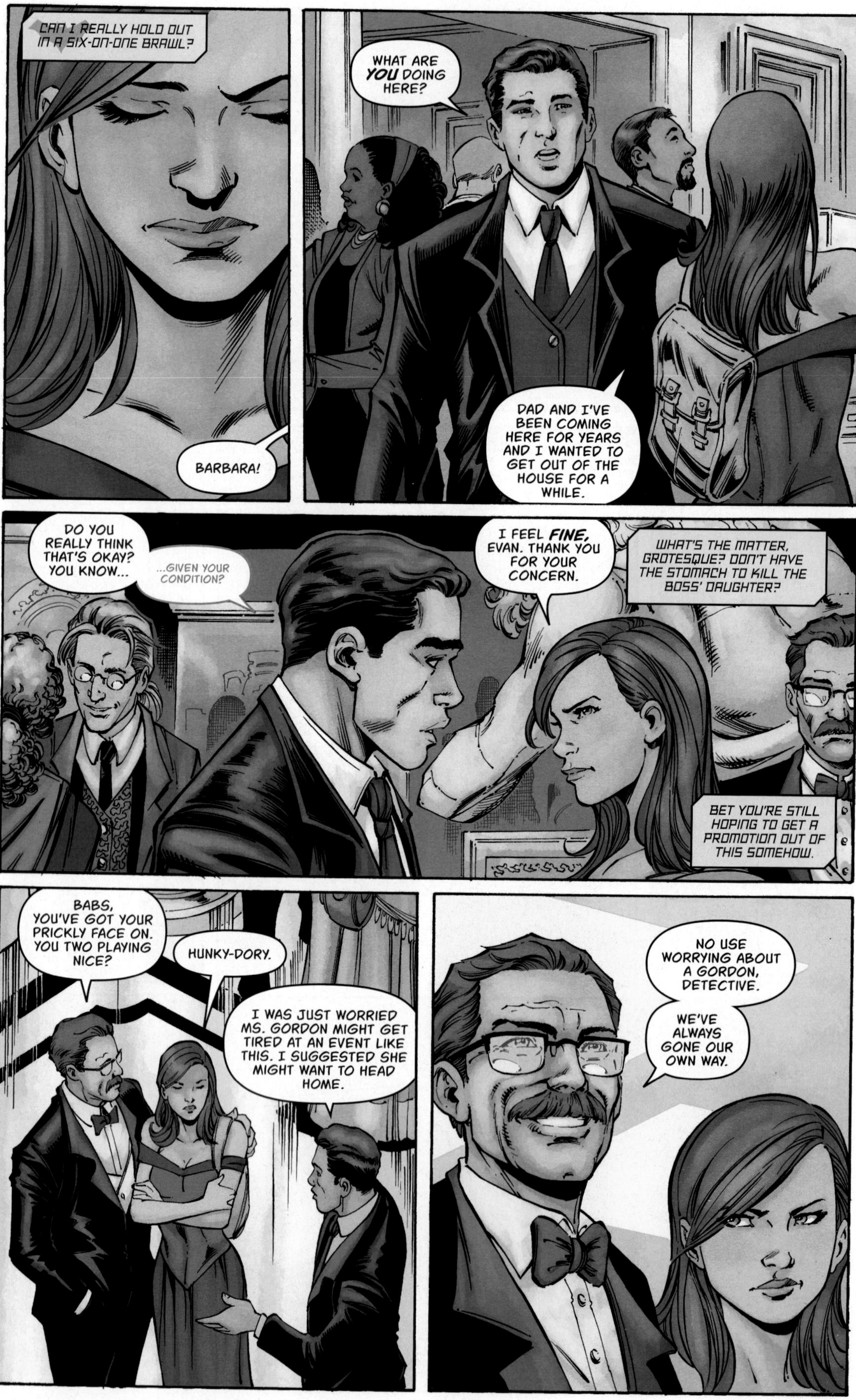
CAN I REALLY HOLD OUT IN A SIX-ON-ONE BRAWL?
BARBARA!
WHAT ARE YOU DOING HERE?
DAD AND I'VE BEEN COMING HERE FOR YEARS AND I WANTED TO GET OUT OF THE HOUSE FOR A WHILE.
DO YOU REALLY THINK THAT'S OKAY? YOU KNOW...
...GIVEN YOUR CONDITION?
I FEEL FINE, EVAN. THANK YOU FOR YOUR CONCERN.
WHAT'S THE MATTER, GROTESQUE? DON'T HAVE THE STOMACH TO KILL THE BOSS' DAUGHTER?
BET YOU'RE STILL HOPING TO GET A PROMOTION OUT OF THIS SOMEHOW.
BABS, YOU'VE GOT YOUR PRICKLY FACE ON. YOU TWO PLAYING NICE?
HUNKY-DORY.
I WAS JUST WORRIED MS. GORDON MIGHT GET TIRED AT AN EVENT LIKE THIS. I SUGGESTED SHE MIGHT WANT TO HEAD HOME.
NO USE WORRYING ABOUT A GORDON, DETECTIVE.
WE'VE ALWAYS GONE OUR OWN WAY.

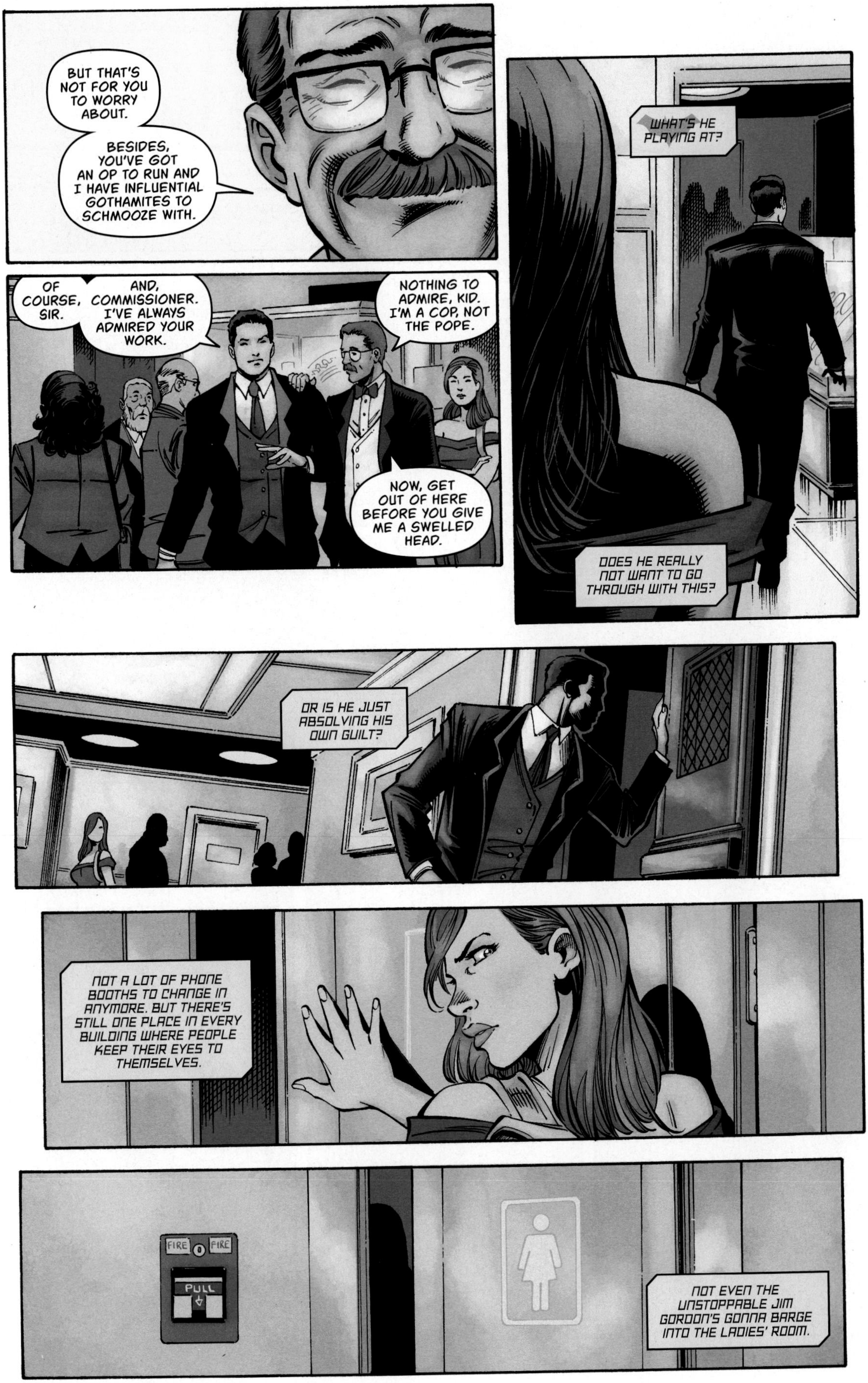
BUT THAT'S NOT FOR YOU TO WORRY ABOUT.
BESIDES, YOU'VE GOT AN OP TO RUN AND I HAVE INFLUENTIAL GOTHAMITES TO SCHMOOZE WITH.
OF COURSE, SIR.
AND, COMMISSIONER. I'VE ALWAYS ADMIRED YOUR WORK.
NOTHING TO ADMIRE, KID. I'M A COP, NOT THE POPE.
NOW, GET OUT OF HERE BEFORE YOU GIVE ME A SWELLED HEAD.
WHAT'S HE PLAYING AT?
DOES HE REALLY NOT WANT TO GO THROUGH WITH THIS?
OR IS HE JUST ABSOLVING HIS OWN GUILT?
NOT A LOT OF PHONE BOOTHS TO CHANGE IN ANYMORE. BUT THERE'S STILL ONE PLACE IN EVERY BUILDING WHERE PEOPLE KEEP THEIR EYES TO THEMSELVES.
FIRE FIRE
PULL
NOT EVEN THE UNSTOPPABLE JIM GORDON'S GONNA BARGE INTO THE LADIES' ROOM.

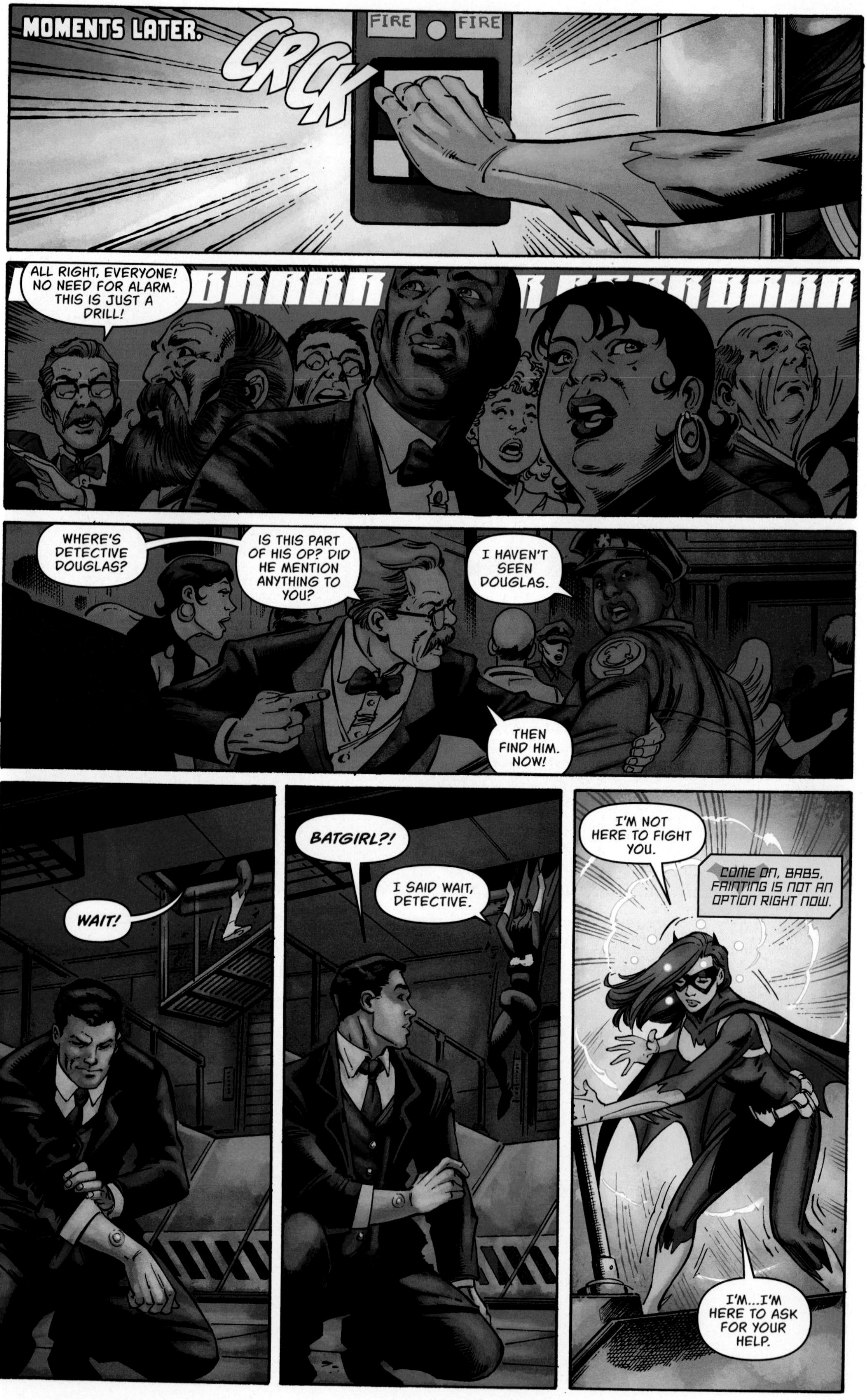

MOMENTS LATER.
CRCK
FIRE
FIRE
BRRRR
BRRRBRRR
ALL RIGHT, EVERYONE! NO NEED FOR ALARM. THIS IS JUST A DRILL!
WHERE'S DETECTIVE DOUGLAS?
IS THIS PART OF HIS OP? DID HE MENTION ANYTHING TO YOU?
I HAVEN'T SEEN DOUGLAS.
THEN FIND HIM. NOW!
WAIT!
BATGIRL?!
I SAID WAIT, DETECTIVE.
I'M NOT HERE TO FIGHT YOU.
COME ON, BABS, FAINTING IS NOT AN OPTION RIGHT NOW.
I'M...I'M HERE TO ASK FOR YOUR HELP.

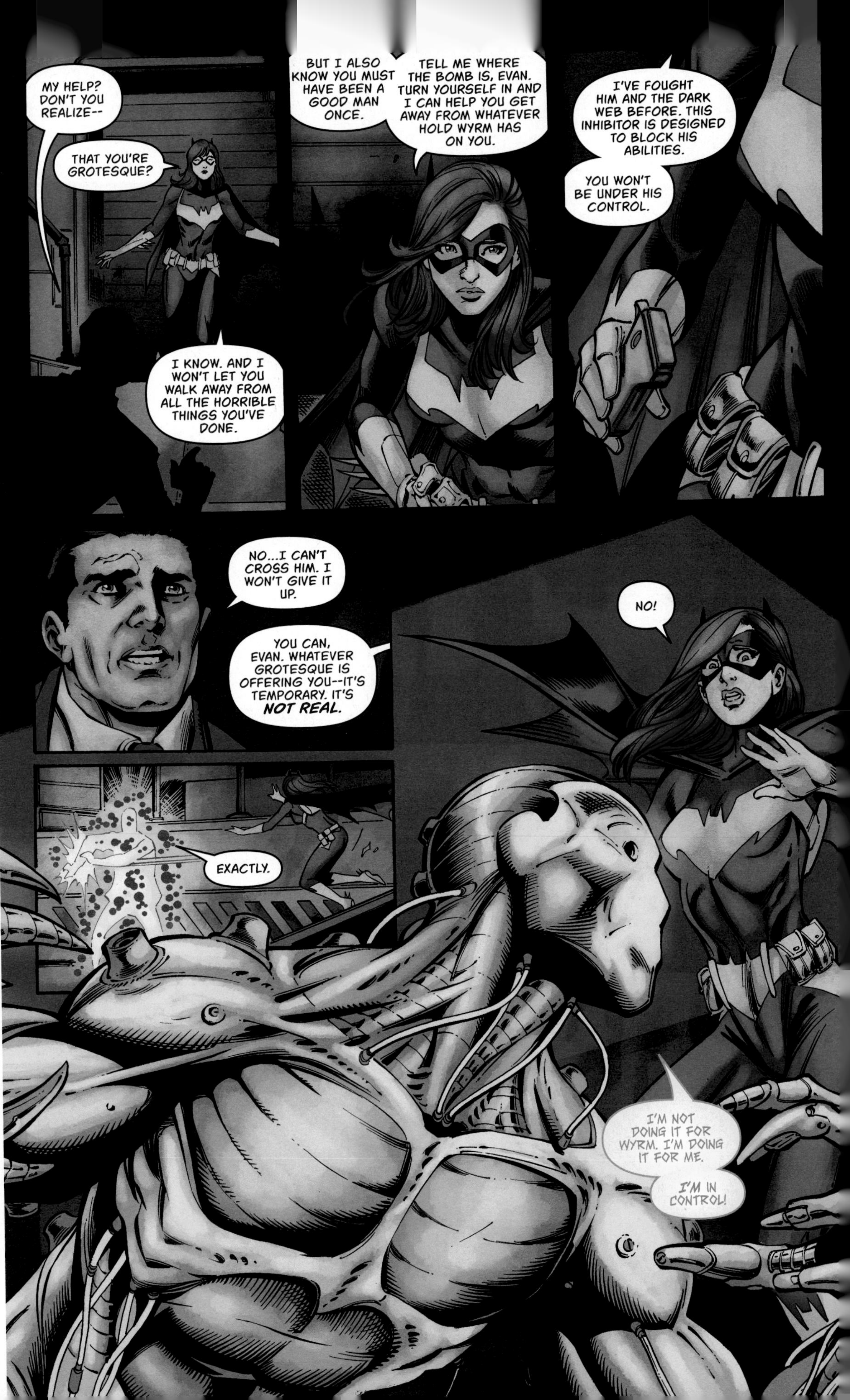
MY HELP? DON'T YOU REALIZE--
THAT YOU'RE GROTESQUE?
I KNOW. AND I WON'T LET YOU WALK AWAY FROM ALL THE HORRIBLE THINGS YOU'VE DONE.
BUT I ALSO KNOW YOU MUST HAVE BEEN A GOOD MAN ONCE.
TELL ME WHERE THE BOMB IS, EVAN. TURN YOURSELF IN AND I CAN HELP YOU GET AWAY FROM WHATEVER HOLD WYRM HAS ON YOU.
I'VE FOUGHT HIM AND THE DARK WEB BEFORE. THIS INHIBITOR IS DESIGNED TO BLOCK HIS ABILITIES.
YOU WON'T BE UNDER HIS CONTROL.
NO...I CAN'T CROSS HIM. I WON'T GIVE IT UP.
YOU CAN, EVAN. WHATEVER GROTESQUE IS OFFERING YOU--IT'S TEMPORARY. IT'S NOT REAL.
EXACTLY.
NO!
I'M NOT DOING IT FOR WYRM. I'M DOING IT FOR ME.
I'M IN CONTROL!

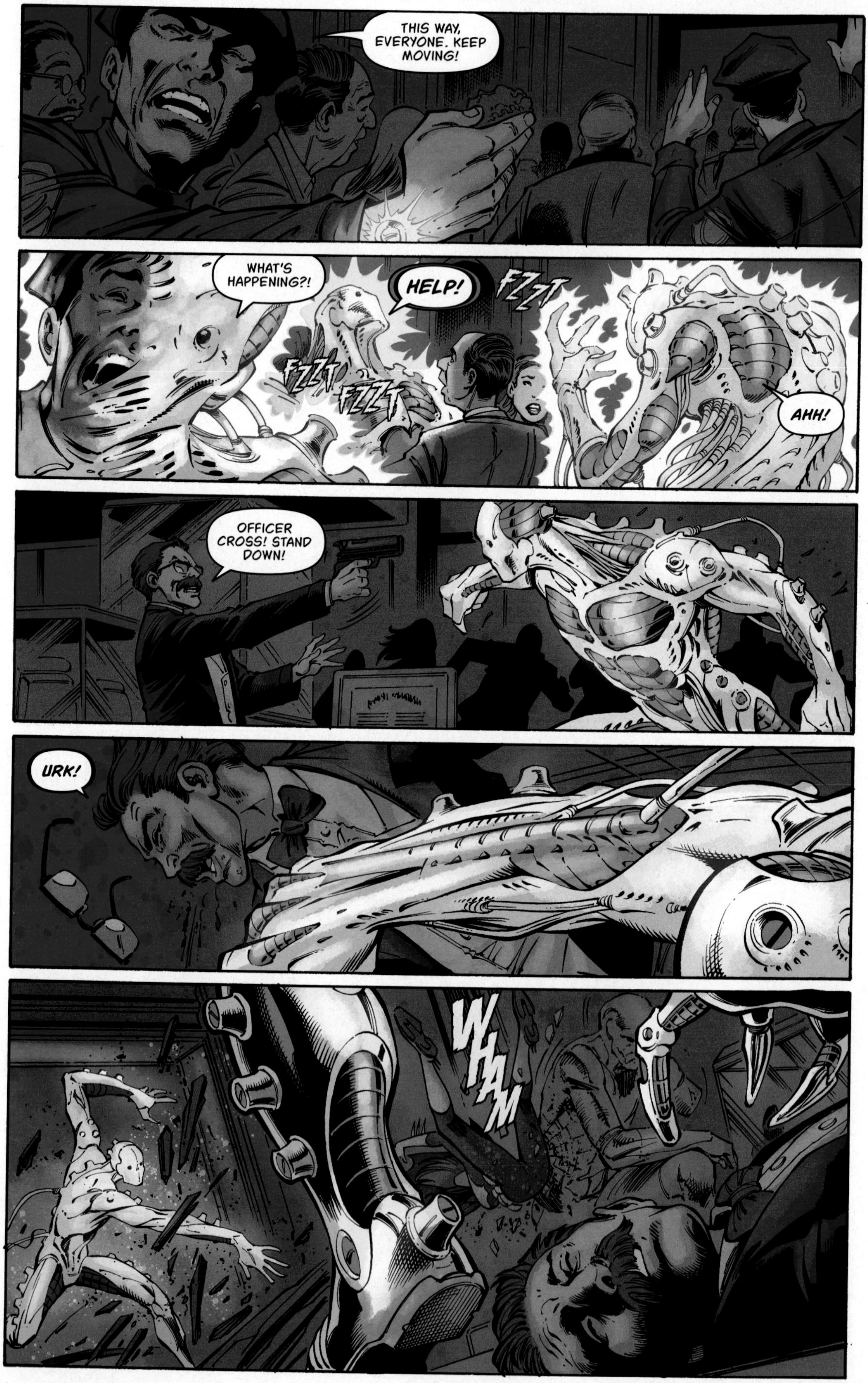
THIS WAY, EVERYONE. KEEP MOVING!
WHAT'S HAPPENING?!
HELP!
FZZT
FZZT
FZZT
AHH!
OFFICER CROSS! STAND DOWN!
URK!
WHAM

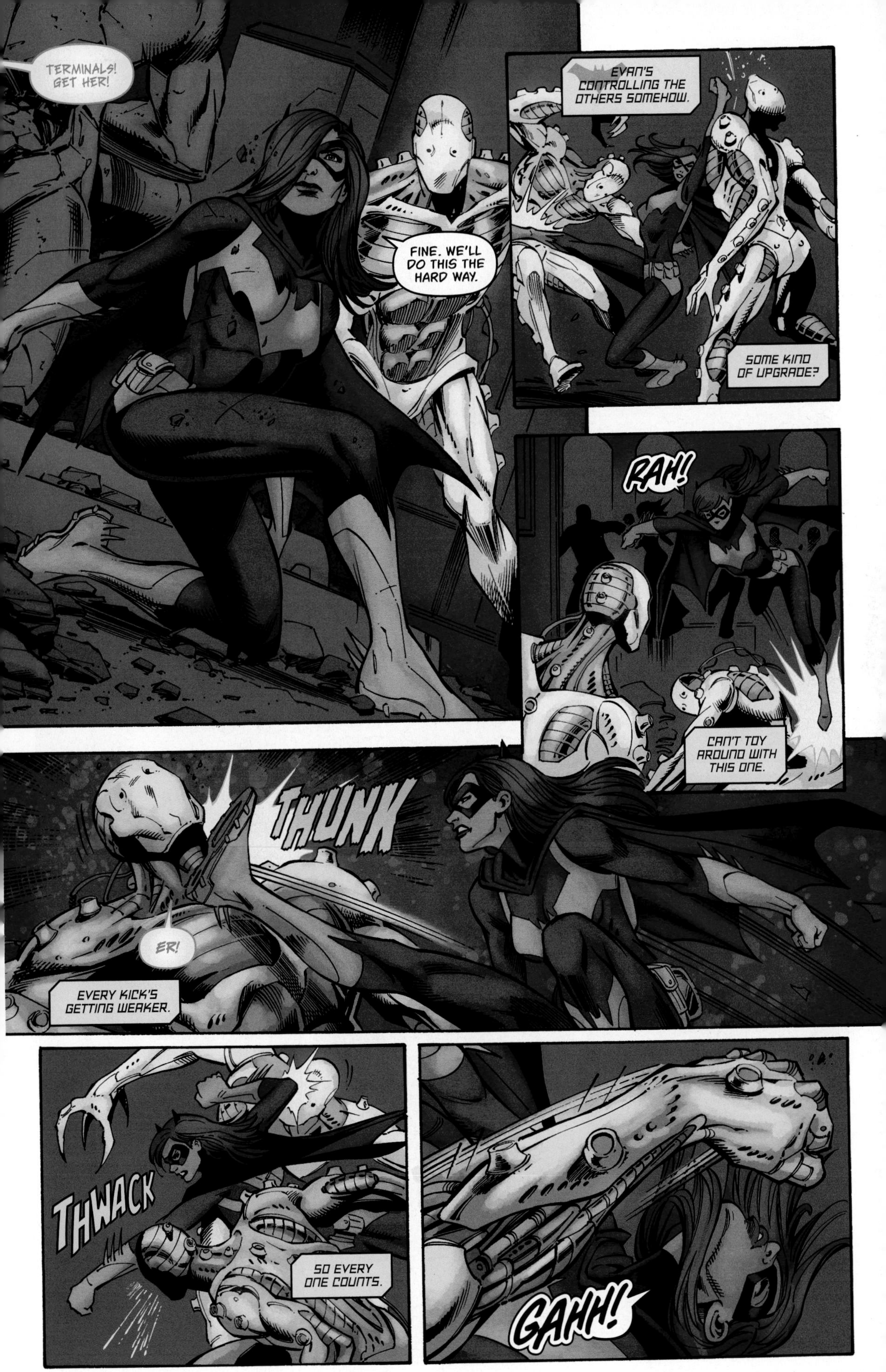
TERMINALS! GET HER!
FINE. WE'LL DO THIS THE HARD WAY.
EVAN'S CONTROLLING THE OTHERS SOMEHOW.
SOME KIND OF UPGRADE?
RAH!
CAN'T TOY AROUND WITH THIS ONE.
THUNK
ER!
EVERY KICK'S GETTING WEAKER.
THWACK
SO EVERY ONE COUNTS.
GAHH!

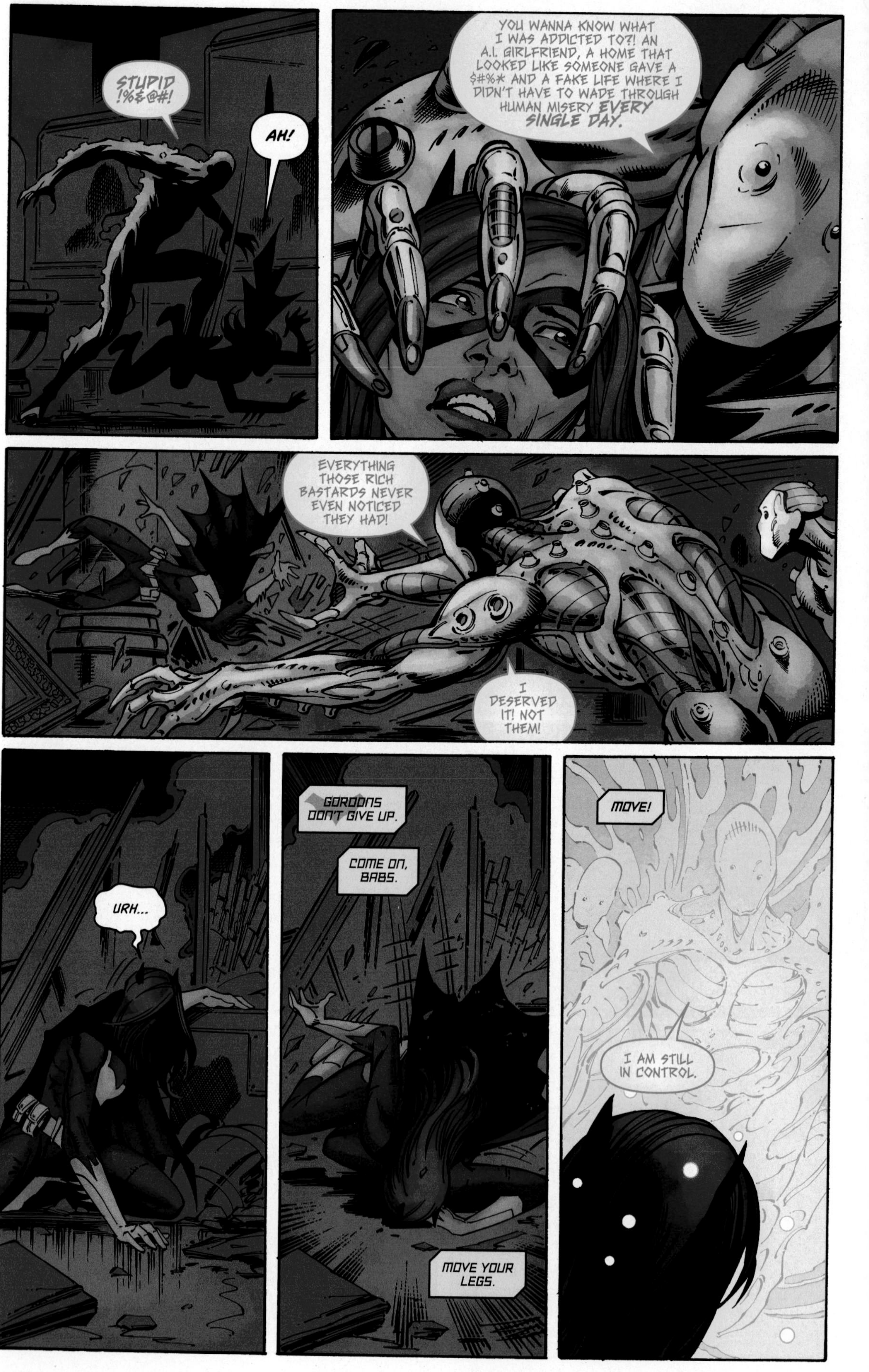
STUPID !%$&@#!
AH!
YOU WANNA KNOW WHAT I WAS ADDICTED TO?! AN A.I. GIRLFRIEND, A HOME THAT LOOKED LIKE SOMEONE GAVE A $#%* AND A FAKE LIFE WHERE I DIDN'T HAVE TO WADE THROUGH HUMAN MISERY EVERY SINGLE DAY.
EVERYTHING THOSE RICH BASTARDS NEVER EVEN NOTICED THEY HAD!
I DESERVED IT! NOT THEM!
URH...
GORDONS DON'T GIVE UP.
COME ON, BABS.
MOVE YOUR LEGS.
MOVE!
I AM STILL IN CONTROL.

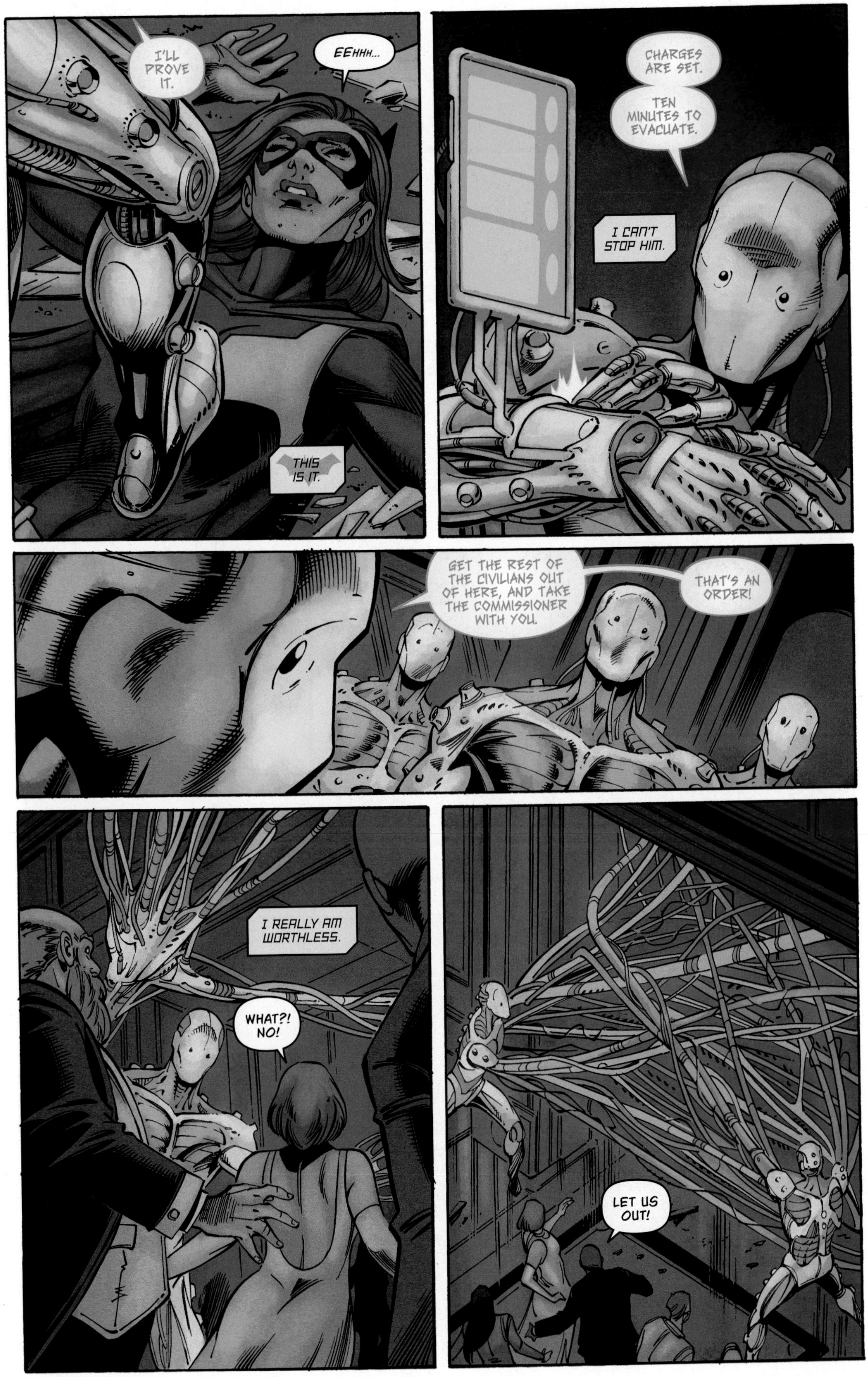
I'LL PROVE IT.
EEHHH...
THIS IS IT.
CHARGES ARE SET.
TEN MINUTES TO EVACUATE.
I CAN'T STOP HIM.
GET THE REST OF THE CIVILIANS OUT OF HERE, AND TAKE THE COMMISSIONER WITH YOU.
THAT'S AN ORDER!
I REALLY AM WORTHLESS.
WHAT?! NO!
LET US OUT!

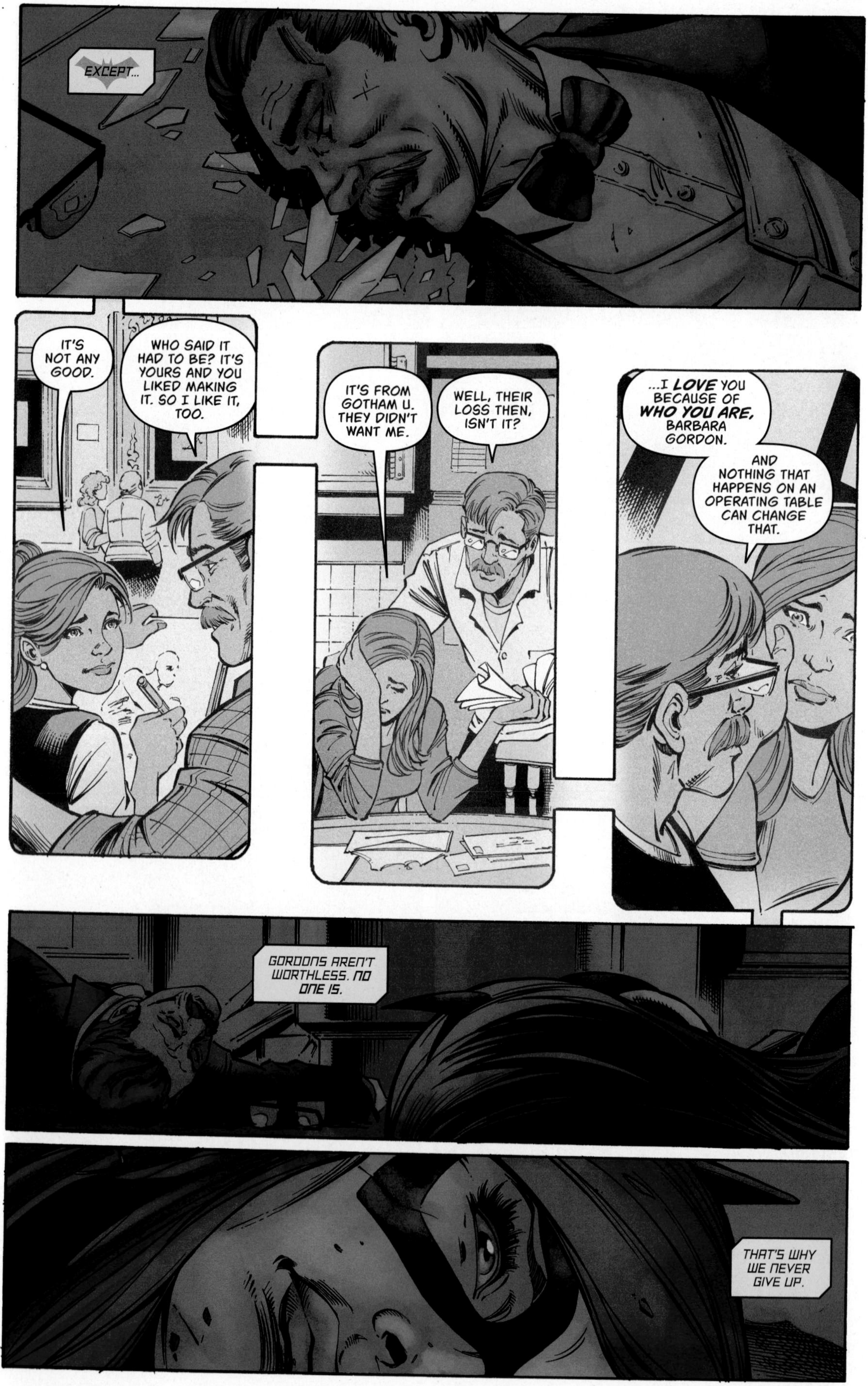

EXCEPT...
IT'S NOT ANY GOOD.
WHO SAID IT HAD TO BE? IT'S YOURS AND YOU LIKED MAKING IT. SO I LIKE IT, TOO.
IT'S FROM GOTHAM U. THEY DIDN'T WANT ME.
WELL, THEIR LOSS THEN, ISN'T IT?
...I LOVE YOU BECAUSE OF WHO YOU ARE, BARBARA GORDON.
AND NOTHING THAT HAPPENS ON AN OPERATING TABLE CAN CHANGE THAT.
GORDONS AREN'T WORTHLESS. NO ONE IS.
THAT'S WHY WE NEVER GIVE UP.

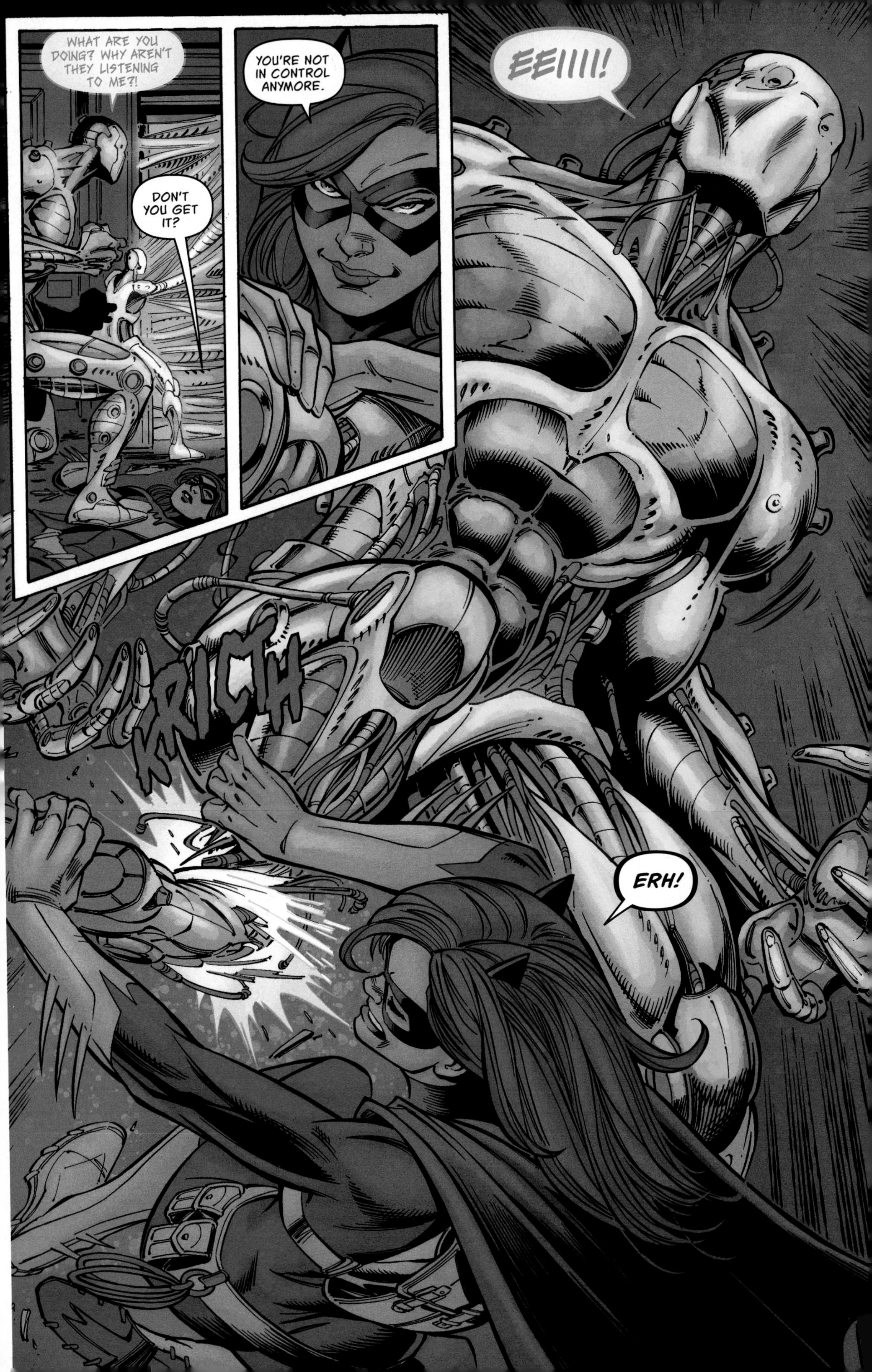
WHAT ARE YOU DOING? WHY AREN'T THEY LISTENING TO ME?!
DON'T YOU GET IT?
YOU'RE NOT IN CONTROL ANYMORE.
EEIIIII!
KRICTH
ERH!

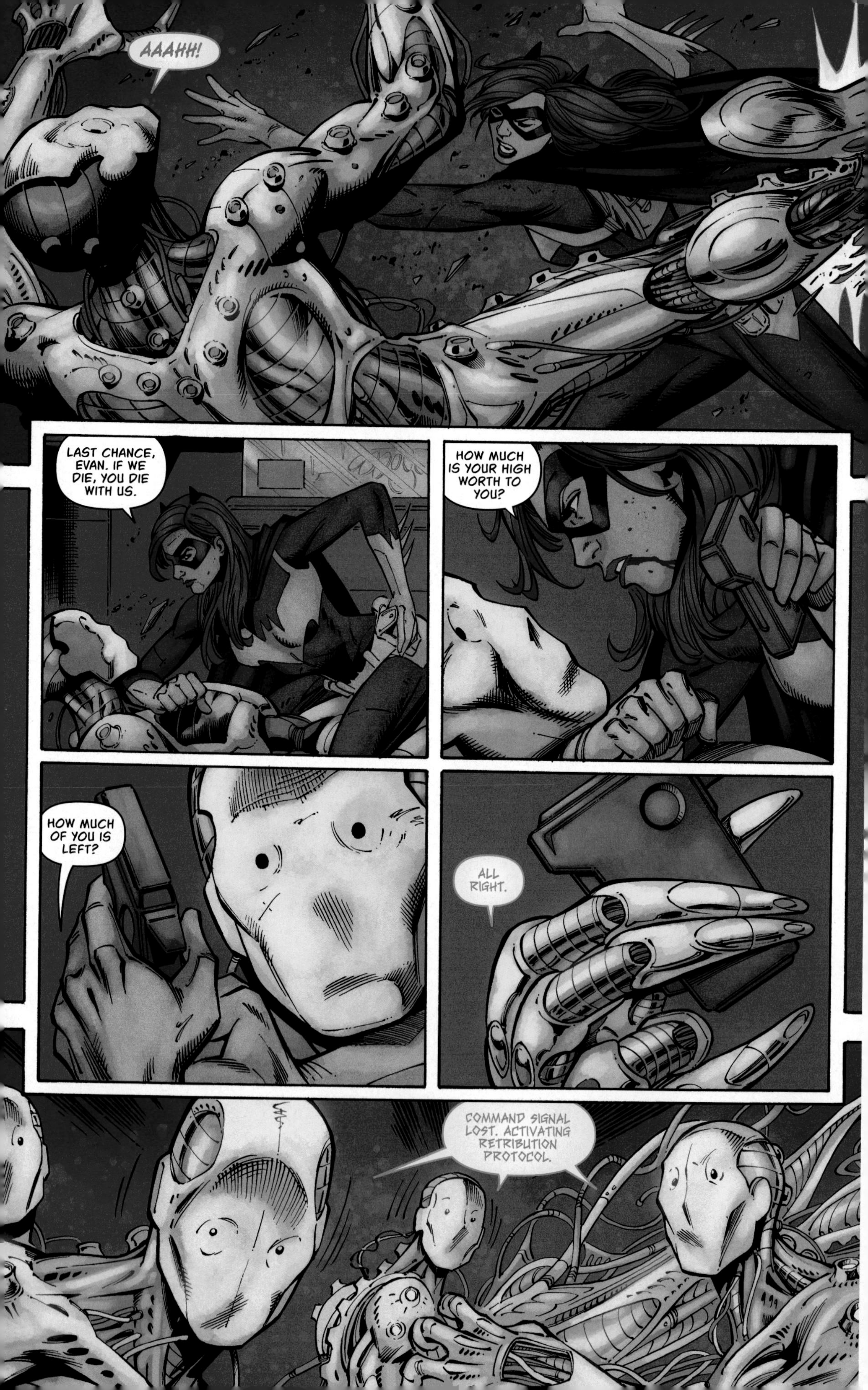
AAAHH!
LAST CHANCE, EVAN. IF WE DIE, YOU DIE WITH US.
HOW MUCH IS YOUR HIGH WORTH TO YOU?
HOW MUCH OF YOU IS LEFT?
ALL RIGHT.
COMMAND SIGNAL LOST. ACTIVATING RETRIBUTION PROTOCOL.

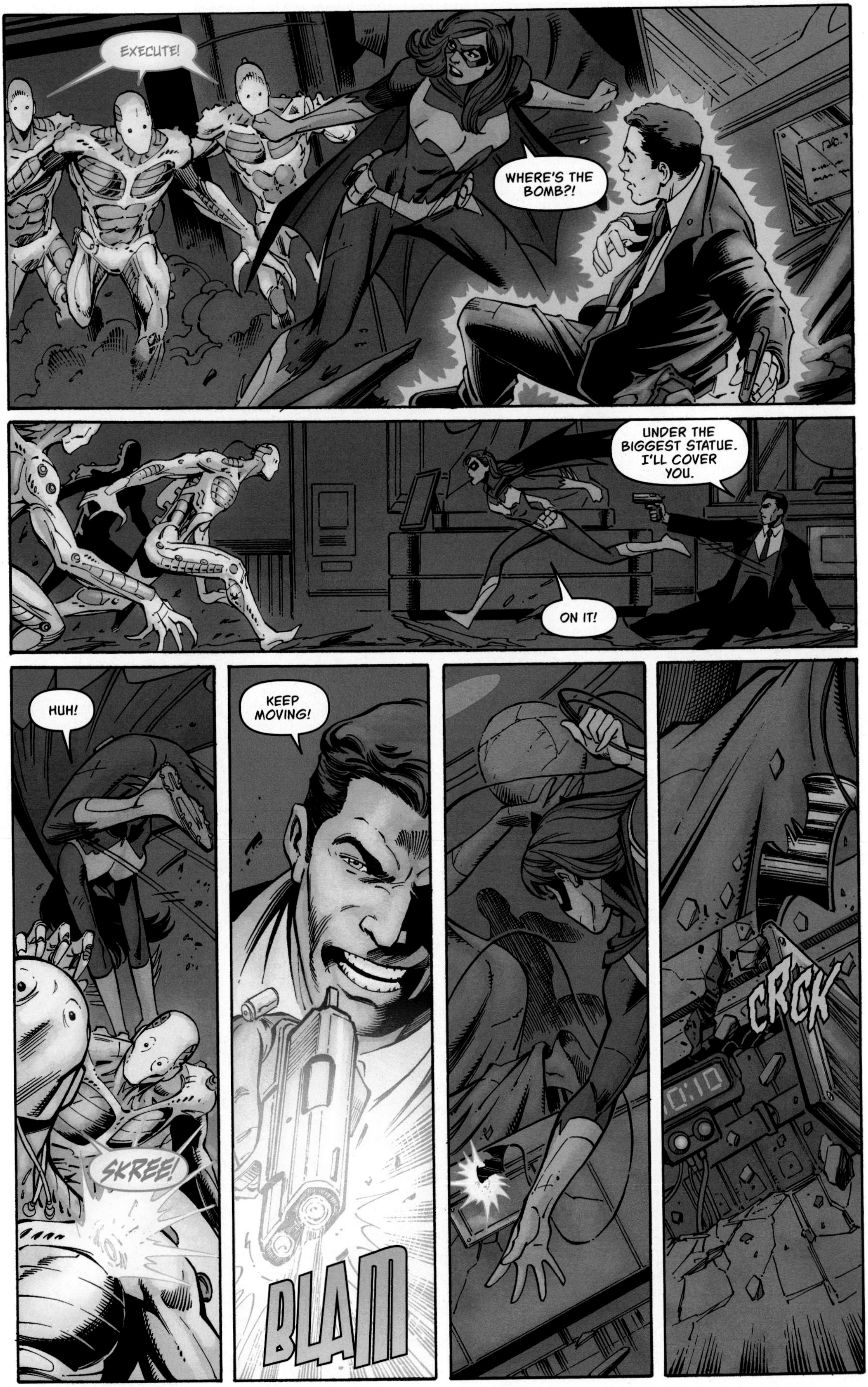
EXECUTE!
WHERE'S THE BOMB?!
UNDER THE BIGGEST STATUE. I'LL COVER YOU.
ON IT!
HUH!
SKREE!
KEEP MOVING!
BLAM
CRCK
0:10

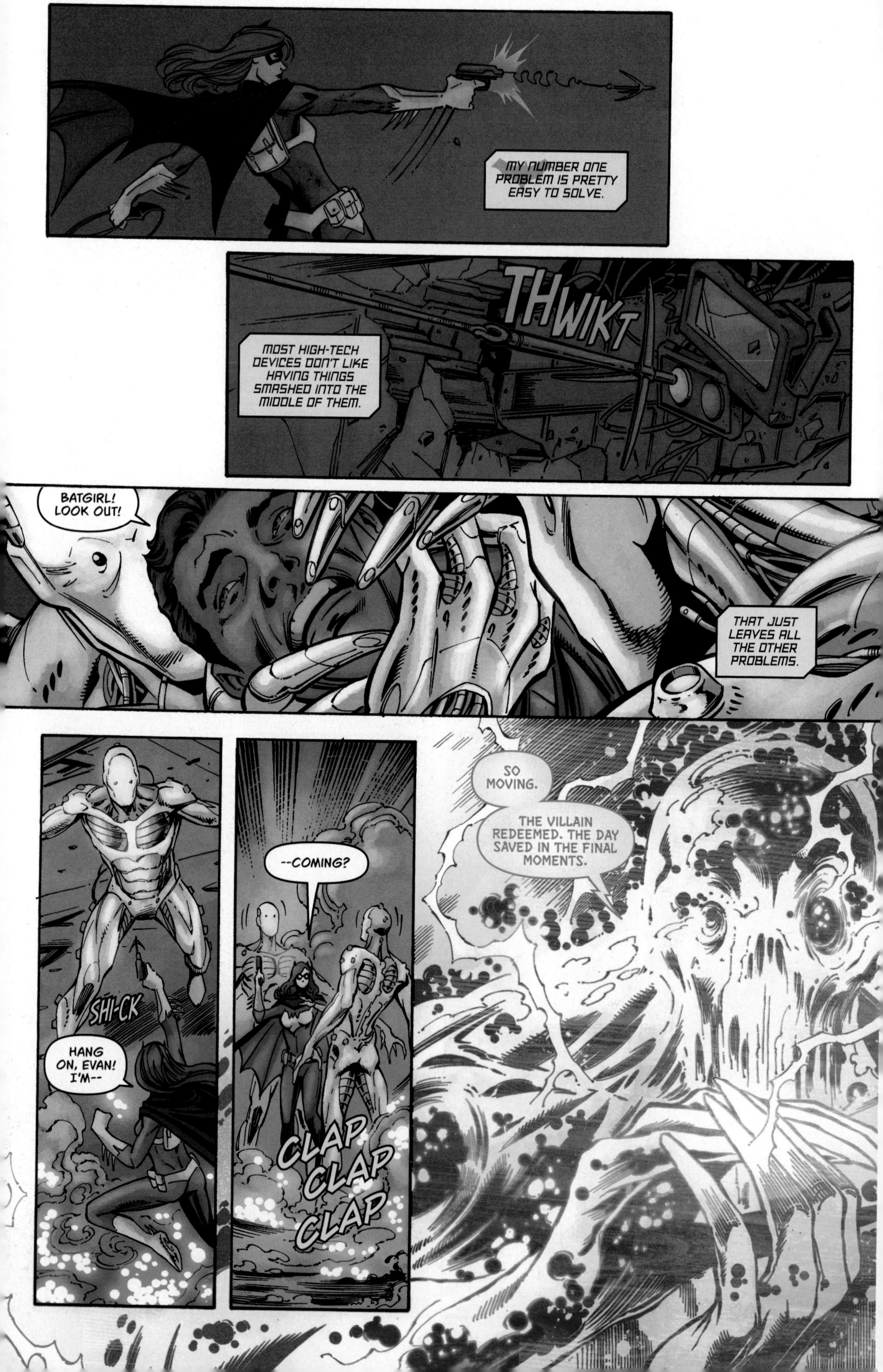
MY NUMBER ONE PROBLEM IS PRETTY EASY TO SOLVE.
THWIKT
MOST HIGH-TECH DEVICES DON'T LIKE HAVING THINGS SMASHED INTO THE MIDDLE OF THEM.
BATGIRL! LOOK OUT!
THAT JUST LEAVES ALL THE OTHER PROBLEMS.
SHI-CK
HANG ON, EVAN! I'M--
--COMING?
CLAP CLAP CLAP
SO MOVING.
THE VILLAIN REDEEMED. THE DAY SAVED IN THE FINAL MOMENTS.

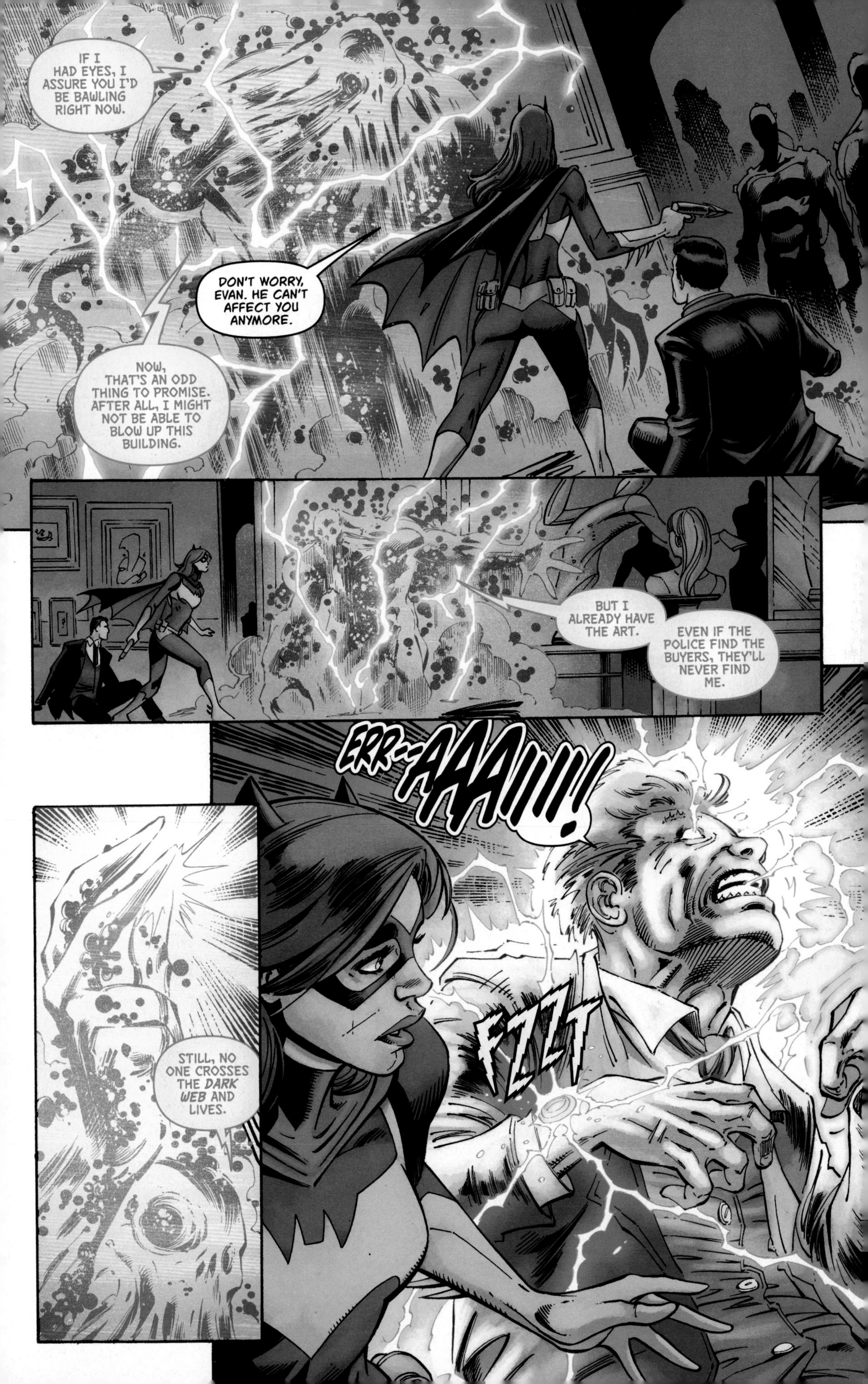
IF I HAD EYES, I ASSURE YOU I'D BE BAWLING RIGHT NOW.
DON'T WORRY, EVAN. HE CAN'T AFFECT YOU ANYMORE.
NOW, THAT'S AN ODD THING TO PROMISE. AFTER ALL, I MIGHT NOT BE ABLE TO BLOW UP THIS BUILDING.
BUT I ALREADY HAVE THE ART.
EVEN IF THE POLICE FIND THE BUYERS, THEY'LL NEVER FIND ME.
STILL, NO ONE CROSSES THE *DARK WEB* AND LIVES.
ERR--AAAIII!!
FZZT

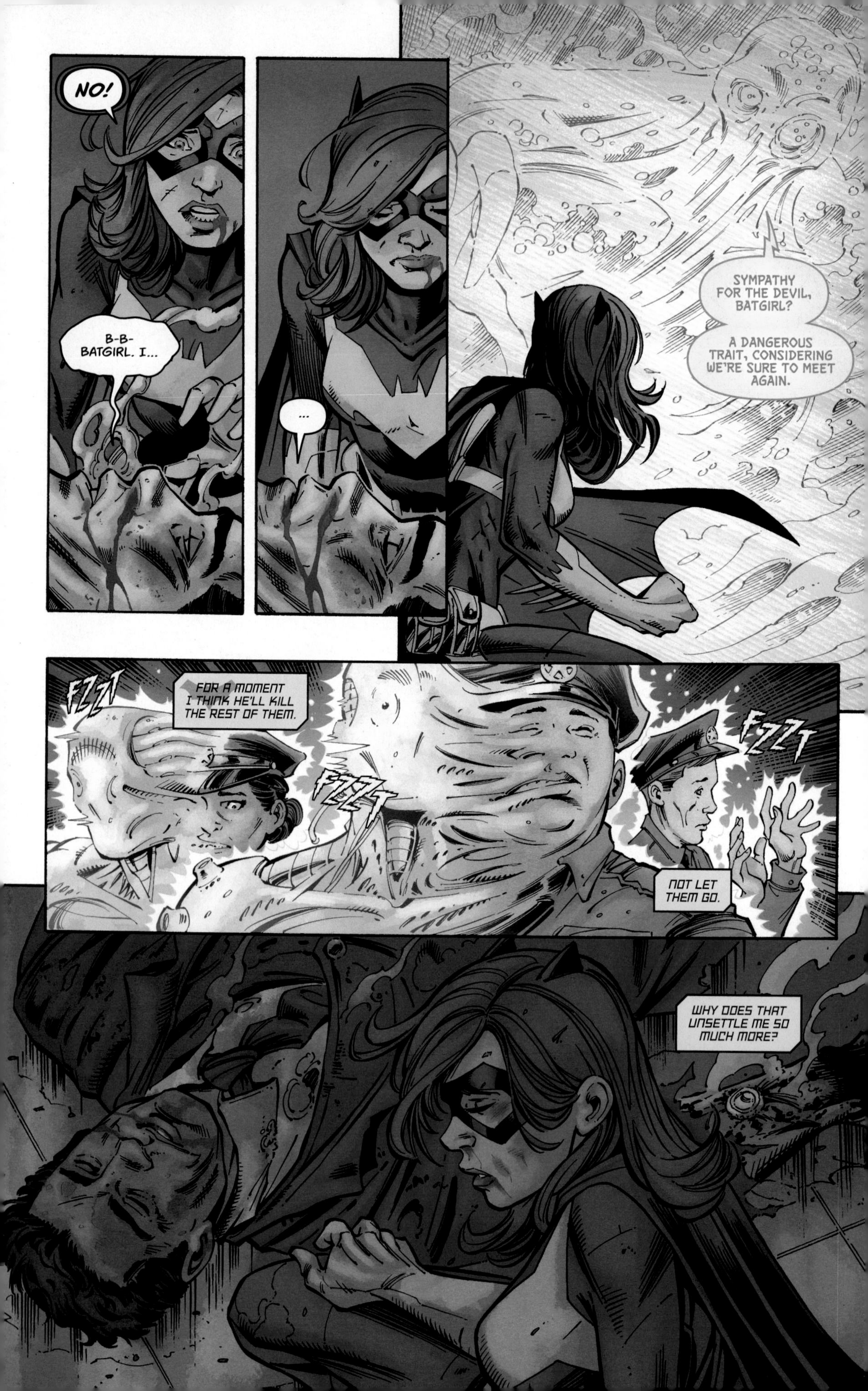
NO!
B-B-BATGIRL. I...
...
SYMPATHY FOR THE DEVIL, BATGIRL?
A DANGEROUS TRAIT, CONSIDERING WE'RE SURE TO MEET AGAIN.
FZZT
FOR A MOMENT I THINK HE'LL KILL THE REST OF THEM.
FZZZT
FZZT
NOT LET THEM GO.
WHY DOES THAT UNSETTLE ME SO MUCH MORE?

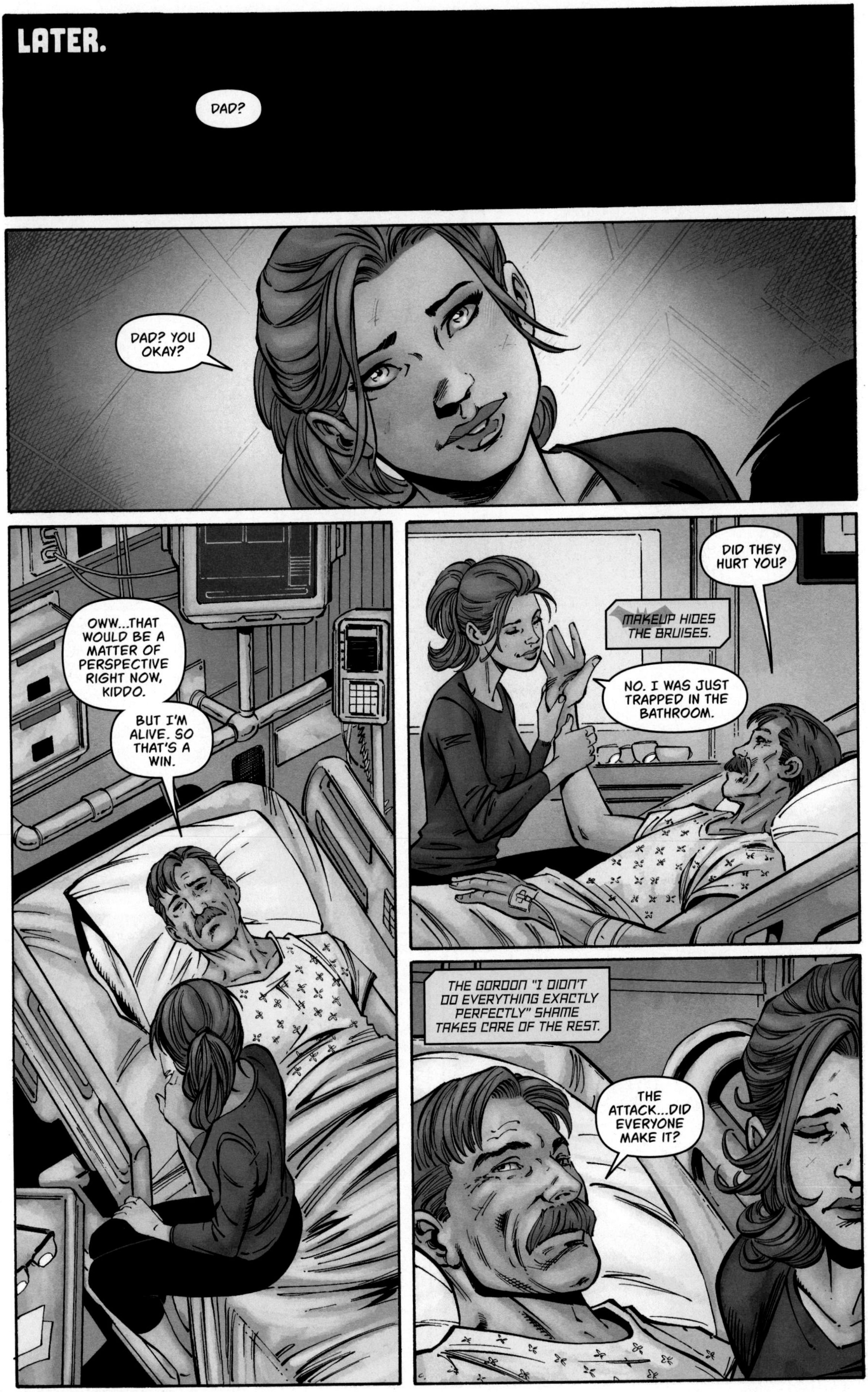
LATER.
DAD?
DAD? YOU OKAY?
OWW...THAT WOULD BE A MATTER OF PERSPECTIVE RIGHT NOW, KIDDO.
BUT I'M ALIVE. SO THAT'S A WIN.
DID THEY HURT YOU?
MAKEUP HIDES THE BRUISES.
NO. I WAS JUST TRAPPED IN THE BATHROOM.
THE GORDON "I DIDN'T DO EVERYTHING EXACTLY PERFECTLY" SHAME TAKES CARE OF THE REST.
THE ATTACK...DID EVERYONE MAKE IT?

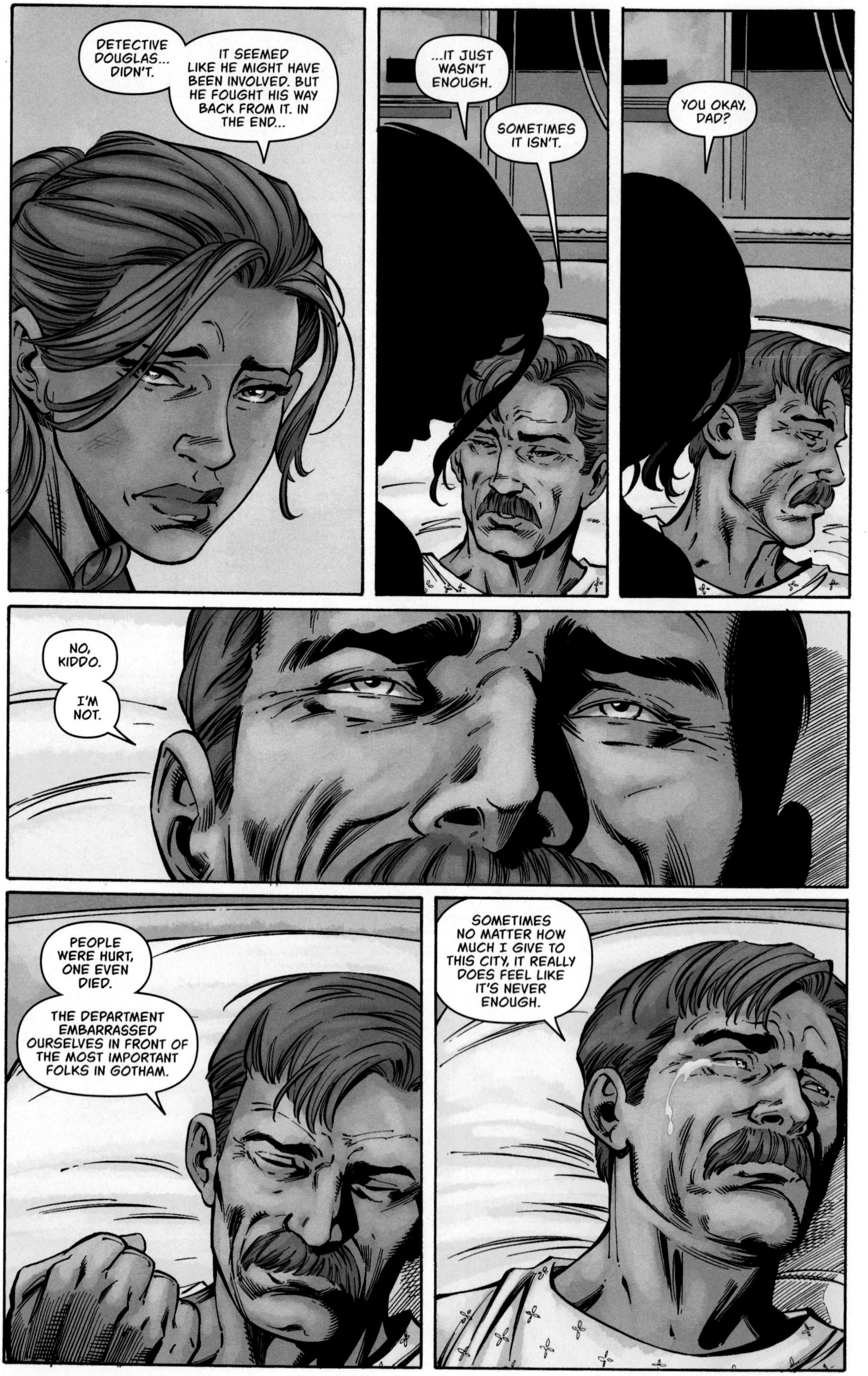
DETECTIVE DOUGLAS... DIDN'T.
IT SEEMED LIKE HE MIGHT HAVE BEEN INVOLVED. BUT HE FOUGHT HIS WAY BACK FROM IT. IN THE END...
...IT JUST WASN'T ENOUGH.
SOMETIMES IT ISN'T.
YOU OKAY, DAD?
NO, KIDDO.
I'M NOT.
PEOPLE WERE HURT, ONE EVEN DIED.
THE DEPARTMENT EMBARRASSED OURSELVES IN FRONT OF THE MOST IMPORTANT FOLKS IN GOTHAM.
SOMETIMES NO MATTER HOW MUCH I GIVE TO THIS CITY, IT REALLY DOES FEEL LIKE IT'S NEVER ENOUGH.

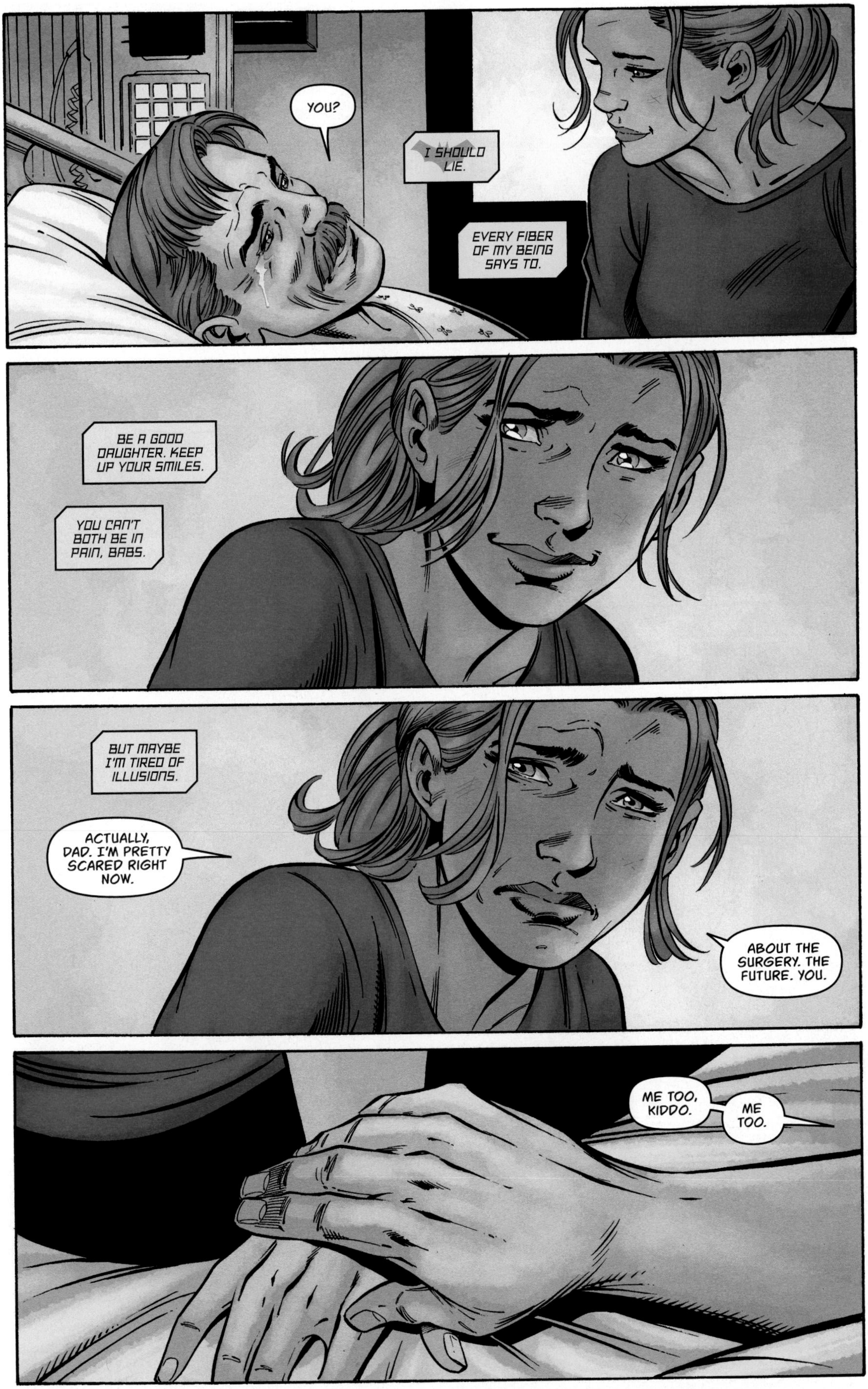
YOU?
I SHOULD LIE.
EVERY FIBER OF MY BEING SAYS TO.
BE A GOOD DAUGHTER. KEEP UP YOUR SMILES.
YOU CAN'T BOTH BE IN PAIN, BABS.
BUT MAYBE I'M TIRED OF ILLUSIONS.
ACTUALLY, DAD. I'M PRETTY SCARED RIGHT NOW.
ABOUT THE SURGERY. THE FUTURE. YOU.
ME TOO, KIDDO.
ME TOO.

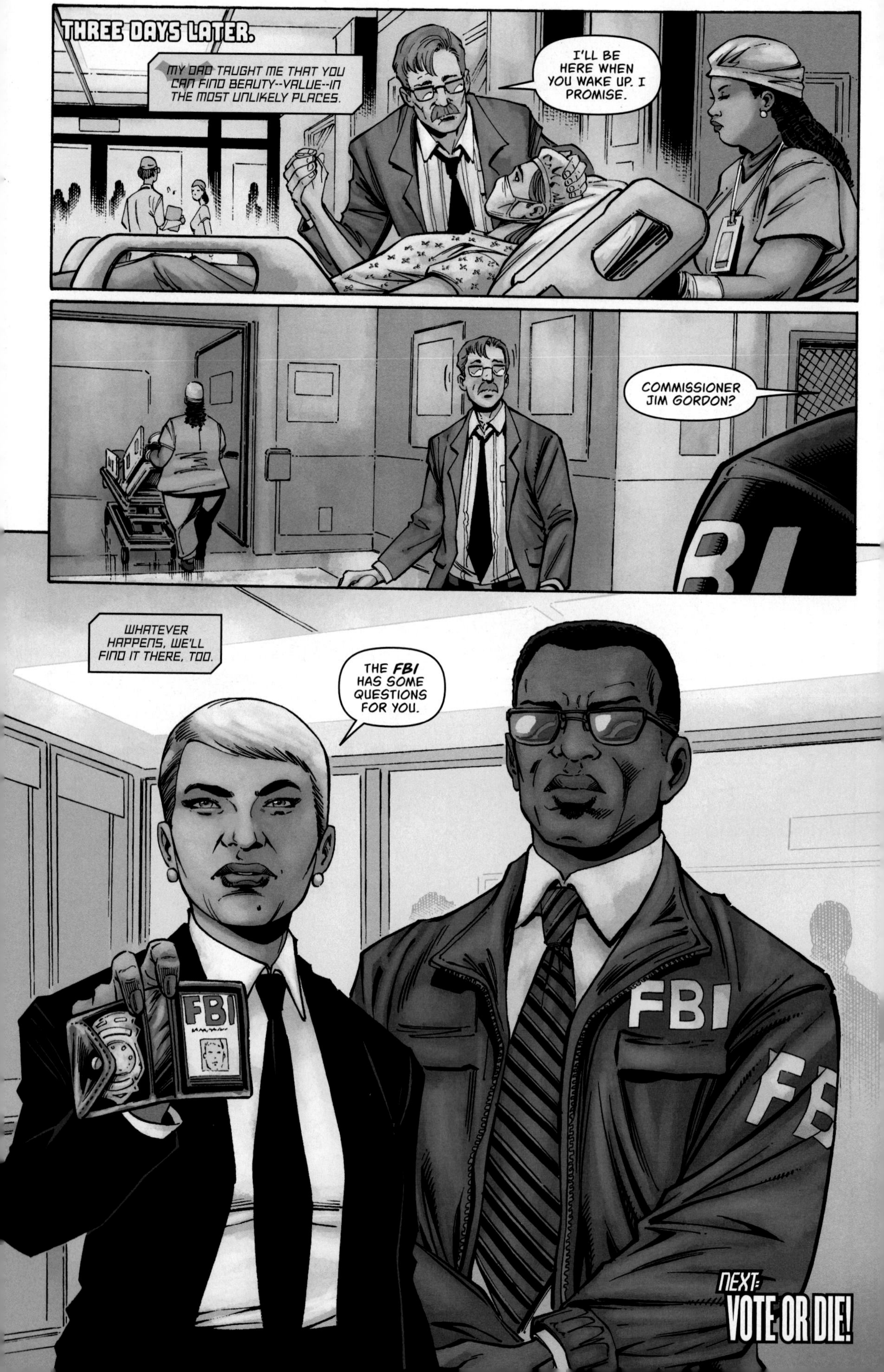
THREE DAYS LATER.
MY DAD TAUGHT ME THAT YOU CAN FIND BEAUTY--VALUE--IN THE MOST UNLIKELY PLACES.
I'LL BE HERE WHEN YOU WAKE UP. I PROMISE.
COMMISSIONER JIM GORDON?
WHATEVER HAPPENS, WE'LL FIND IT THERE, TOO.
THE FBI HAS SOME QUESTIONS FOR YOU.
FBI
FBI
NEXT: VOTE OR DIE!

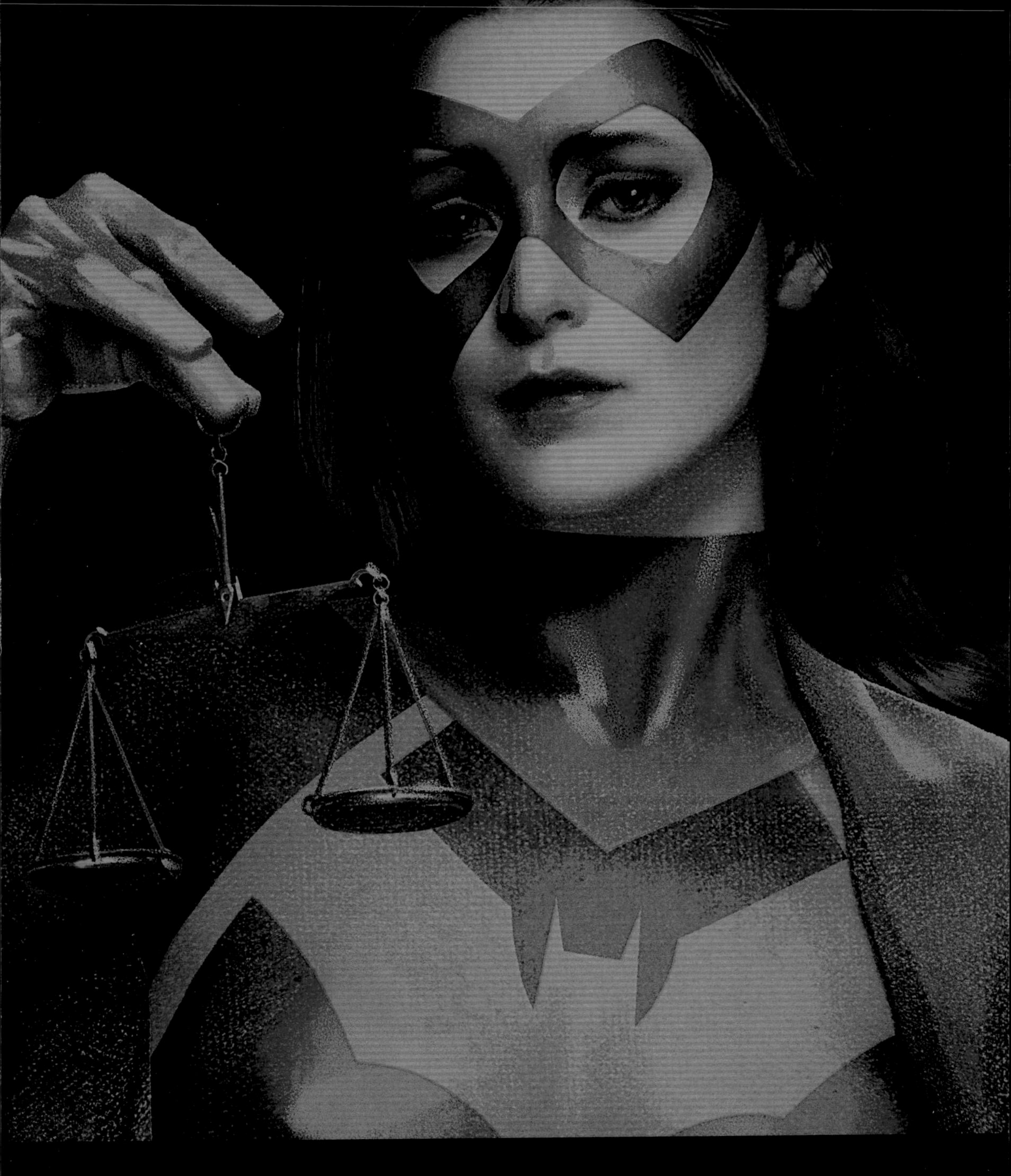

# VARIANT COVER GALLERY

BATGIRL #25
variant cover by JOSHUA MIDDLETON

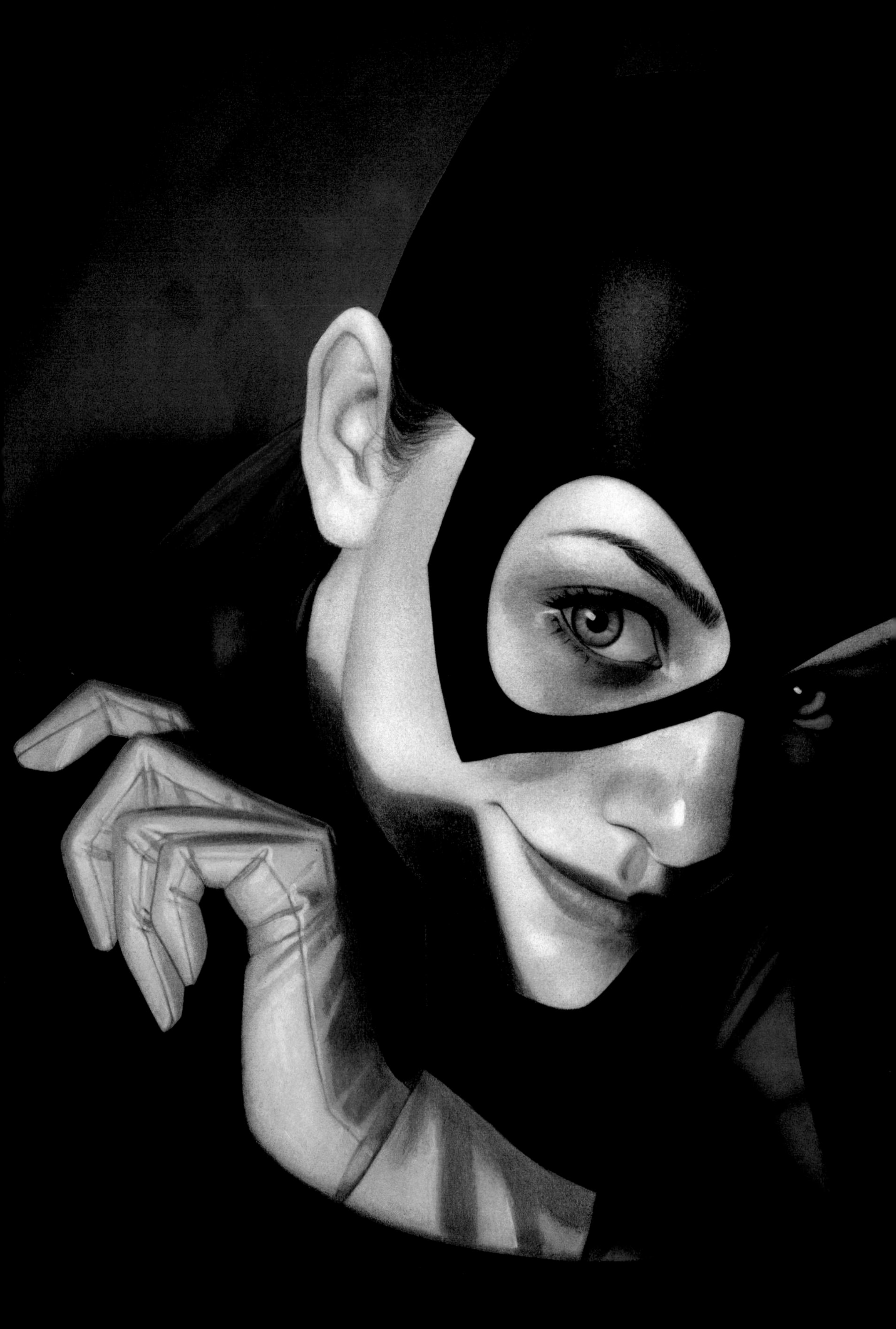

BATGIRL #26
variant cover by JOSHUA MIDDLETON

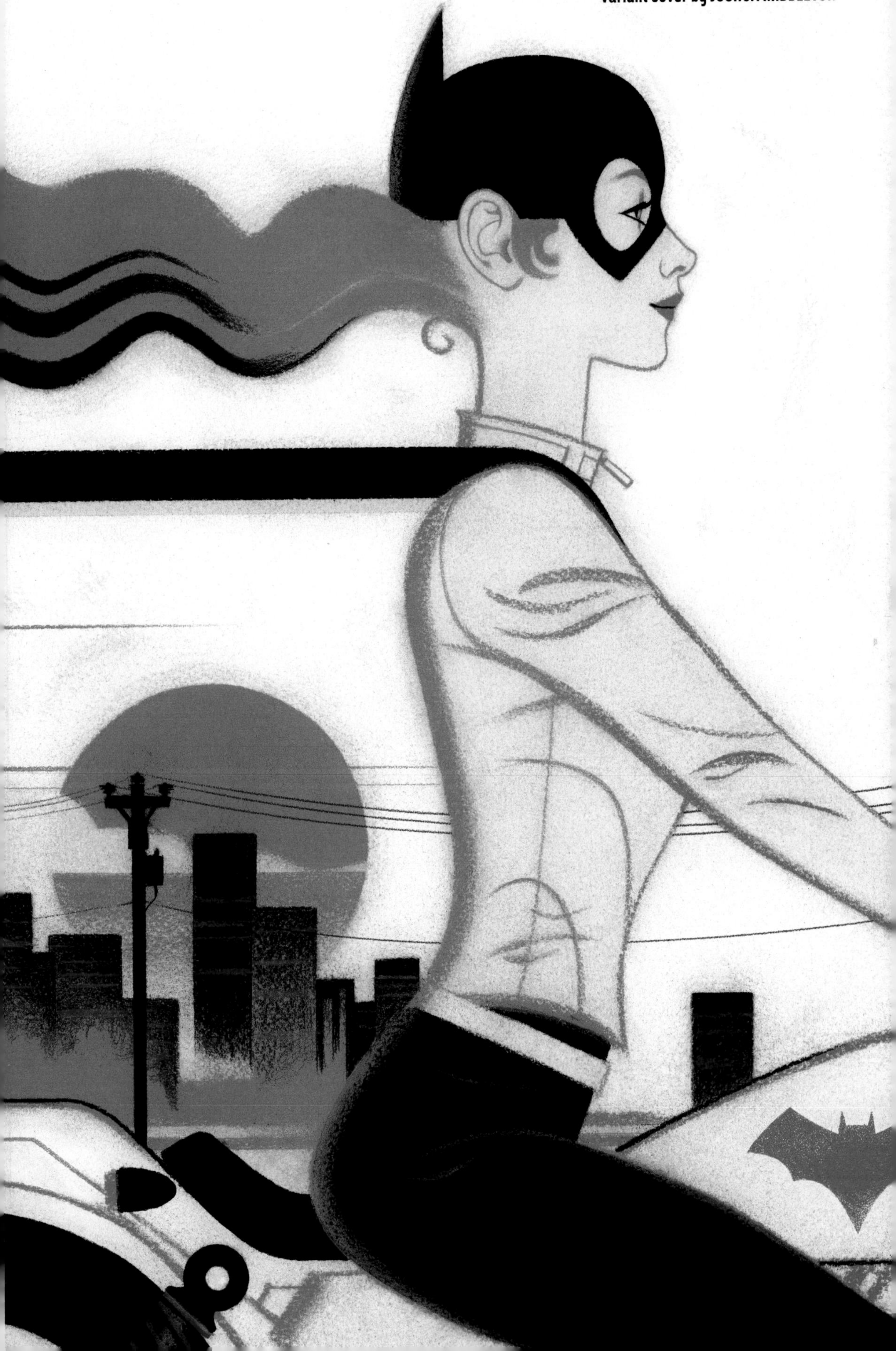

**BATGIRL #27**
**variant cover by JOSHUA MIDDLETON**

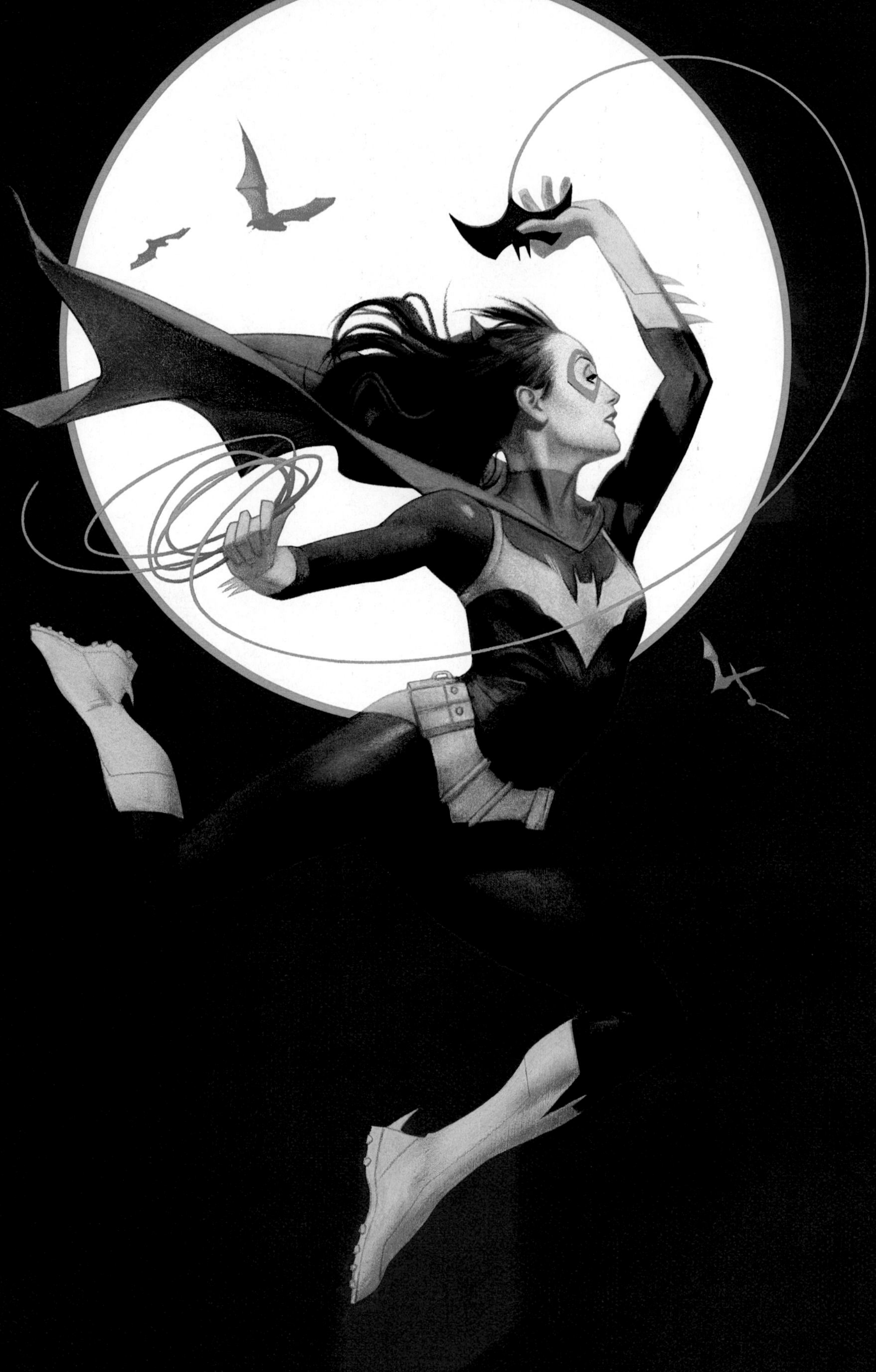

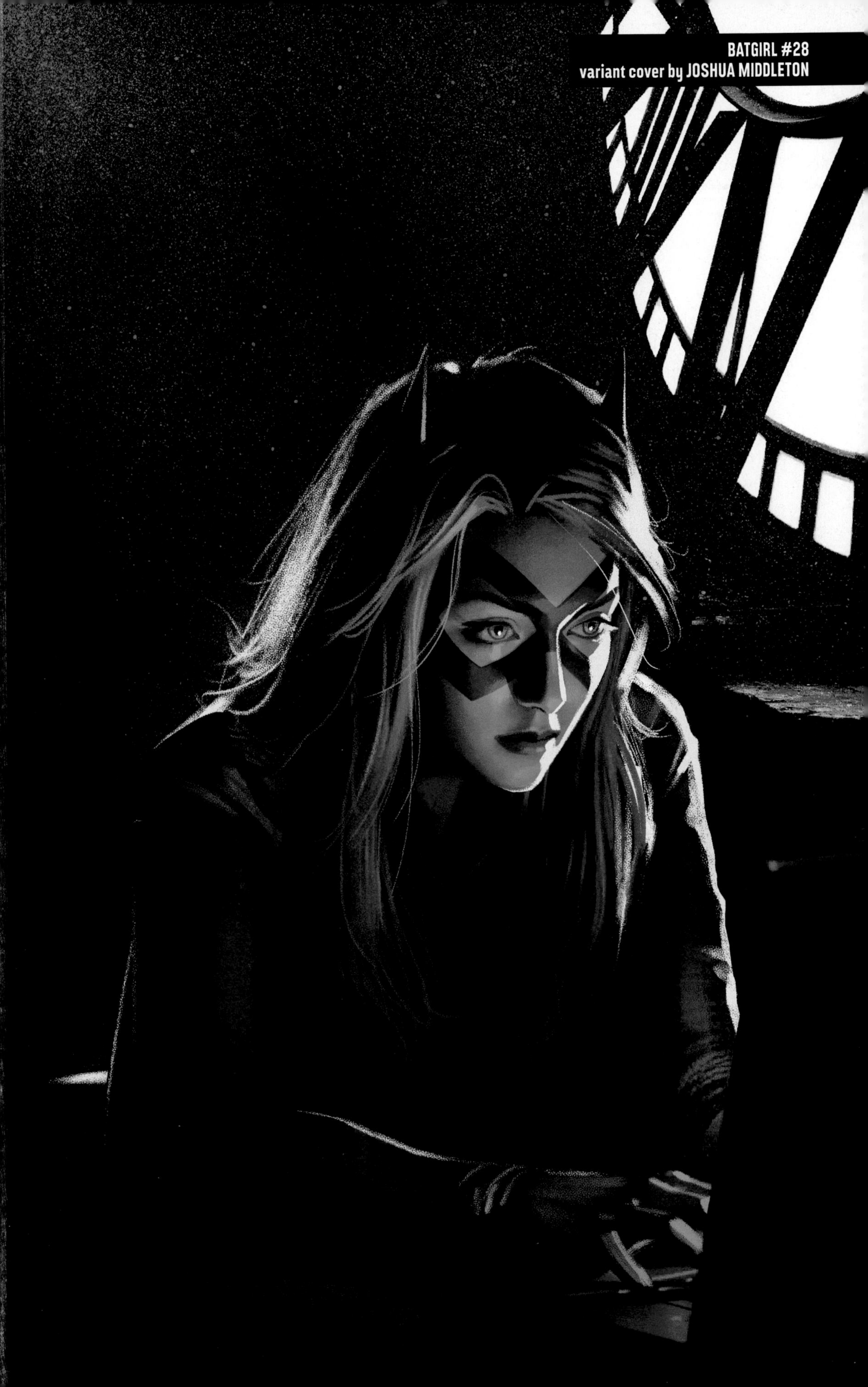

**BATGIRL #28**
**variant cover by JOSHUA MIDDLETON**

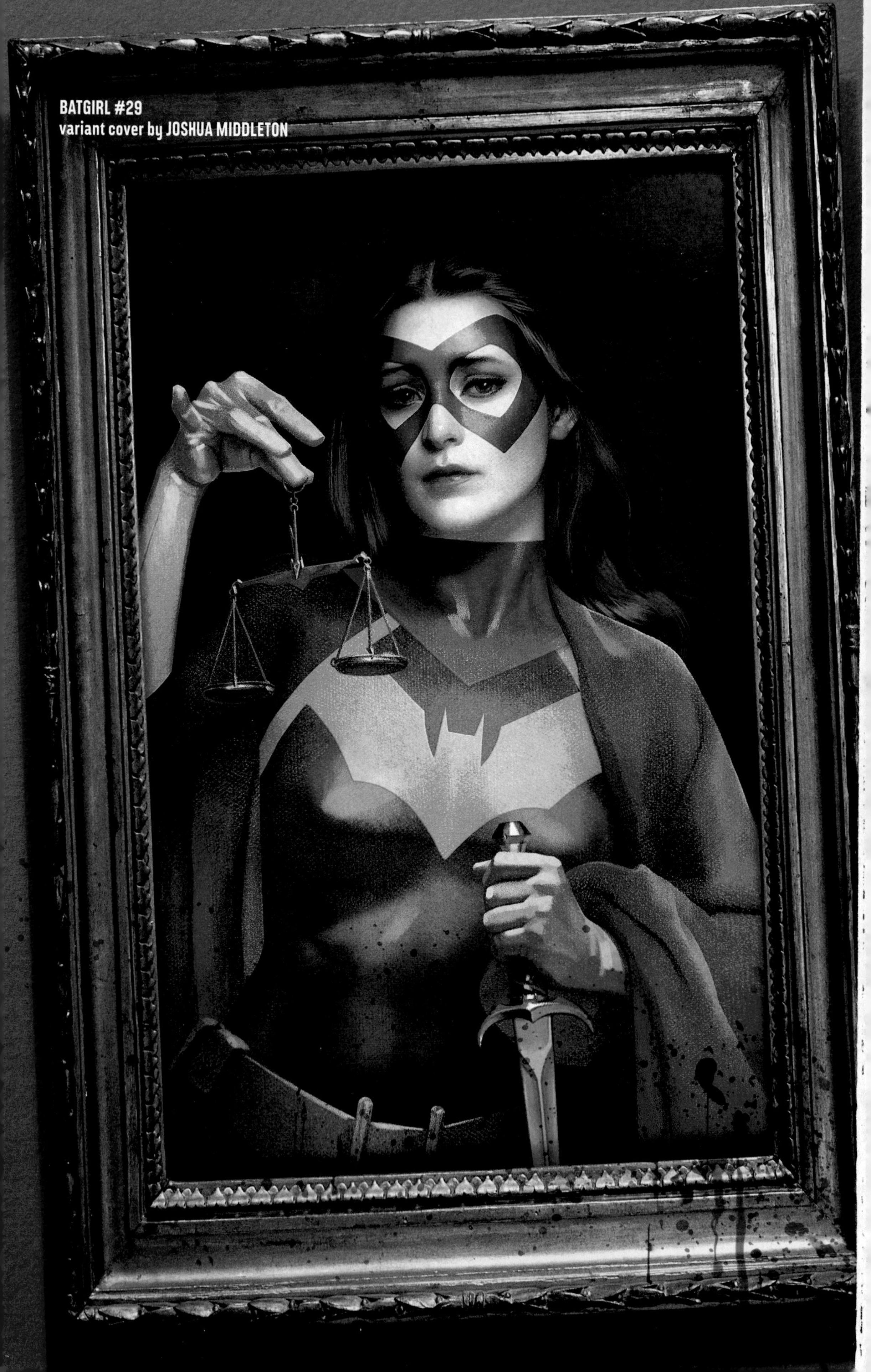

BATGIRL #29
variant cover by JOSHUA MIDDLETON